# CONFESSIONS
## *of an* EX-SECRET SERVICE AGENT
### The Marty Venker Story

# CONFESSIONS
## *of an* EX-SECRET
## SERVICE AGENT
### The Marty Venker Story

by GEORGE RUSH

DONALD I. FINE, INC.
*New York*

Library of Congress Cataloging-in-Publication Data
Rush, George
Confessions of an ex-Secret Service agent.
1. Venker, Marty. 2. United States. Secret Service—
Officials and employees—Biography. 3. Presidents—
Protection—United States. I. Venker, Marty
II. Title.
HV7911.V427A3 1988 973.92'092'4 [B] 87-81421
ISBN 1-55611-054-5

Manufactured in the United States of America
10 9 8 7 6 5 4 3 2 1
Permissions to come

To Viola

To Peg and George

# AUTHOR'S NOTE

This book comes to you courtesy of the sure-fire, ever-dependable serendipity of New York. It happened like this. Three years ago *Forbidden Broadway* producer Jeff Martin was getting ready to open his first nightclub, on the island of Aruba, when it occured to him that he needed a disc jockey. Who knows why, but Jeff remembered that three years earlier he'd served jury duty with a guy who was a DJ—a guy named Marty . . . Marty? . . . Marty *Venker*! Jeff tracked down Marty Venker, and though Marty wasn't keen on flying, he agreed to go to Aruba and at least start the disco rolling.

One day Jeff and Marty were at Jeff's place, plotting their musical invasion of the Caribbean, when Jeff's friend, Russell Levine, dropped by. The three of them happened to get talking about politics. In passing, Marty mentioned something that he usually didn't bring up—that he used to protect the Presidents of the United States. Russell and Jeff blinked several times. Marty, dressed in a T-shirt and some amusing lace-up Spartacus shoes, looked like he didn't own a tie. This character? Guarding Presidents? Get outta here!

Nevertheless, Russell, a screenwriter, started asking Marty what it was like to work in the Secret Service. Back then, Marty didn't think much about it. A few years before a prominent literary agent

7

had tried to persuade him to work with a handsome TV anchorman on a book about his Secret Service years. Marty had turned the offer down. He'd said he wanted to get on with the rest of his life. But now enough time had passed, and Russell seemed like-minded enough, that Marty felt like talking. Russell asked him if he'd be willing to be interviewed for a magazine article. Marty said okay.

Russell and I had met just once before when he called to ask if I'd like to work on this article. When I came over to Russell's to meet Marty I realized that we were already acquainted—in the sense that at least twice before, from on high, Marty had made me dance. That established, Marty, Russell and I turned on a tape recorder and began to talk. In time, we finished an article for *Rolling Stone*. Approached by book publishers, I decided to keep asking Marty questions. Obligingly, he kept answering them.

Few agents still in the Secret Service are willing or able to talk freely about their life's work. Marty's old friend Gordon Heddell was one of several agents who, when I asked them for an interview, said they'd like to talk, but then begged off. "The Secret Service speaks through one voice," Haddell explained, "and that's the office of Public Affairs." White House correspondents will confirm that the people in that office have some of the tightest lips in Washington. Public Affairs abides that an assassin can fashion even the smallest shard of information into a weapon. True enough. Of course, the Service's official mantra of No Comment is also its way of body-guarding itself—of keeping Capitol Hill critics at bay, of preserving the mystique of the granite agent.

Memoirs by elected and appointed officials have long been a fact of Washington life. Every President knows that, once they are freed from office, his aides and cabinet members will, like the President himself, take the opportunity to pass along a little learning, set the record straight, settle some old scores and maybe make a buck or two. Several former directors of the Secret Service have recorded their adventures in books that celebrate their tenures. The Public

Affairs office includes these books on its recommended reading list. It seems unlikely, though, that this book will ever make that list. Shortly after I sent the agency several pages of questions, I received a call from spokeswoman Jane Vezeris. She informed me that the office wouldn't be spending "much if any" time on my queries because "this isn't a project we endorse . . . I mean, what do *we* get out of this?" Vezeris was kind enough to give me some budget and personnel figures and she did address a few questions that, she said, "I can answer off the top of my head." But, never mind the memoirs of past directors; Vezeris insisted that "the Secret Service doesn't approve of any agent recounting his or her experiences in print. Particularly not an agent who went out the way that Marty did." Under the Freedom of Information Act, a request was made to see Marty's permanent file. That request did yield a few enlightening letters of commendation. It also dredged up several hundred sleepy-making pages of expense reports and bureaucratic paperwork. Livelier stuff, no doubt, resides among an unspecified number of pages that, according to another Secret Service officer, were "withheld because the documents in the requested file contain information compiled for law enforcement purposes."

Given this official undertow, I'd like to applaud those broadminded agents—retired and still working—whose thoughtful replies deepened my understanding of their job. Besides being helped by agents who spoke on background, I was aided by Mike Endicott, Steve Garmon, Jim Kalafatis, Jerry Parr, and Chuck Rochner. Thanks to them all.

I am also grateful to those who've known Marty outside the Service: Tim Alger, Tom Birdy, Barbara Bowers, Paul Costello, Frank DeCurtis, John Glover, Debby Johnson, David Jurman, Dr. Bertrand Newman, Janet Paist, Frank Roccio, Rose, George Sarantakis, Sue Simmons, Steve Venker, Viola Venker, Kirke Walsh, and Judy Weinstein.

Among the writers whose work strengthened my work are Jack

Anderson, Robert Sam Anson (*Exile*), Raymond Bonner (*Waltzing With Dictators*), Fawn M. Brodie (*Richard Nixon: The Shaping of His Character*), James W. Clarke (*American Assassins*), Brad Gooch ("Club Culture" in *Vanity Fair*), Dick Hebdidge (*Subculture: The Meaning of Style*), and William Manchester (*The Death of a President*).

Some friends whose insight, faith, shelter, and indulgence I'll always remember are: Steve Bloom, Vivian Bobka, Jill Brooke, George Coleman, Eileen Daspin, Frank Devine, George Dubose, Pam Glick, Todd Harris, Richard Johnson, Tony Keats, Stuart Krichevsky, Brant Mewborn, Jonathan Roberts, and Amy Rosmarin.

Thanks again to Russell Levine, whose tact and guile brought and kept us together. And *music maestro, please,* for Martin Joseph Venker, for uncommon candor under questioning. May he find his perfect beat.

*George Rush*
*May, 1988*

# CONTENTS

11

# Contents

# CONFESSIONS
## *of an* EX-SECRET
## SERVICE AGENT
### The Marty Venker Story

# CHAPTER ONE

## *An Internal Matter*

ONE night in New York in 1980:

"There I was, lying in the foyer of Richard Nixon's townhouse, and thinking, 'God, this is it, this is the weird way I'm going to die!'

"Let me back up a minute. This was about 10:30 at night. I'd just finished supervising the last shift and three new agents had just checked in. I was down in Nixon's basement. That's where we set up the Secret Service command post, right next to the wine cellar where Nixon used spend hours—caressing his vintage years. That night I was getting ready to go home. So I looked up at the video monitor. It showed what was going on out on East 65th Street. The pastor of the church across the street, he'd let us stick a camera on the church's roof. And this camera—it was sort of like the eye of God, you know, always watching, all day long, looking down through the trees with a zoom-lens and night vision, like the Holy See, never letting Nixon out of its sight.

"Anyway, I looked at the video monitor and it showed the coast was clear. So I climbed the basement stairs to the foyer. I unlocked the front door. I bent over to pick up my flight bag, at the same time that I pressed down on the door latch. That's when it happened. Bam! This fat lady burst in.

"She blindsided me. Knocked me right on the floor. She must've weighed two hundred and fifty pounds.

"Now twenty feet down the hall, past the vase of flowers, Nixon was in his study, talking on the phone. The fat lady started yelling, 'I got to see him now!' She was blathering something about Cambodian socialism and the Pope being gay. Which was standard. I mean, she used to loiter outside the townhouse. David Rockefeller, the Chairman of the Chase Bank, he lived right next door to Nixon. And when Rockefeller would step out of his limo, this fat lady would tell him she used to be his wife. Right then when she was on top of me, I didn't care if she used to be his brother, Nelson. I just wanted to know if she had a gun or something. She had this tattered coat, and naturally, she stunk to high heaven, drooling into my face, swimming around on my chest. That's when I started thinking, '*This* is the weird way I'm going to die. Not shot in a motorcade, but smothered by this maniac woman.'

"So I got mad and lifted her off me, then I pushed her back out the door. Out on the front landing, I pinned her to the steps. Now I'll tell you, over the years I'd questioned a lot of deranged people who'd threatened to kill the President. And if I learned anything it was that crazy people may be crazy, but they're not stupid. They know when they're jerking you around. So I caught my breath, and I shook this woman real hard, and told her, rather loudly, 'Don't you *ever* fuckin' come back here again! Go bother someone else!'

"Of course by this time, the other agents had heard the commotion. All of a sudden, the fat lady was staring down the barrels of an Uzi submachine gun and a Remington .870 pump shotgun. We gave her a second to compose herself. Then she climbed up the steps and wandered down the street. Back into the night.

"Next day, Richard Nixon phoned the command post and asked if I'd come up to his study. About seven years before this I'd questioned a guy who'd written Nixon threatening letters and who'd turned up at an airport to greet Nixon—armed with a hunting rifle.

This fat lady hadn't been armed, but she'd probably gotten as close to Nixon as any of these people ever had. So Nixon wanted a briefing.

"I walked into his study and there he was—the face that sold a million Halloween masks. He said, 'Well, what was the problem?'

"I told him.

"He said, 'It's a shame. You didn't have to hurt her, did you?'

" 'No, sir.'

" 'Well, what did she want?' "

"I told him what she mumbled about the Pope and Cambodia.

" '*Cambodia?*'

"Now he was curious. See, Nixon had been real reclusive when was living in San Clemente. And even now that he'd come back to New York, he wouldn't show much of himself to the reporters who used to lay for him outside his townhouse. But inside, you knew Nixon was plotting. You know, targeting the East Coast power circles. Checking the pulse of the citizenry.

" 'Well,' he said, 'what did she think about Cambodia?'

"I said, 'What?' He made her sound like she'd been a guest on "Meet the Press." I did a double-take. I looked at him sitting next to that *fireplace* of his—even if he had to turn on the air conditioning, Nixon had to have a blazing fire.

"He said it again, 'What did she think about Cambodia?' I don't mean to make *too* big a thing of this, but it struck me as funny. I mean, here's this guy who, as vice president, used to have the Secret Service drop him off at a Park Avenue psychotherapist. The doctor's name was Arnold Hutschnecker, and apparently Nixon liked him— he even talked Gerald Ford into seeing Hutschnecker. But publicly, after word got out that Nixon was seeing a 'shrink,' Nixon cut off the sessions and started dumping on psychotherapy. He used to say, 'People go through that psychological bit nowadays. That sort of juvenile self-analysis is something I've never done.' But I'll tell you, right then, while he was waiting to hear what the fat lady felt, I was wondering if the doctor made housecalls.

"So I said, 'I don't know what you mean. Sir, *she–was–crazy.'*

"Nixon sort of collected himself into a Presidential posture. Like he was replaying the tape of our conversation. Then he said what he always said: 'Of course, of course!' "

The fat lady, when she landed on Marty, seemed to carry the full weight of the decade he'd spent training and working for the Secret Service. Marty's job had come to seem, like that lady, gargantuan and bizarre. True, he'd left behind the asylums where he'd interviewed unhinged threat-makers. But the White House just seemed to cater to a more sophisticated patient. The Presidents sometimes needed protecting from themselves. But if Marty had his own assumptions shattered, he also roughed up some assumptions about what a Secret Service agent should be.

He had faced mobs all over the world. Yet the most riotous crowd existed within Marty himself. In the auditorium of his mind, the man in the gray flannel suit kept being hassled and drowned out by this wild leather-jacketed dude who kept breaking into song. In college Marty had led a band called the Soul Seekers, but for several years after he joined the Service, he'd lost interest in music. He decided, like so many of his generation, to "grow up," and become a professional.

He picked one of this country's more peculiar law enforcement jobs. There is other "police" work—much less glamorous than that of the Secret Service agent—which gives a person a much better chance of getting killed. No other law officer in America, though, makes a more explicit vow of suicide. Secret Service agents promise to step in front of the President, puff up their chests, stretch out their arms and catch a spiraling bullet as though it were a touchdown pass on homecoming weekend. The agents' oath is at once patriotic and un-American. The democracy where all men are created equal still puts the life of its elected emperor above the lives of all others. It gives a small cadre of samurai the chance to become martyrs. To keep their nation speeding into the future, a few Americans preserve the code of a medieval palace guard.

In exchange, those guards see the emperor as a man, unguarded. Richard Nixon, Gerald Ford, Jimmy Carter and Ronald Reagan were just a few of the people whose court intrigues glued Marty to the Service. He watched as Menachem Begin, hands in his pockets, and Anwar Sadat, smoking his pipe, unexpectedly crossed paths in the Camp David woods and began to walk in the same direction. He also saw the real-life sound stage for "Dr. Strangelove"—the underground nerve center in the Maryland mountains where, when the Doomsday missiles flew, the President would go to run what was left of America. Unforgettable moments of war and peace postponed Marty's burn-out.

But, eventually, he did snap.

"Other agents have come a lot closer to dying than I have. There're some real heroes in the Secret Service, and I'm sure they've got stories better than mine. All of them, every agent, worked for a different Secret Service. This is the one I worked for. These are some of the weird things that happened to me. Mostly by accident."

For five years after he left the Service, Marty himself kept most of his memories classified. Few people in his present life knew what he'd done before. But silence and secrecy aren't what Marty is about anymore. Right now he feels ready to play some old records.

# CHAPTER TWO

# *The Last Chance Jukebox*

"BACK when I was seven I wore a big 'S' across my chest. I'd been sent from my father's planet of Krypton to uphold law and order in America. Only thing was, I had more fun when I kept my red and blue Krypton costume covered up. The temperature could top ninety, but I'd keep my cape tucked inside my shirt and jeans. I'd race into my family's one-story red brick house in south St. Louis and my mom, Viola Venker, would be talking with my two older brothers. She'd say, 'Uh, what do you think, Superman?' Then catch herself: 'Oh, Clark, I didn't mean to say that!' "

Marty would grin at her appreciatively.

"We were trying to keep his identity secret from his brothers," explained Viola.

"As I got older I could pick up any old flute and get music out of it. So my mother gave me money for trumpet lessons. And I won a trumpet prize. Then I taught myself the guitar. By the time I was eighteen, me and three of my classmates at Affton Senior High School were pretending to be the Supermen of 1964—the Beatles. We practiced the Fab Four's hits, purchased the requisite rayon Beatle wigs and, when the day of the Affton talent show arrived, bounced out on stage. I was supposed to be John Lennon. When we sang

'Ticket to Ride,' believe it or not, the girls were screaming like we really *were* the Beatles.''

The Beatles drew on rhythm-and-blues, but Marty wanted to dig even deeper into that bag, into that really stinky soul music called funk. Downtown, at a record store near the bus station, Marty would pick up the smokier, grittier sort of r&b that radio relegated to its Jim Crow time slots.

"I always liked the hard beats, the music that got people off their seats. The college where I enrolled—Southeast Missouri State—was basically a cheap party school and a way to stay out of the war. I figured that a party school needed a good party band. So some other guys and I started one called the Soul Seekers.

"We had a dream of getting all kinds of people—black and white—into the funk. One nation under a groove. We'd play covers of songs by James Brown, Otis Redding, Wilson Pickett, B. B. King. And as we got better, the guys, who were studying music, started writing and arranging more of their own charts. We started out playing at SMS, but pretty soon we got an agent who booked us into places all over Missouri and Illinois and Arkansas. We'd get to some of these gigs, though, and find out our agent hadn't made it exactly clear who the Soul Seekers were. The black people in the band would walk into these honky tonks in the Ozarks and these rednecks would just about choke on their J.D. And *then* we'd launch into J. B.— 'Pappa's Got a Brand New Bag'—and it was like how fast can we get back to the van?

"But most of the shows went better. Not a bad way to make your tuition nut—and then some. But my girl friend, Barbara, wasn't impressed. At least not at first. Maybe it was my wardrobe—green custom-made superbad bell-bottoms with three-inch elephant cuffs and a hip-huggin' seat. I used to go all the way into the north St. Louis ghetto, to Joe's Clothes, to find those freaky got-to-get-over

threads—those two-tone Pyramid shoes with heels as high as hous-
ing projects and shimmering shirts with plaids as loud as police bull
horns."

Outlandish as some of his outfits were, Barbara found that
"Marty, when I got around to talking to him, was rather shy, but
very bright." And the more they talked, the more Barbara felt as if
Marty was "the most honest person I'd ever met. Once you get to
know Marty, you fall in love with him. Which is what I did."

Cape Girardeau, the home of Southern Missouri State, wasn't
New York City, but it wasn't your typical honky-tonk town on the
Mississippi either. The Cape Girardeau citizens had held on to some
of their ancestors' lively French spirit. Their local university had
attracted enough militants to support regular protests by the Students for a Democratic Society and other consciousness-raisers. But
even with these radicals running around the quad, Barbara thought
Marty stood out.

Marty: "I'd done the protest thing—traveled to Berkeley, to
march in the Free Speech Movement demonstrations. I'd also
brought her to a James Brown concert where, as far as Barbara could
see, she and I were the only white people. That was nothing new for
me. For a while now, I'd been a regular at inner city nightspots in
St. Louis, joints like The Dyna-flo Inn, The Blue Note, The Nosebag,
The Red Top. Other students, even black ones, couldn't believe that
I stuck my head into such places—dingy neon lounges near the
Collinsville Racetrack and the docks of the Mississippi. But then I
had a guardian angel and patron saint named Benny Sharp. He was
a bandleader with a wide Redd Foxx grin. Benny, who was in his late
thirties, was best known as a guitarist, but he used to tell the guys
in his band, 'I could outcroon all you motherfuckers if I wanted to.'
Back in '65 and '66, Benny scored some smallish national hits when
he and his group, the Sharpees, released 'Do the 45' and 'Tired of

Being Lonely.' And after Ike and Tiny Turner took to the road, Benny pretty much took over the r&b throne of St. Louis.

"Benny's had a signature song called the 'St. Louis Sunset Twist.' He named it after The Sunset, this club in a 'dusky' neighborhood, where I first heard him. I'd catch Benny's first set at The Sunset and then I'd follow him to the after-hours ghetto clubs. After a while I'd be dropping by Benny's house, three, four times a week. He'd teach me things on the guitar. Man, could he play! Never glanced at his strings, he just felt it. He's still probably the feelingest guitarist I've ever seen. When James Brown played in St. Louis, he'd be at the nightclubs, checking out Benny. A lot of nights, when Benny did his one A.M. set, he'd let me sing for an hour, hour and a half. People in those clubs were almost always real friendly toward me. One night there was a little trouble at The Nosebag. Some guys trying to get heavy. But Benny just opened up his guitar case and pulled out his chrome-plated .45 with the pearl handle. Just showed it to them. That seemed to focus everybody's attention back on the music.

"On weekends, me, Barbara, and our friends would pile into my '58 Chevy and drive all the way from Cape Girardeau to St. Louis to hear Benny at The Chatterbox. We could usually make the trip in three hours. I'd spot a toll booth up ahead and put the pedal to the metal. The toll collector would have his arm stuck out, ready to take a dime—until he saw that Chevy wasn't stopping. We'd blast through doing seventy."

They'd all still be revved up when they sat down at a big table at The Chatterbox and ordered their first round of beers. By one-thirty A.M., when a flock of long-necks would be nesting on their table, Benny would ask Marty to come up on stage.

"Go on!" Barbara would say, nudging him. Marty would tuck his chin into his chest and scrunch up his shoulders like a kid pretending he didn't hear his own name. Of course, Barbara knew he was dying to get up there and torch that place. She'd seen how a song could torture him with pleasure, make him tug on his own hair like a crazy man. And so now came his moment at The Chatterbox, and well, okay, why not. He consented.

"I'd tell the Benny's guys, key of —I think it was G. I'd be a little nervous at first, but once Benny counted down, 'one, two, three,' and we jumped into it, I'd get lost in the song. I used to sing 'The Tennessee Waltz.' Really. This funky version like you've never heard. And I used to sing Eddie Floyd's 'Knock on Wood'."

"If you closed your eyes and listened to his singing," Marty's friend George Sarantakis recalled, "you used to swear he was a black guy."

And did the crowd move? "Oh, yeah," remembered Marty. "That crowd was dancing."

"After a year at SMS, Barbara transferred to St. Louis University. We'd been getting pretty serious. But when she'd bring up marriage, I'd tell her I didn't feel I could commit. She started dating some other people, but she still drove down from St. Louis to see me. One weekend I told her that I'd invited a local girl to a Soul Seekers' party. She was furious. In the middle of the night, she headed down to SMS. When she got there, she found the other girl in my bed—by herself. I was asleep in Barbara's old bed next door.

" 'I can't believe how loyal you were!' she said."

"But I think the whole business told us that this long-distance relationship was developing a bad connection. After a while I stopped getting phone calls from her."

A bigger problem loomed beyond southeast Missouri—in Southeast Asia. Marty's brother, Steve, had been on one of the first troop planes sent to Vietnam in 1966. "I didn't really question our government," said Steve. "At the time I just thought it was right. But I didn't think Marty was the type to get stuck in the Army for two years. I just didn't think he was cut out for the military."

"I agreed. From all I heard, it sounded like a lot of poor schmucks were getting suckered into fighting for a country that didn't exactly want to be 'saved.' Who was going to run this country if we *did* win? Every time you opened the paper, Saigon had some new bozo in office. By the time I was a senior, William Westmoreland was ordering up 200,000 fresh bodies. I wanted to make sure I wasn't one of them. So I signed up for six years in the Army Reserve. I became a 'weekend warrior.' Spent six months in basic training at Fort Leonard Wood. It was quite a bit different from staying up all night long at nightclubs. But the training sort of appealed to my communist tendencies. The Army was the great leveler. I liked seeing people who'd never taken an order in their lives being told what to do.

"At least the Reserve put some starch into my life even as it was taking on more and more wrinkles. Benny Sharp had told me to stick with music. But Benny himself was losing interest in it—beginning to drift toward the day when he'd become the minister of his own church. Even the Soul Seekers were breaking up. The other people in the band somehow put me in charge of setting up the rehearsals and getting us to the gigs on time. But some of the guys were graduating and our best player was strung out on every kind of drug. We were playing an outdoor party once and he was so high he fell down into a puddle. I'm surprised he didn't electrocute himself. But even when he was lying there in the water he just kept on thumping that bass."

Marty's parents could've told him that's where all that goofing around with music got you.

"Believe it or not, my parents were part of my musical influence," Marty says now. "They used to have square dances in our basement.

That may have been my first 'underground' dance experience."
When was Marty going to straighten up and fly right? Marty's dad,
Harry Venker, wasn't bringing home so much money as a warehouse
manager that the family could afford its very own resident pop star.
Marty's oldest brother, Bud, had begun his charge up the corporate
ladder, and Steve, just back from Vietnam, was already working
toward an engineering degree. At least Marty had majored in marketing management, and for all his carousing, had kept up a B
average. To Marty, though, working in business "was like selling
your soul." A couple of times he'd taken off his Mr. Superbad
threads, put on a tie and met with some corporate recruiters. But
their firm handshakes and slide-rule smiles only saddened him. The
authorities had arrived. They were busting up the dream party where
Marty just kept on making people dance for the rest of his life.

No girl friend.

No band.

No idea when his Reserve unit might be called up.

But 1968 would get grimmer still.

"Four weeks before my twenty-second birthday, I was hanging out
in a campus pub called The Last Chance. I was sitting on a stool
feeling sorry for myself—you know, thinking about how the jukebox
wouldn't ever have a record by 'Marty Venker, Northern Southwest
Sales Representative.' Then I noticed the TV over the bar. They were
breaking in with a special news bulletin. Robert Kennedy had been
shot in Los Angeles. The bartender turned up the volume on the set.
People started gathering around, watching the commotion in that
hotel kitchen: Bobby crumbling to the floor. People screaming, *'Get
the gun!'* Rosey Grier and Rafer Johnson tackling Sirhan Sirhan. All
this disembodied crying and moaning. Bobby was staring up from a
pool of blood, with a busboy kneeling next to him. They kept showing the film over and over. People in the bar were biting their lips

and sobbing. And I'll tell you, nobody looked like they could name the record on the jukebox.

"I remember I was in high school, in the middle of my algebra class, when the principal's office announced President Kennedy had been shot. My teacher started crying. I'd just turned eighteen, but Kennedy seemed like the first person I could vote for. He was a tough sonofabitch, but he was also compassionate.

"Then came Martin Luther King. When you heard him, you could feel him making history. I could see the hope he was giving to black friends of mine. I never saw them so mad or sad as when King got murdered. It was like it was back to square one—the plantation owners had put down the slave uprising. We didn't know it then, but the whole thing had been hatched in St. Louis."

(In 1979, the House Select Committee on Assassinations concluded that James Earl Ray had killed King to collect $50,000 put up by St. Louis patent attorney John H. Sutherland and his associates on the White Citizens' Council.)

"It wasn't long after King got shot that Bobby Kennedy spoke at SMS. He made a big impression. It really seemed like he could end the war. He had so much energy it was as if Jack Kennedy had come back to life in someone closer to our age. You couldn't help but be inspired. Then a couple of weeks later, I saw him dying on the TV set. I thought, Jesus! Is this ever gonna stop? What's happening to us?

"It was right after Bobby died that I read about Congress providing Secret Service agents to all the candidates. And about how the Service was going to be hiring more agents. I started thinking more and more about applying. Then I wondered, if I wasn't hot on the Army or the corporate recruiters, how was I going to handle being a soldier in a suit and tie? But I felt like, what the hell, I couldn't put off maturity forever. My friend, John Glover, he'd become a cop. We used to go out cruising in his squad car and I got off on that. John was real honest and he used to hang out with me at the black clubs where Benny played. Becoming a cop hadn't turned John into a pig. He still liked to party.

"Also, I was already hitched up to the Reserve for six years—I figured I might as well be working for a part of the government I liked. I knew I didn't want to pull black-bag jobs for J. Edgar Hoover. I knew I couldn't become some mole for the CIA, getting us into a new Vietnam. The Secret Service had the only mission I could justify to myself. It kept dissenters like Robert Kennedy alive. Or it tried to. I figured that there had to be a next wave of candidates who'd pick up where Kennedy left off. Somebody would try to kill them. That was the new order of things.

"I don't want to make myself out to be a martyr. As much as anything I joined because I didn't see anything better to do with my life. I was also going through this thing in my head about my old girl friend. I think I wanted to show Barbara—and everybody else—that I was finished with my teenage rock 'n' roll fantasy. I was going to be 'a man' now.

"I told my parents I wanted to guard the president of the United States. At first they figured I'd completely gone off the deep end. My dad thought it was a scatterbrained idea. I'm not sure what his reasons were—other than that he thought it wasn't a stable job and that people who worked for the government were lazy.

"My mother said, 'You hated the Reserve. You're going to do this?'

"I'm sure she was worried about me getting hurt. But she'd worked for the government as a secretary in the Army, and she also had this adventurous streak."

"I had to feel proud," said Viola. "It was a very patriotic thing to want to do. At the same time, Marty was definitely the most, let's say, *eccentric,* of my sons. So when he told me, I was probably the most surprised person in the world."

# CHAPTER THREE

## *The Order of St. Jack*

"I was eating dinner with my family one night, bugging everybody out with my plan to protect the President, and Tom Kenyon—my brother Bud's father-in-law—mentioned that one of his best Army friends was an agent with the Treasury Department. Tom said he'd give him a call for me. So I went downtown and met Gene Overturf. Gene was this husky, balding guy in his forties who worked for the Bureau of Alcohol, Tobacco and Firearms. He'd won all kinds of medals in World War II, and in the Bureau he was known as a real cowboy. On busts, he was always the first guy through the door. But even Gene said, 'If I had to do it all again, I'd go into the Secret Service.' Problem was, when I was applying, the Service didn't have any openings. So Gene told me to start out in ATF—Alcohol, Tobacco and Firearms. He said, 'Build up your grade, then you'll make more money when you jump over to the Service.'

"So that's what I did. I passed the Treasury's basic law enforcement exam, and in November of '69 I started working in the ATF's St. Louis office. Mostly I worked on confiscating automatic weapons, sawed-off shotguns—illegal arms. I just watched and kept my mouth shut. Right away, I started having second thoughts about this brilliant idea of joining the government. I mean, the bureaucratic mind

29

can be truly mind-boggling. One time I was driving this older agent around and I flicked on the turn indicator while we were waiting at a busy intersection. This agent got all upset and told me, 'Turn off that damn indicator! Don't you know those things only have so many blinks in them?'

"I worked in St. Louis for a little over a year, picked up some training in bomb disposal in Chicago and then flew to Washington, D.C., to enroll in the Treasury Law Enforcement School. Along with agents from the IRS and the Customs Service, I learned how to get a search warrant, plan a raid, make an arrest, sketch a crime scene, testify in court."

His firing range scores earned him the highest marksmanship ranking of "Expert." After three months he graduated and flew out to the Los Angeles ATF office.

"The agents in L.A. didn't waste any time. They picked me up at LAX and I told them, 'I'm staying at the Sheraton.' But then they drove right past the hotel. I said, 'Hey!'

"One of the guys in the front seat turned around and said, 'Listen, we want you to help us on this nut job. It'll just take a few minutes.' The agent gave me a photo of this middle-aged guy with a beard and long greasy hair and said the guy was suspected of owning a machine gun.

"The agent in front said, 'Last time we talked to him, he said if we didn't stop fucking with him, he'd blow us away.' No big deal— they heard that all the time.

"So we got to this middle-class suburb. Tract houses with neat lawns. People were working in their gardens. The house we pulled up to, though, had peeling paint and a lawn that looked like it hadn't been cut in months. We got out of the car, and one of the agents said, 'Marty, why don't you hang out by that tree?' There was a real big tree on the front lawn. The other agents rang the door bell and a woman, this guy's wife, answered. She told the agents her husband wasn't home. Then she closed the door and the agents walked back to their car. A black and white squad car pulled up and the agents started talking with the cops. Then one of the agents looked like he saw something behind the house. So they jumped into the squad car and took off. They left me standing behind this tree.

"A few minutes passed, then I heard somebody in the backyard say, 'Come out with your hands up.' Then I heard gunfire.

"A woman screamed, 'I've been shot!'

"My first time in the line of duty, I pulled out my pistol. Now it was dead quiet, and I was thinking, Should I stay put or should I try to move around to the back? I looked down the street. The neighbors who'd been gardening were lying face down in their flower beds.

"Then suddenly, I saw the guy from the mug shot. He was peeking around the corner of the house. My finger started tensing around the trigger of my gun. But then the guy fell forward. He was handcuffed. Lucky thing I didn't kill him.

"What happened was this: When the agents looked into the backyard of the house, they saw a German shepherd sniffing around a big dollhouse and wagging his tail, like his master was inside. Sure enough, the guy was on all fours in there. The agents told him to come on out, but when they snapped the handcuffs on him, when the guy felt that cold metal on his wrists, he freaked and commanded his dog to kill. The dog started chewing up the agents, so they shot it. One of the bullets went through the dog's head and hit some gravel that sprayed up and cut the wife's leg. She wasn't shot but she was yelling her head off.

"After that we went inside the house. The guy had an altar draped with Nazi flags. The altar also had these different sized artillery shells, arranged like a cathedral pipe organ. In the bedroom he had a huge swastika flag for a bedspread. Oh yeah, bolted to the living room floor was a provocative piece of sculpture—a fifty-caliber machine gun."

All in all, the day made fine training for Marty. Interviewing would-be assassins was one of the Secret Service's regular activities. So it was useful for Marty to remember that when knocking at a survivalist stronghold, always cock your ears for growling noises: The standard right-wing nut kit comes complete with attack dog.

"My time in L.A. apparently qualified me for more trips to the lunatic fringe. I got sent out to Kansas City to try to infiltrate the White Citizens' Council—the people who were supposed to have put out the contract on Martin Luther King. The Bureau believed that the Council had an arsenal of machine guns and explosives. So I rented an apartment in Kansas City, and my bosses tried to figure out how a twenty-four-year-old guy like me could blend in with this paranoid clique of middle-aged little Hitlers with pot-bellies. I sat for months in that apartment, reading, watching TV and 'establishing my cover.' Finally the bosses gave up on the idea."

After a year and a half in the ATF, Marty was a strong candidate for the Secret Service. The Service could be choosy, since it got many more applications than it had openings. Quite a few applicants got ruled out just because their bodies didn't measure up. Candidates, who were between twenty-one and thirty-five years old, had to have twenty-forty vision, correctable to twenty-twenty. A good number of agents were former athletes, but applicants couldn't be so tall or so brawny that they couldn't slip gracefully in and out of limos. Martin Joseph Venker stood six feet, weighed 180 pounds, had fine vision, ample cardiac reserve, no varicose veins and no flat feet (he'd be doing some running). The agency's medical examiner declared him to be in good physical condition and he was emotionally stable.

* * *

"The Service puts you through its own series of interviews and exams—a lot of which test your powers of observation. I passed them and then I waited to see if the official background-checkers would find out about the time the cops booked me back in college. The Soul Seekers gave a house party where everybody got too loud and rowdy and that was the night the neighbors called the police. Everybody else was climbing out the windows of the house, so it was up to me to welcome the cops to the party. Anyway, the Service never did turn up the arrest, and I was accepted for training as a Special Agent. I got lucky."

Marty's ATF record spoke well of him. But his background didn't exactly start him on the fast track. Quite a few of the protection candidates had law and graduate degrees. The star agents were often Ivy Leaguers, frat presidents, dreamy quarterbacks who might've turned pro. That dashing executive-type whose Brooks Brothers suit didn't pinch at the shoulders, who spoke well, with a deep, assured mid-Atlantic accent—*he* was the man who made it to the White House, the one who radiated class as he toured the world paving the way for the President of the United States.

Of course the Service also hired guys who were more like your burly "let's-move-it!" city cop. These guys went through the protection training, too. And then, like almost all new agents, they got shipped out to the field offices (of which there were sixty-two in 1971). The field office boys guarded the candidates during campaign years and they helped out the White House detail when the President passed through town. Mostly, though, they did criminal investigation and intelligence work. They kept tabs on the crackpots and the radical groups that the Service deemed dangerous to the President. They also chased down counterfeiters who printed money and forged government checks and bonds, and commercial credit cards. Capturing phony greenbacks was the reason the Treasury minted the Secret

Service back in 1865—three months after the murder of Abraham Lincoln. Busting counterfeiters was still the Service's most consistently treacherous job.

A lot of the "street guys," as the field office agents proudly called themselves, wouldn't trade their jobs. They liked the steadier hours. And after working undercover in slums, they crowed that they were the toughest bastards in the Secret Service. Yet the street guys also knew that the White House agents rode the Secret Service showboat. When Air Force One flew into town, the street guys were supposed to drop everything and take orders from those Washington mannequins, who had probably never kicked down a door in their lives. A street guy could really burn watching those glamour boys just basking in that TV camera light. Secretly, that door-stomping field office joe could be nagged by the thought that somewhere along the line some East Coast bigwig decided that a guy who butted heads with wiseguys didn't have the polish to stand outside the Oval Office. Under their breath, the street guys could get nasty. They'd call the White House detail "the blow-dried protection faggots."

Of course, with the passage of time, the Service Secret affirmed equal opportunity: The East Coast bigwigs came to promote not only women and minorities but also that burly, burping street guy. Today, agents who once might have been considered overly coarse are working at 1600 Pennsylvania Avenue—thanks partly to the rise of some California field office agents who made themselves indispensable to Ronald Reagan.

But back when Marty joined, the distinctions between prince and prole were more rigid. And, after he was given the once over, it seemed as if Marty could be at home in either role. He had that taut, handsome face that looked good on TV. He was articulate and reflective. But coming out of the underside of St. Louis, he also had the street-wise, knock-around attitude of the lug who bounced around the field offices. With Marty, there was no telling when something—anything—would strike him as complete bullshit. And so, he was a self-contradiction from the onset.

"I flew to Washington, D.C., in the fall of 1971 and checked into the Park Central Residence Hotel near the White House. I started six weeks of classroom training. During the day I'd listen to lectures in state and federal law, in fire fighting, in atomic, biological and chemical warfare, and so on. They taught us 'ten-minute medicine'— how to keep anybody alive for ten more minutes. Special attention was given to stanching bullet wounds.

"They showed us the Technical Security Division, which is sort of like the Service's version of 'Q' in the James Bond novels. The Tech people come up with all this state-of-the-art equipment for sniffing out bombs and bugs and scrambling phone calls. Whenever DuPont or somebody comes up with something like the bullet-proof fabric Kevlar, Technical gets it first. They've tried out bullet-proof clip boards and attaché cases—the idea being that agents would hold them up near the President's head to cut down on the line of fire. The Tech people also keep trying to refine a metal detector that can find a gun by shooting a beam into a crowd.

"We'd learn about diplomatic protocol—how to stay cool around power mongers who had some of the thinnest skin in the world. How to cool them down. We studied crowd phenomena. We learned about 'the mind of the mob,' and I don't mean the Mafia. You learn how to guess what a crowd will do next, how to gauge the crowd's boiling point—when you can calm the people down and when it's time to *get out of there.* The instructors always emphasized the intellectual solution to a problem. If somebody in a crowd acted up, you were always supposed to make the move that attracted the least attention. Arrests and brute force, all that was for the police to handle.

"We got a crash course in psychology. We'd go over to St. Elizabeth's, the federal mental hospital in D.C., and the doctors would

give us tips on how to pick out the truly violent types from the ones
who were just crazy. We got this psychological profile that was
supposed to help us spot a would-be assassin. It was distilled from
the profiles of everybody from John Wilkes Booth to Sirhan Sirhan.
History's most famous failures—you got to know their miserable
lives by heart.

"At night came the strenuous stuff. We'd drive out to Beltsville,
Maryland, where the Service has its training center. It's concentrated
on about sixty acres and a bunch of one-story brick buildings. It
looks sort of like a junior college." (The Service talked in 1982 about
building replicas of the White House and Blair House out at Beltsville so that the agents' training maneuvers would be more realistic,
but the 1.6-million-dollar plan was eventually shot down.)

"We used to run through basketball-style plays for moving the
President through a crowd. It was called 'working the man.' One of
us would play the President and four others would form a diamond
around him. We'd pretend we were moving him through a hotel
lobby and out to his car. There'd be a crowd of other agents. Then
there'd be a mock-attack. Somebody would shout 'cover and evacu-
ate!' We'd all form a sort of wigwam around the 'President' and get
him inside his car.

"We learned a special blend of martial arts that the Service culled
from all over the world. The idea was to bring your attacker down
with the smallest effort and in the most discreet pain. We spent a lot
of time running around this make-believe city out there. It had a
freeway, an overpass, a shopping mall. We'd practice escape driving,
weaving through cones and skidding around on oil slicks. We'd
spend hours skipping on and off the running boards of moving limousines. You also had to get in and out of moving cars without running
boards. You had to use just the right steps or you'd find yourself
under the wheels. A lot of guys got hurt even in training.

"You'd learn to shoot the guns you were issued. Those included
an Israeli nine-millimeter Uzi submachine gun and a Remington .870

pump shotgun, modified for the Secret Service. Your basic weapon was a Smith and Wesson Model 19 .357-caliber pistol. I usually wore it on my left hip. I was a pretty good shot, but I always hated wearing a gun. It was a burden, physically and mentally. I never even liked guns when my father wanted to take me hunting. As far as I could see, the Service tried to weed out the gun nuts. The whole idea of the job was to prevent gunfire.

"For laughs, though, some of the agents would put a photo-target of another agent up on the firing range. The whole time you were out there you went through a sort of carnival funhouse of reaction tests. You'd stand in a pitch-black room with a pellet gun and watch a film that they'd project against white paper. On screen you'd see this cheering crowd, and then suddenly a guy with a gun would turn around and aim it at you. If the gunman pulled his trigger before you pulled yours, you were dead. If you fired first, your gunshot froze the movie and then you checked to see if your pellet hole was in the gunman or in some innocent bystander. We also used to walk and drive down a pretend city street called Hogan's Alley. There life-sized cardboard people popped out of windows and doors. They were programmed by computer and they could be a terrorist with a rifle or a lady with her baby. You'd have to think fast. Firing a pistol on foot wasn't so bad. But firing a shotgun inside a car—the reverberations could throw you off. The baby might lose an ear.

"We'd also watch films of real-life assassinations. Naturally, the featured attraction was the home movie Abraham Zapruder shot in Dallas on November 22, 1963. They showed you the gruesome version that the public usually didn't see, where parts of President Kennedy's brain sprayed all over Jackie. Again and again, I watched that film. The instructors didn't want us ever to forget it."

It was Kennedy's staff that had rejected the bubble-top cover that the Service had wanted to put over the President's Lincoln Continental—known as "the Queen Mary," or SS 100X. The politicos didn't want to insulate their candidate from the city whose votes they needed. John Kennedy, who wouldn't even wear hats, had vetoed the idea of agents riding on his limo's rear bumper—where one of them might've stopped a bullet. Less than a month before his murder, he'd said, "If anyone wants to do it, no amount of protection is enough. All a man needs is a willingness to trade his life for mine."

So, in a way, part of the blame for JFK's death rested with the man himself. And yet the night before the shooting, nine Secret Service agents had stayed out late, and some had been drinking. The Service had failed to check out the occupants of parade route buildings such as the Texas School Book Depository, where one Lee Harvey Oswald had worked. What's more, the Service's intelligence division was prehistoric. Records of threatmakers weren't kept in a computer, but on index cards.

Yes, agent Clint Hill had made a breathtaking leap to push Jackie back inside the limo just as it was racing off. Yet even the First Lady, though she came out of mourning to watch Hill (always her favorite agent) get his Treasury award, had reportedly fumed to friends about the agent who'd been at the wheel of the Presidential limo. The driver's reactions were so geriatric, Jackie allegedly told friends, that "he might as well have been Maud Shaw" (the Kennedy children's hoary nanny). If that agent had hit the gas before the third shot, she supposedly griped, Jack might still be alive.

Senator Ralph W. Yarborough, who'd ridden in Dallas in the VP limo, complained that the agents had reacted too slowly. After seeing a Secret Service man lying across the trunk of the President's car as it sped toward the hospital, Yarborough recalled that the agent "beat the back of the car with one hand, his face contorted by grief, anguish and despair."

There was no question about one thing: those had been dark days for the Service. There'd even been talk of disbanding the Secret Service and giving the job of protecting future Presidents to the FBI. The rival agency had been assembling a thick file on Oswald for months before the shooting; but those tightwads hadn't peeped a word about him to the Secret Service. Give the job to Hoover—that's the thanks the Service deserved after it'd checked out something like 2,500 death threats sent to Kennedy in 1963? After its agents had headed off loony Richard P. Pavlick, who'd planned on smashing his dynamite-loaded car into Kennedy's car? The agents—a lot of whom were Irish—had lived and breathed for "Lance" (JFK's code name). They'd helped him spirit his girls in and out of the White House, and they'd gotten him to Sunday mass on time. Lance's chief agent, James Rowley, used to take his vacation in Hyannisport, just so he could stay close to the Kennedy compound.

In the end, the Secret Service kept its job. But the Warren Commission Report branded the agency's procedures as "seriously deficient."

"We were told to read the Warren Report from cover to cover—all twenty-five volumes. Then, in 1979, the House Select Committee on Assassinations concluded that the Warren Commission hadn't probed the possibility of a conspiracy deeply enough, and that organized crime 'probably' plotted to have Kennedy killed. The committee said acoustical evidence showed a 'high probability' that a second gunman fired from the grassy knoll on the parade route. A Secret Service agent in the motorcade said he heard a shot from the knoll. So did a Dallas cop who ran to the knoll and there met a man who said he was a Secret Service agent and who quickly flashed a badge. Later, the Secret Service confirmed that no agent had been anywhere near the knoll.

"And yet three of the twelve members of the select committee dissented with its findings, and subsequent acoustical studies by the FBI and the National Academy of Sciences contradicted the second-gunman theory. At least in the case of the Kennedy assassination, I sided with the dissenters.

"I'm no conspiracy buff. Sometimes some guy in a bar would find

out I was with the Secret Service and he'd want to talk my ear off
about what *really* happened in Dallas. I'd say, 'Sorry, I have to run.'
The job was hard enough without the possibility that I was up against
the Mafia, or some rogue arm of my own government. But a little
time on the job taught me something: Random evil is a lot more
sinister than any conspiracy. People don't want to believe that some
desperate loner can just walk into a gun store, walk out and stop the
country. But he can. Oswald, Sirhan, most of the others—they were
losers who got lucky for once in their lives."

Jerry Parr, who joined the Service in 1963 and who headed the
White House detail under Carter and Reagan said, "Dallas kept us
alert. Every generation has an opportunity to have its ass tested
somewhere down the line. You can't transmit experience to another
generation. But it's important to pass the culture on—even knowing
that it won't fit the new age. Certain values need to be passed on."
    Of all the Secret Service catechism passed on since the ascension
of St. Jack, there was one inviolable article of faith: that no agent's
life weighed more than the sorrow that would crush the nation if the
Service ever lost another President.

"Years later I would see on posted announcements for jobs that
called for years of experience a reminder to the applicant that 'any
failure to properly and effectively perform his duties could have fatal
consequences. Mistakes, errors in judgment or inattention to duty
could cause acute embarrassment or inconvenience to the Principal
and reflect adversely on the Secret Service.'
    "To the Beltsville Instructors the vow the new agents took was one
of simple logic. Cops learn to crouch down in a shootout. But the
instructors would ask, 'What good does it do if you crouch? The
bullet goes over your head and hits *him!*' So the idea was to stand
up straight, make yourself a bigger target—do anything possible to
distract the shooter. That was fine with me. I wanted to safeguard

the electoral process. That sounds highfalutin'. But I think most people are looking for a strong commitment to something. I wanted to have some purpose to my life, other than making money and having a new car. Somebody kills a President or a candidate—it affects lives you'll never know about. It instantly changes the course of history. It's the saddest sign of chaos in a country that we keep hoping, someday, will be a real democracy. Also, I have to admit that if it wasn't that serious a sacrifice, if the stakes weren't that high, I probably wouldn't have gotten interested in it.

"Once I was accepted, I reported to a doctor who injected warm plastic into my ear, forming a mold. A few days later, I was given my first earphone. It had a wire that ran down to a radio 'transceiver' on my belt; another wire ran from there to a flesh-colored mike on my wrist. I was tuned to the same frequency as the other agents— strong young men with hearing aids. Eventually we hardly needed the earphones, so unified were we in our thoughts.

"After almost a year of training, I packed my earphone and pistol and headed for the field office in Springfield, Illinois, where senior agents would observe me. At about the same time, though, I heard that Gene Overturf, the St. Louis Treasury agent who'd encouraged me to join the Secret Service, had committed suicide. He'd been having problems. He'd get drunk at parties and hold a gun to his head or stand out on a balcony like he was going to jump. He was an underdog who became a big wheel. I think he hired me because he thought I was a lot like him . . ."

# CHAPTER FOUR

# The Stern Mask and the Simpering Grin

"I'D only been reporting to my first field office for a couple of months when I got sent out onto the campaign trail. Four years had passed since the last election, which had motivated me into a suit. Nineteen seventy-two was going to be the first year the Secret Service would guard *all* Presidential candidates right out of the starting gate. We were ready for the worst. Watching them pack smoke grenades and gas masks, hearing them discuss which hospitals could best handle bullet wounds, I thought, it's like we're planning for war.

"It'd been bad enough in '68, when the agents had stood their ground at the Chicago Democratic Convention—holding off battalions of Yippies who flipped them the bird and whipped tennis balls studded with nails. But since sixty-eight the ranks of Americans fed up with the Vietnam War had grown. In 1970, rocks thrown by antiwar protesters in San Jose, California, had left ten dents in the limousine of the President. Now dissidents were stitching together new effigies of The Man, to burn for 'News at Eleven.' Our Intelligence Division was getting word that the college whiz kids were wiring smarter bombs. Who knew what to expect? America was beginning to look like a tropical nation of juntas and coups where the victorious candidate was the one who survived till voting day.

* * *

"I would ride in a motorcade's follow-up car. Just behind me would be the war wagon, a suburban family car that carried the heavier firepower; ammo taped to the ceiling and an Uzi-armed agent peering out the rear window.

"On a typical morning you'd be shivering in Madison, Wisconsin. There'd be snow on the streets. Four cities later, you'd be in Beaumont, Texas. Your wool suit would feel like a cooking pouch. Over on one side you'd have the hippies shouting, 'Out of Vietnam!' On the other side you'd have the guys in workshirts yelling, 'Stand up for America!' They all sounded like they were screaming at us.

"Then the candidate's limo would put on the brakes and the shift leader would radio, 'Arrive, arrive.' The candidate would jump out. Then I'd turn around to hold back some photographers and *boom!*— fifteen camera strobes would explode in my face. All those little dots of light would start bouncing in front of my eyes like ping-pong balls.

"The shift leader would radio, 'Let's get him inside.' But the candidate would be dawdling. He was there to press some flesh . . . to make the news. Off he'd wander, down the ropeline, grinning, winking, bending down to take a bite of somebody's hotdog, closing his eyes to inflict a kiss.

"I'd catch up with him. I'd move ahead on the ropeline, keeping my eyes low, watching the hands. You'd always keep your jacket open, ready to draw. You'd always be waiting for your earphone to blurt out, *'Gun left'* or *'Gun right!'* An agent at my side would be ready with an Uzi in a briefcase. I might lift up my eyes. For a second I might glance up at the glowering windows of the hotel, where one busboy might be making the most of his coffee break by squinting through the cross-hairs of a hunting rifle. That's when it would happen—when you were looking someplace else. Suddenly an arm would appear, there'd be a flash of metal and a goofball teenager would jab a pen knife into the belly of a donkey or an elephant emblazoned on a star-spangled balloon. Our hearts would go pop.

"You started to view crowds like excitable animals. They could stampede at any moment. You never knew what would spook them. People act differently together than they do as individuals. They flip out all the time. They don't realize they're claustrophobic till they feel their feet getting lifted off the ground. The crowd starts to carry them off, and they know that if they ever fell down they'd never get up.

"You'd see people at their worst in crowds. Crippled people in wheelchairs get pushed up to the ropeline so they can see. But then the candidate finally shows up and the crowd doesn't care about crippled people. I'd find paraplegics getting strangled by the rope. I'd try to untangle them and the people behind them would just keep shoving. I'd get pissed off and shove them back.

"You tried to avoid losing your cool like that. For one thing, you get distracted. For another thing, you attract attention to yourself."

Marty's goal was to float through the human marsh, camouflaged in gray, sweeping for "mines." He knew what they might look like. He'd reviewed photos of the active threat-makers, the "look outs" whom the field office agents had interviewed, or tried to.

"Mostly you relied on your sense of human character. You learn to look for the face that doesn't belong. The guy who's nervous and perspiring when most people around him are having a good time. The guy who's grinning at some solemn event like a memorial service. You can usually tell when someone's having a psychotic episode. When I thought somebody came off as suspicious, I'd walk right up to him and start talking, real casual. 'Howya doin'?' Or I'd jostle them and say, 'Oh, sorry.' I'd have frisked them. I'd stand on the candidate's receiving line, watching the eyes of the people coming by, checking to see if they had their hands in their pockets or their purse. If we saw a guy make a sudden move we'd grab him by the elbow and escort him to another room. Ask him some questions.

Maybe he was just pulling out his camera. All you could do is say you were sorry."

Counterfeiting agents could show off the bushels of phony bills they'd captured. Customs agents could pose for a picture next to their latest haul of cocaine. But the protection agents could only take pride in nonevents—"uncelebrated victories." Who knew on any given day how close a candidate came to dying? How many times had his plane disappeared into the sky, leaving behind a cranky gunman who'd chickened out after getting "looked off" by a Secret Service agent?

The *look,* the fierce stony face—that was an agent's essential helmet. Sunglasses helped. With his shades on, an agent could give a dozen people the feeling he was staring them dead on. The shades also stoppered any tenderness or confusion that might leak out of an agent's eyes.

"I didn't wear sunglasses as much as some agents. I wanted people to see my eyes. You tried to put out every signal you could to say, 'Don't mess with me. I'm ready for you.' You'd conjure up your own fantasy of someone who'd intimidate *you.* Someone more frightening, more cold, more high-tech than a cop. A gray-suited cyborg, who had executive privilege to shoot to kill. Fact was, the Secret Service hadn't returned fire since those two Puerto Rican nationalists tried to kill Harry Truman in 1950. But that's why the *look* was so important. People had to imagine you had some laser-beam belt buckle—some hidden power.

The face, White House detail leader Jerry Parr explained, "is not taught. The agents imitate each other. It's a cultural thing, and I'm not sure it will ever change. There's a strain in knowing someone out there might do you in, and it keeps you very serious. The agents get very, very hyper looking for those eyes that are glittering with hatred. Terrorism and counterterrorism become mirror images of each other."

"Sometimes we had to take off those masks or we'd all go nuts," Marty remembers, "We had this running gag. I'd turn to the other guys in the follow-up car and say, 'Again, what is our official response to an assassination attempt?' The other guys would throw up their hands like ninnies and scream, *'Hoooooly shit!'*

Since 1902, nineteen members of the Secret Service have died in the line of duty. The Service lost eight of those people since 1972. The odds of dying were improving. But dread of death or injury may be the Service's best-kept secret.

"As long as I was on the job I never heard anybody—and that includes me—say he was afraid of anything. The truth is, I don't think we trusted each other—at least in terms of confiding fear. It's a competitive job, and traditionally the agent who gets promoted is the square-jawed, silent type.

"Of course there were times when I felt like a moving target. But you just had to assume, 'Hey, it won't happen to me.' You couldn't get morbid, or you'd be paralyzed. I wondered, and I'm sure every agent wondered, if when the time came to take the bullet I'd go through with it. But you know, heroism and self-preservation don't always conflict with each other. If some nut pulls a gun, shrinking away from it is what'll get you killed. You only have one chance to dive on it before it goes off. Later, if you're still alive, you can shiver and say, *'Hooooooly shit!'*

"Which is what we were saying in May of '72. We were only halfway into the campaign when George Wallace got shot. I'd been guarding him just a few weeks before. When I saw that TV footage of Arthur Bremer, I said, 'It's that *guy!*' I'd spotted him before at a Wallace rally. Really strange-looking guy. You know, he had that red, white and blue outfit on, the silver sunglasses, that simpering grin. He was covered with more buttons than even an honest enthusiast would wear."

A few days before he planted a bullet in the Alabama governor's spine, Arthur Herman Bremer, a lovelorn oddjob man from Milwaukee, had written in his diary:

> It bothers me that there are about 30 guys in prison now who threatened the Pres & we never heard a thing about 'em. Except that they're in prison.
> Maybe what they need is organization. "Make the First Lady a Widow, Inc." "Chicken in Every Pot and Bullet in Every Head, Com., Inc."
> They'll hold a national convention every 4 years to pick the exacutioner. [sic]

Bremer had started out stalking Nixon. The twenty-one-year-old drifter had looked forward to the performance he would give the Secret Service after he'd plugged the President. "I was concerned with my appearance & composure after the bang bangs," wrote Bremer, who imagined he was the son of actress Donna Reed. "I wanted to shock the shit out of the SS men with my calmness." But after seeing Nixon six times without getting close to him, Bremer grew frustrated with the "overly beefed-up security" brought on by the "radical commies" who protested Nixon. More and more impatient, he thought about emptying his .38-caliber revolver into some Secret Service agents. He wanted "SOMETHING to show for all my effort." When he finally did open fire, one of his bullets tore through the throat of agent Nick Zarvos, blasting open his larynx and settling into his left jaw. Zarvos eventually came back to work.

But like the cripples Marty had untangled along the ropelines, George Wallace would watch future rallies from a wheelchair. In the 1968 campaign Wallace had boasted that he received more death threats than any other candidate. Again, in 1972 he'd traveled with a retinue of Alabama state troopers and a three-sided steel rostrum that gave him chest-high protection.

On May 15, he chose to take off his bulletproof vest because the day was a scorcher. He'd decided to give forth at a shopping mall in Laurel, Maryland, even though the Secret Service had warned him against speaking at shopping malls. Wallace hadn't listened. At least the agents had kept Nixon clear of Bremer. But that was cold comfort. Once again, the Secret Service hadn't been able to keep the executioner from voting.

# CHAPTER FIVE

## Taken in by Appearances

"CALL it hindsight, but I felt I'd been on the money about Bremer. I'd spotted a killer in the crowd. No question about it now—they *were* out there. The day after the Wallace shooting newspapers around the country carried a photo of me escorting a 'grim-faced' George McGovern out of Detroit. I also looked grim, with reason. Bremer's first infatuation, it turned out, had been with McGovern."

Yet even as the Bremer attack molded the fierce Secret Service mask to Marty's face, Marty found himself guarding men whose candidacies tempted him to laugh.

"Baby doctor Benjamin Spock was running against the war. I'd been reared with the help of Spock's book, and was all for the doctor's cause. But even Spock admitted that basically he was running as a PR gimmick, to get the press to show up at his speeches. The pediatrician had tiny hope of snatching the Democratic nomination. But how could the Secret Service risk the chance that some unloved former child might slay Dr. Spock? We were his sitters.

"Then there was Congressman John G. Schmitz, known as 'the Bob Hope of the ultra-right,' though his lip hair made him look more like Wayne Newton. Schmitz's district included San Clemente, California—meaning that, officially, Schmitz was President Nixon's representative. But Schmitz, who'd been a fighter pilot in the Marines and one of their classroom instructors on the Communist system, never forgave the 'fumbling, bumbling' Nixon for going to China. At 'Schmitz for President' rallies in high school gyms, I would stand around while Schmitz, running on the American Independent Party ticket, did his shtik for right-thinking citizens.

" 'The Democrats and the Republicans are just two wings of totalitarian socialism,' Schmitz would say. 'America has the choice between Richard Nixon, the candidate endorsed by Moscow and Peking, or George McGovern, the candidate endorsed by Hanoi and the Manson family.' Schmitz, who also said, 'It takes courage to run with a German name and a moustache,' hoped to scoop up the voters who'd backed George Wallace. A longtime John Bircher, Schmitz told all who'd listen that the attack on Wallace came out of a Communist conspiracy and that Washington was withholding evidence that would prove that antiwar activists in Milwaukee trained Arthur Bremer.

"Schmitz would take his bows, and then we'd escort him to his car. Schmitz would be on the road with some agents and he'd ask them to pull over at a liquor store. He'd go in and buy a cold case of beer. His agents would toss it in the trunk and then Schmitz would plop back into the car and pop open a frosty one. He used to sit back there smoking a stogie and just grooving on the idea that he had his own private police force. We had to scope out the men's room everytime he wanted to take a leak. I'd be in the front seat of his car and he'd call up to us with his campaign slogan: *'When you're out of Schmitz, you're out of gear!'* Burp. I'd just shake my head and think, what a waste of the taxpayer's money. The only legitimacy some of these jokers have is us. Most of these candidates had never run a national campaign before. We'd practically end up working on the candidate's staff—smoothing out his travel plans, keeping him on time. And, of course, giving him that Presidential aura."

Marty didn't know how complicated casting *just the right* Secret Service agents would get in future election pageants. When George Bush campaigned in the 1980 Iowa caucus, he asked to waive Secret Service protection. He didn't want to look like a big shot. He wanted "to roll up his sleeves and talk with the people." Eventually, though, Bush accepted protection. Bush's campaign managers thought he looked good with agents. But when the time came for Bush to shoot some TV ads, his managers decided that his real agents weren't tall enough to make Bush look sufficiently Presidential. So the media wizards suited up a detail of hunk actors.

Granted, some of the field office agents weren't everybody's pinup of the Secret Service man. Some of the men sported brown polyester blazers, patterned shirts and fat houndstooth ties. But the Service did have agents who were real clothes horses—all day long, straightening their ties, touching up their hair, adjusting their sunglasses. The slickest of them would come to earth on "Angel" (Air Force One) when Nixon decided it was once again time to listen to the Silent Majority in his beloved city of Peoria, Illinois, just north of Marty's old Springfield office. All week long the papers in Peoria would run pictures of Secret Service advance agents laying the groundwork for the royal circus from "Crown" (the White House). Finally, the big day would come. "Angel" would touch down. "Stagecoach" (the President's limo) would rumble out of its cargo plane. The White House agents would pile into their War Wagon. They'd gallop onto their customized limos with the gleaming running boards. The air would ring with the metallic snap of handcuffs and wedding bands smacking against limo hand bars. And then, flanked by a squadron of local motorcycle cops, the agents would cruise into town, striking all these dramatic, romantic poses as the citizens of the heartland stood bedazzled.

However, even as Marty avidly performed in the chorus behind the White House's stars, he couldn't help but wonder if little redundancies crept into the theatrics.

"When we'd stop to catch our breath. I'd ask another agent, 'Why are we running alongside armored limousines?' The guy would look at me like I was off my rocker. But I said, 'Come on, don't tell me some of this shit we do isn't PR. We're supporting actors.' Which didn't mean I didn't like it. I was completely susceptible to the mystique of the White House agents. Their demeanor, their diplomacy, everything about them was different from the field office agents. I'd study a guy like Bob Taylor, the head of the White House detail. Real handsome guy—an agent's agent. A reception hall would be buzzing with politicians and campaign contributors, and Taylor would come through a set of double doors. He'd close the doors behind him and everybody would quiet down. Taylor would double-check the eyes of the agents all around the room. He'd wait for each agent to give him a nod, and then, only then, would he turn on his heel and snap down that door handle and present . . . *the President of the United States.*

"At our best, when we were operating as a team, the Secret Service was a thing of beauty. I was really proud of the way the Service disdained brute force, and the way it impressed upon agents the idea of freedom of speech, the right of all people to protest their grievances. Particularly after I saw what other law enforcement agencies were like. You'd be in some town where a demonstration would be heating up and you could see the local cops were just itching for some action. Hippies would be carrying signs that showed Nixon with bloody fangs. They'd have placards with swastika skulls that said,

'Re-elect the President.' I'd tell the cops that the protesters could hold the signs, just so long as they didn't have sticks that they might use as javelins. Some of those cops would look real disappointed. So later on, I'd see some cop tearing a sign without any stick away from some demonstrator. I'd run over and say to the cop, 'Hold up! Cut it out!'

"The cop would say, 'But a Secret Service agent told me to do it.'

"I'd ask, 'Who? Which Secret Service agent? Point him out.'

"The cop would start searching through the crowd, telling me, 'The guy had a radio and a lapel pin.' Finally, the cop'd find the guy. The guy did have a lapel pin—only he turned out to be one of Nixon's staff people. Your Jeb Magruder type.

"You could show cops the difference between lapel pins, but they still had their own power to 'maintain the peace.' I'd see them twisting the arms of protesters, shoving them into police vans. I'd think back on that summer I had marched at Berkeley, and the time I'd worked undercover in Kansas City. Back when I was waiting around to infiltrate the White Citizens' Council the office had me work some Nixon event. I was supposed to put on my jeans and pretend I was a demonstrator. So I was in a crowd of demonstrators and the cops told us to 'move it.' We started to, but the cops said we weren't moving fast enough. Fuckers started hitting us with nightsticks, knocking us down. I'm lying there on the ground wondering, which side am I on here?

"I kept that to myself. But, politically, my heart was with the left-wingers. Even when I was in a suit, I'd sort of hope for peaceful demonstrations. I liked watching Presidents get tested. A little screaming, name-calling, dramatic tension—that's America to me. I'll take a semi-unruly mob to a dinner of fat cat Republicans any day.

"Of course that wasn't exactly a widely held view in the Secret Service. A few of the other young agents thought like I did. Some of the older agents, too—you know, your lunchpail Democrats who remembered JFK—they'd cuss out Nixon if you got them alone."

But law and order were the guiding principles of most agents. "Like most law officers Marty knew," agent Chuck Rochner said, "agents tend to drift toward conservatism—just from what they're exposed to."

Jerry Parr, who'd been around since 1963, points out, "The Service has made strides in hiring Hispanics, blacks, and women. But it still tends to be a real conservative organization. There were some big struggles during the war years, with the so-called long-haired hippies."

"A lot of protesters probably saw me as some goose-stepping automaton," says Marty. "And hell, I did feel like a robot, with that wire coming out of my head. But what could I do? If the antiwar people didn't know why I got into this job, I couldn't worry about it. I knew where I was coming from. Fact is, I sort of laughed to myself when I saw the hippies sneer at me like the hard-hats sneered at them. I've always been fascinated with the way people get taken in by appearances.

"I know a lot of reporters and protesters thought we were bullies and goons and flunkies. But I made friends with quite a few reporters. After all, they all want you to tell them something. Which is why you had to be careful. They're paid to snitch. They complain if you don't let them in someplace, and then if you do, you see a story about 'lax security' in the paper the next day.

In his *Fear and Loathing on the Campaign Trail '72,* gonzo journalist Hunter S. Thompson reported that he'd once walked into the dining room of Chicago's Sheraton-Schroeder Hotel and spotting McGovern's political director Frank Mankiewicz, had rushed toward him—to have a word. Suddenly, Thompson saw four Secret Service men shift into the "Deadly Pounce position":

> [The] four thugs with wires in their ears were so alarmed at my high-speed appearance that they were about to beat me into a coma on pure instinct, and ask questions later. . . . I was not accustomed to working in a situation where any sudden move around a candidate could mean a broken arm. Their orders are to protect the candidate, period, and they are trained like high-strung guard dogs to react with Total Force at the first sign of danger. Never hesitate. First crack the wrist, then go for the floating rib . . . and if the "assassin" turns out to be just an oddly dressed journalist—well, that's what the SS boys call "tough titty" . . . everybody is a suspect.

"Thompson's got a gift for comic exaggeration, but he's right—everybody *was* a suspect. Especially 'oddly dressed' people who raced into rooms. There were times when I had to plow people over, throw a body block. You regret it, but you wind up in situations where you're one person against a herd of people. I don't think agents were out to crack ribs. The art was in how we could get through a crowd using subtle nods, visual signals."

During the '72 campaign, demonstrators complained of Secret Service abuse at Nixon rallies in Pekin, Illinois, and Nashua, New Hampshire. Protesters in Charlotte, North Carolina, sued eleven Secret Service agents, charging that the agents had illegally barred them from a Billy Graham rally attended by Nixon. The plaintiffs, who asked for one million dollars in damages, said that even though they'd held tickets to the 1971 rally at the Charlotte Coliseum, they'd been thrown out and told that their tickets were counterfeit.

In his initial hearing of their complaint, U.S. District Court Judge James B. McMillan said the eighteen plaintiffs had indeed been

"abused, manhandled and excluded . . . without apparent just cause"
in a "wholesale assault on [their] civil rights and liberties." He told
the Secret Service to lay off nonviolent dissenters. Then, two years
after the judge said that, he dismissed the agents as defendants. The
agents had explained in court that White House staffers asked the
Secret Service to keep Nixon-baiters out of the rally, but that the
agents refused. Four years after the rally, the court convicted White
House Chief of Staff H.R. Haldeman of planning the whole thing.

All through 1972, the Secret Service fought off Haldeman's efforts
to turn its agents into Nixon's image-police. The White House staff
asked to listen in on Secret Service radio messages. Agents told them
to get lost. Before a rally in Cleveland, White House advance men—
the "roadrunners"—asked the Service to turn away protesters.
When the agents told them no, the Nixon staff did it themselves,
setting up two "checkpoint" chutes—one that funneled Nixon
Youth types into the rally and another that flushed the long hairs
into the parking lot. The protesters sued; charges against the Secret
Service agents were dismissed.

"A lot of the agents might have been conservative in their personal
views but they knew the Service had to stay above politics. Even
among each other, agents didn't usually talk about politics, except
to goof on politicians. We all saw what went on backstage. One party
was as shifty and as inept as the other. You can't be distracted by
politics. When Sirhan Sirhan opened fire, Bobby Kennedy had some
big athletic guys standing right there. But they were caught off-guard
because they were Bobby's supporters—they were caught up in the
happiness of him winning the California Primary.

"You have to stay detached. The Secret Service has been in the
White House a lot longer than any of the guys who've moved in there
for a while. The Service isn't going to see itself get screwed in
anybody's four-year experiment. They have support on Capitol Hill
and they can go to the press. That's why the relationship with the

President is so tense. He and his men aren't sure how far they can push the Service. When a new President arrives, the Service lays out how it'd like to keep the guy alive. But the agents can only make recommendations which the President can ignore. For a while the President's staff may be cooperative. But then they start getting cocky. They want to get their man more exposure, put him in the best possible light. Like JFK's staff—they didn't want any bubble top on his car. It'd block the view of the candidate."

Nobody played politics with the Secret Service like Nixon's staff. Nixon hadn't been in office long when his aides began to cast a suspicious eye on Rufus Youngblood, who had thrown himself over LBJ the day Oswald opened fire. LBJ called Youngblood's move "as brave an act as I have ever seen anyone perform," and the Secret Service made Youngblood its deputy director. Such notoriety was enough for the Nixon staff to peg Youngblood as "a Johnson man," even though the agent had served six years under Eisenhower.

"Nixon aides suggested quietly to the Secret Service that [Youngblood] be moved out of the White House," reported Jack Anderson in October, 1971. "He was given a desk across the street at Secret Service headquarters. Thereafter, he was subjected to petty harassment until he quietly resigned last June after reaching eligibility for his twenty-year pension. At 48, he was at the peak of his career."

The agents found Haldeman's fingerprints on most of these machinations. He'd walk right up to agents and dare to tamper with The Face—their protective mask.

"Haldeman would say, 'I think you should start smiling more.' He'd say, 'Do you realize when I'm talking to you, I am the President?' The ballsier agents would tell him to get lost. The agents used to joke that if anybody ever started shooting at the President, Haldeman better duck because a Secret Service bullet might find him.

"I loved seeing Henry Kissinger bust Haldeman's chops. One time Nixon's entourage was walking from their cars into a hotel. And being the supreme ass-kisser that he was, Haldeman was lugging in Nixon's bags. So Kissinger was walking past him when he stopped, and looking at Haldeman loaded down with suitcases and dripping with sweat, said in that imperious German accent, "Haldeman, you look like a bell hop."

But there were times when Nixon called upon the Secret Service to do his personal bidding and the agency had hopped to it. During his second term, Nixon admitted that the Service had bugged the phone of his brother, Donald, and had assigned agents to shadow his younger sibling. The White House said the wiretapping and surveillance were "related to the protective functions" of the Service. But the Service has no authority to protect a President's brother, who himself said that he'd never been explicitly told about the bugging. Nixon eventually admitted that he'd been worried about his brother's financial dealings with a free-wheeling Howard Hughes lieutenant who'd been indicted for tax evasion. The President had wanted to keep an eye on Donald, lest he embarrass the White House.

The Secret Service also snapped to when Nixon asked for protection for former Vice President Spiro T. Agnew. For four months after Agnew pleaded no contest to income tax evasion, twenty-one agents continued to guard him, at a cost of more than $100,000. Agnew and his guards were spending a sunny weekend at Frank Sinatra's Palm Springs estate when the General Accounting Office announced that protecting the out-of-work VP was a violation of the law. The Controller General ordered funds for Agnew's protection cut. Nevertheless, the Service said it would only comply if Nixon cancelled his request. Not eager for another fight, Nixon did. "It is revolting that a penny of public funds should be spent on this impenitent felon as he lives the high life," Anthony Lewis wrote of Agnew.

. . . [How] can we wonder that Americans are cynical about their political system?"

The '72 campaign saw the Secret Service keeping a long, long "potential assassins" list that picked up where Nixon's "enemies list" left off. National Archive documents show that the Service had as many as a million names in its "threat" file in 1963. That figure, however, was misleading in that back then every person who either dined at the White House, obtained a press pass or was introduced to the President on a trip ended up in a central file. By 1969, the Secret Service had become a little more discriminating. That year the agency issued some "liaison guidelines" regarding intelligence to local police, the FBI and the CIA. The Service said it wanted to know about any efforts to "embarrass" high officials, about any people who made "irrational" and "abusive" remarks about those officials, about any people seeking "redress of imaginary grievances," and about all "anti-American and anti-U.S. Government demonstrations." Even with those guidelines, though, the threat file was still estimated to contain between 100,000 and 180,000 names.

The Service kept its eye on right-wing factions like the John Birch Society and the National Youth Alliance. But it spied most on would-be trouble-makers on the left. If you opposed the Vietnam war, or happened to be black, you stood excellent chances of making the Secret Service's list. Among the unlikely assassins whom the agency kept CO-2 (Central Office) dossiers on were Muhammad Ali, Joe Louis, Harry Belafonte, Cesar Chavez, Joan Baez, Jane Fonda, Tom Hayden, Tony Randall, Carl Reiner, and Groucho Marx. The CIA provided the Secret Service with lots of steamy rumors about singer Eartha Kitt's Parisian love life. The Service had begun to investigate Kitt after she embarrassed Lady Bird Johnson by asking blunt questions about the Vietnam war at a White House luncheon.

Individual files explained why certain people might be dangerous or "disruptive to the protectees": Marlon Brando had "made statements sympathetic to black militant causes." Dick Gregory "often speaks critically of the protectees and Administration but refrains from making threatening statements." Father James Groppi had been seen "demonstrating against welfare cuts" and "in front of a building where VP was speaking."

Baseball great Jackie Robinson was deemed "not dangerous" but still of "protective interest" because he was part of a group that approached a White House gate to ask about the President's black capitalism program. The agency kept a separate "black nationalist" list of 5,500 names, which included leaders Ralph Abernathy, Roy Innis, and Roy Wilkins. And even though a federal study of assassination attempts showed that the assailants were almost always loners—not joiners—the Service watched more than four hundred organizations, from the NAACP and the Southern Christian Leadership Conference to the Gay Liberation Front and the Chinese Hand Laundry Alliance.

Any critical letter sent to the President apparently started a file. Pickets in front of his house provoked the Visual Intelligence Branch to snap pictures of the sign-carriers. The Secret Service itself didn't always seem sure why it listed a group. The National Welfare Rights Organization, for instance, had a file listing, "Interest in Protectees—None." Nixon himself was a Quaker; still, the pacifist Quaker Action Group needed watching, evidently because it was "opposed to war and the use of nuclear weapons." At least the Service had an easy time keeping tabs on one potential threat. Its own agents were protecting Dr. Benjamin Spock.

On every front, the Service faced charges that it was becoming the genuflecting palace guard of the imperial President. Secret Service director, James J. Rowley, had to explain to Congress why Nixon's two vacation homes needed 1.9 million dollars in "security improvements" that included an ice-making machine, a new furnace, a swimming pool cleaning machine and more than a $100,000 worth of landscaping.

Rowley testified that the Service had decided Nixon's old heating system at the Western White House in San Clemente (code name "Storm King") was a fire hazard and that the grounds needed land-scaping to camouflage electronic intruder-detectors. The Service had gone along with Nixon's aides and cronies on other spending. The agency scrapped its original design for a fence running around Nixon's Key Biscayne house after his pal Bebe Rebozo insisted that the President wanted a "conventional" fence—like the one that en-circled the White House. The White House-style fence cost an extra $20,000, but you couldn't really tell because the Service concealed it behind a "security hedge." The Service also said that neither Nixon nor his people had mentioned that a wall built around his San Clemente house also enclosed property that Nixon planned to sell to private buyers.

But the worst splotch on the Secret Service's vaunted apolitical independence came when it had to admit that an agent guarding George McGovern had passed confidential info to the White House. The agent, James C. Bolton Jr., told his father, who was an aide to Republican Congressman Glenn Davis, that McGovern had met with an alleged "subversive" one weekend in Massachusetts. It wasn't true. But Bolton's father leaked the story to the White House, where a staffer circulated a memo saying that the agent "has promised to keep his dad informed of these and other kinds of activities."

In August of 1973, the Service announced that Bolton Jr. had resigned. The Watergate inquiry dredged up charges that the private schedules of other Democratic candidates had passed from agents to the White House. CBS News reported that the Secret Service was looking into claims that one of its top officers also shoveled dirt about McGovern into the ears of Nixon's people. It was said that back in 1968 an agent had kept Lyndon Johnson apprised of Nixon's move-ments. The Service said it could find no evidence supporting these other charges.

By 1976, the Service reported that it had winnowed its watch list down to 39,000 names.

"When I heard about the original list and the other revelations, it really ticked me off. I understood that after the Kennedy assassination, the agency probably thought it was better to have too many names on its list than too little. I knew that it was the FBI that dished up the names of the so-called subversives. But keeping all those ridiculous FBI names just made the Service a party to Hoover's witch hunt—COINTELPRO and the rest. I think Secret Service agents knew that it wasn't the guy opposed to Vietnam that we had to worry about. It was the guy who thought Nixon was an agent of the Kremlin.

"I think most agents were upset by the leak from McGovern's campaign. It made us all look bad. The other places where headquarters caved into Nixon—bugging his brother, guarding Agnew, obeying Bebe Rebozo—all of that hurt the morale of the agents who'd been taught to stay nonpartisan. At least it chipped away at my dedication.

"But you kept on keeping on. Most of the '72 race I spent on the McGovern campaign. I thought McGovern was a decent guy. Once when some protesters and reporters said McGovern's Secret Service detail was a bunch of thugs, McGovern called a press conference and defended us. He thanked us for risking our lives. I basically agreed with his politics. He would've ended the war immediately. But he lacked charisma. And I didn't think he could unite people behind his beliefs. He also surrounded himself with people who hurt his cause. Maybe he thought Warren Beatty could plug him into the Hollywood money and teach him how to deal with the cameras. But I don't think your average American wanted to see the President hanging out with kooky limousine liberals. Beatty once told some reporter that McGovern wanted to legalize pot. McGovern spent the rest of the race getting out of that one. Then there was Gary Hart, who ran the campaign. Worse than anything, he wanted to be Warren Beatty. Hart would never look you in the eye. You could see he was an opportunist. To me, he represented the most distasteful part of American liberalism."

Marty also wasn't impressed with the way McGovern flip-flopped in his support of his running mate, Senator Thomas Eagleton, after Eagleton admitted that he'd received psychiatric treatment.

"The agents could leave that alone. The business about Eagleton's shock therapy. The agents kept asking each other if somebody had packed the jumper cables in the car—'so we can get Eagleton started if he stalls.' When Eagleton did stall, his replacement, Sargent Shriver (former Ambassador to France and John Kennedy's brother-in-law) recharged some of my own sense of purpose. You couldn't help but like the guy. He'd seen the polls. He knew McGovern's chances weren't good. But it rolled off his back. At least he was going to enjoy the fun of the chase. Of all the campaigns I worked on, I think I got closest to the people on that one. Shriver's plane, like most of them, looked like a sprawling trailer park that somebody had crammed inside one Winnebago. People had family snapshots taped to the walls. There was constant typing. People were doing their laundry in the bathroom sink. But on Shriver's plane we also had . . . a duck. When the plane took off, somebody would let the duck out of its cage and it'd flap around the cabin. The duck would quack wildly as it soared to an altitude it had no hope of reaching again. It was the perfect mascot for McGovern and Shriver.

"When Shriver flew home to D.C. I stood post at his Maryland estate. Waiting for hours in a place where danger looks remote was an agent's most tedious job. I was going through two packs of Kents in a day, standing post, even though I had to sneak my smokes on post.

"Yet even standing still could be exhausting when it involved watching the Kennedy clan in action. It was their first Presidential election since Bobby's death. Shriver may have been McGovern's second choice. But Chappaquiddick had kept Teddy out of the race, and the Kennedy's were happy to have any of their own in the running. Campaigning was their lifeblood. Teddy and Rose and Ethel, all their kids, they'd all huddle together at the Shrivers' place. The Kennedys sort of treated the Secret Service like extended family. Even when I was off duty, I used to go over to the Shrivers' to play touch football with them. Maria Shriver was just a teenager then, and she had that great raven-black hair. I used to call her 'the Indian princess' and she'd write little notes to me and Larry Buendorf, who was one of the coolest agents. At night I used to walk through the Shrivers' house and look at the doodling that JFK had done on Oval Office notepaper. They had it framed on the walls—notes from when Shriver was the first head of the Peace Corps. That really was one of my happiest times in the Secret Service. For a while it brought back the feeling that the New Frontier was still out there."

A few months before the November voting, Shriver and McGovern were ready to revisit the Great Society. The Democrats were looking for the endorsement, or at least the advice, of the thirty-sixth President, Lyndon Baines Johnson.

"It was the first advance I'd been put in charge of. I was told to set up the visit to the LBJ ranch, which, appropriately, was code-named 'Volcano.' I'd heard the stories about LBJ. How he'd never call an agent by his name. He'd just yell, 'Secret Service!' How you'd always find him pissing outdoors. In the Rose Garden. Or in the middle of the night, he'd get up to piss off the porch of his ranch house. The agent standing post would hear something and shine his flashlight over on LBJ in midstream. The longhorn President. He'd bark back at the agent, 'What the hell are you looking at?'

"One time his daughter, Linda Bird, fell down while she was waterskiing. LBJ blamed the Secret Service. He ordered one agent to arrest another agent. So the agent handcuffed his partner to a tree.

The two of them broke up laughing, which set off a chain reaction. All the agents on the ranch started handcuffing each other. Another time, Johnson kept whacking this agent in the front seat of his limo with a newspaper. The agent told Johnson to cut it out. Which immediately made LBJ whack him again. The agent told the driver to stop the car. Then the agent got out of the car, opened up the back door and punched Johnson in the eye. He had a shiner for a couple of days.

"At one point, I had this job of arranging for McGovern to kiss Johnson's ring, which was sort of tarnished by then. As far as I could tell, neither Johnson nor the candidates were too keen on this meeting. Johnson apparently thought Ed Muskie was the only Democrat who could beat Nixon. He thought McGovern was an extremist. Of course McGovern had been one of the loudest critics of Johnson's Vietnam policies. A lot of Democrats wanted to distance themselves from Johnson, but I guess McGovern hoped Johnson could get him some Southern votes.

"Okay, so here I was, trying to set up this shindig—making my first phone call to a United States President. Johnson came on the line and I told him that McGovern and Shriver would be arriving at his ranch via Army helicopter. Right away, he blew up. '*What!* You bring military helicopters onto my property and I'll cancel the whole fuckin' thing.'

"He shouted at me for a while, and then he hung up the phone. I honestly didn't understand. I looked at the military liaison and said, 'Why'd he cuss me out?'

"But then it dawned on me that Johnson was really into symbols, as most politicians are. He'd gotten funny in his old age. Back in his last days as President, about the only place where he could safely shake hands was on a military base, with a crowd of soldiers. But now, you know, he was wearing his hair long—shoulder-length—I guess as some show of empathy with the long-hairs who used to chant, 'Hey, hey, LBJ, how many kids did you kill today?' I guess he didn't like the symbolism of McGovern and Shriver, those two liberal losers, coming to haunt him at his ranch with Vietnam helicopters. Maybe he thought it would remind everybody why *he* didn't run for re-election. Or maybe he was thinking of McGovern and Shriver. He might not have wanted all the pundits to make the association that the Democrats got us into the war.

"Anyway, I had to call back the Army transport people in Washington. I told them to paint over the insignias on the choppers and to dress their pilots in civilian clothes. All this was super Top Secret.

"So McGovern and Shriver came to Texas. But before they choppered to LBJ's ranch, they wanted a parade through Austin, to wave to the Dixie-crats. So they put together one of the longest motorcades of the campaign. This thing stretched for miles. I was riding in a police car at the head of it, just praying everything'd go smoothly. I kept checking the side-view mirror and telling the cop at the wheel to slow down a little. He was more nervous than I was. He kept slamming on his brakes, jerking me into the dashboard. He was sweating. I said, 'Just take it easy.' All the while I was talking over the radio to the car that had McGovern and Shriver. They were in the middle, waving, slowing down, speeding up. The whole motorcade was like a giant anaconda with indigestion. So I told the cop, 'Let's pick up a little speed.' But the car just kept poking along. I said, 'How 'bout a little speed?'

"The cop said, 'I'm giving it gas.'

"The cop and I watched the car's speedometer drop to zero miles per hour. I got on the radio: 'We've got a problem here.' The car right behind pulled around us. Then another car, and another car. The mayor, the congressmen, finally McGovern and Shriver—they all passed us by. The head of my detail saw me standing there like an idiot next to this broken-down squad car. It was so humiliating. I thought, 'How much bigger of a screw up can there be?' The other cars didn't even know where they were supposed to go. I was sure this was the last advance I headed.

"So I radioed for another police car to pick me up. When it got there, I jumped into the front seat and I exploded. I picked up the CB mike and started swearing. 'Why the hell doesn't somebody check these cars out! How stupid can you get?' Then I looked around to the back seat and saw this reporter holding a tape recorder. The tape was rolling. I said to him, 'You're *not* going to use this, are you?' Of course the guy nodded yes. Next day, the paper had an article: *Agent Expresses Dismay with Motorcade.*

"Fortunately my supervisors laughed it off. It was just one of those things. The squad car's electrical system had blown. Who knows? Maybe it was Eagleton getting back at us for those jokes.

"At least McGovern and Shriver got to the ranch okay in their unmarked helicopters. They had lunch with LBJ under a big oak tree. Apparently LBJ told McGovern to lighten up on the Vietnam rhetoric and talk more about his roots, his rise from poverty. He also told McGovern that he had his support. Whatever that was worth at that point. Then LBJ started feeling sick. He'd already had one coronary. McGovern and Shriver stayed a little while longer, then they climbed back into their helicopter. They didn't look happy. A few months later, LBJ had another coronary. His Secret Service agents tried to get his heart started, but they couldn't."

Meanwhile, in the final months of the '72 campaign, the agents on the White House detail were trying to subdue Nixon and his elves. It'd always been a challenge guarding the grandstanding Nixon. In 1958, when he was Vice President, he leapt onto his car and told a rock-throwing mob in Lima, Peru, that they were "cowards." After the 1970 rally in San Jose, California, when a mob of one thousand demonstrators strained against police lines, Nixon climbed onto another car and taunted the protesters with the V-sign that he considered his "political trademark." Nixon said to a nearby aide, "That's what they *hate* to see!" Apparently the protesters started hurling rocks and eggs and vegetables. Nixon felt that face-offs like these were excellent for image building. So what if they tempted fate? "If somebody is going to make an attack," Nixon wrote after Bremer diverted his aim from Nixon to Wallace, "he will be able to do so even though [Secret Service agents] are surrounding me."

Eager to please his boss, H.R. Haldeman was always on the lookout for new gutsy confrontations. Before the Billy Graham rally in Charlotte, a White House advance man sent Haldeman a memo warning that Nixon could expect violent demonstrations. In the margin of the memo, Haldeman wrote, "Good."

Marty had heard about the tension that had been building all through Nixon's first term between Haldeman and Bob Taylor, head of the White House detail.

"Three days before the voting, Nixon was supposed to appear in Providence, Rhode Island. So Haldeman told his advance guys that when the President came off Air Force One, they should lower the ropes so Nixon's supporters could rush across the tarmac. It'd be a 'spontaneous' show of affection. It'd make great TV. Haldeman also told the roadrunners not to tell the Secret Service about any of this.

"But Bob Taylor got wind of it. And the day of the event, he yelled at Haldeman over the radio, for all the agents to hear, 'If you order those ropes dropped, I will personally arrest you.' Arrest the White House Chief of Staff! Haldeman backed off in Providence, but the next day, at the airport in Greensboro, North Carolina, the White House advancers followed through on the rope scheme. The ropes came down, and a couple hundred people mobbed Nixon's limo. The agents had to form a shield around him to get him back onto Air Force One.

Somewhere along the way Taylor got so steamed at Haldeman that he grabbed him around the throat. So Haldeman started pressuring the Secret Service to have Taylor booted off the White House detail.

Taylor went way back with Nixon. Back in 1958 Taylor was one of the agents who surrounded Nixon's car when a mob in Venezuela started stoning it. Taylor also took the heat in April, 1972, when Nixon met with the American Society of Newspaper Editors at the White House. As they stood in a receiving line, Alan Romm, editor of the Middletown (Connecticut) *Times-Herald-Record,* and Romm's wife got ready to tell Nixon to "stop the bombing." But even before they could shake Nixon's hand, Romm reported, Bob Taylor called them out of the line, told them he'd heard that they were going to try to talk with Nixon and he asked them not to. Taylor told them the reception line was running late, Romm said. Later, Romm made a stink about this "censorship," and the White House apologized for Taylor's action, saying that Nixon did listen to "substantive comments" from the press.

"I just can't believe Bob Taylor would interfere like that. I don't think he'd even care how fast a receiving line was moving. But he did look out for Nixon. The day Nixon took the oath of office for the second time, it was freezing. Taylor put his own overcoat over Nixon's shoulders. And that was the same day that Nixon refused to close his car window and left himself wide open for people throwing eggs. Even after Taylor did all that for Nixon, Nixon let Haldeman have his way. A month after the inauguration Taylor was out. Headquarters announced that he was moving to the Foreign Dignitaries Protective Division. They also had to announce that Taylor's second-in-command, Bill Duncan, had asked for a transfer. Director, James Rowley, said it was all 'in keeping with our policy of rotating supervisory personnel.' Taylor went down in flames," says Marty, "and we all admired him for it."

Nixon had won the election by a landslide. The man who'd been the original target of Arthur Bremer (and also of Lee Harvey Oswald) had once again found an ally in an assassin. With George Wallace out of the race, conservatives who couldn't stomach

McGovern swung their votes to the Republican President. It wasn't till a few days before his defeat that McGovern finally lost his self-consciousness. A Secret Service agent heard him lean down to a heckler at a rally and whisper, "I have a secret for you—kiss my ass."

Maybe McGovern was gutsier than Marty had thought. But in the end, Marty Venker, who'd joined the Secret Service to "protect the electoral process," voted for no one.

"I'd seen too much of his campaign to believe in McGovern. But it wasn't just that. I couldn't vote for anybody. I was no fan of Nixon's secret bombing, or the rest of his deceptions. But the Service told you to swallow your opinions, and that's what I did. It's strange. The job's supposed to be so patriotic, but to do it you have to learn to be apathetic. More and more, I'd read the newspaper and I'd just skim by the trade measures, the arms treaties, what have you. I wanted to disassociate myself from the whole deal. I thought the country could get along without my vote. Goddam, I was protecting these guys. Once you got your feelings involved, it made it that much harder to step in front of a bullet. You might think at the last minute, 'How do I feel about this guy?'

"I'd just as soon not know what he stood for."

# CHAPTER SIX

# *Brain Rays from Washington*

FOR six months—half his first year—Marty worked that campaign without getting even one day off.

"A lot of agents did it. Every day was another 'unusual situation' that called for extra men. Forget about your weekend, that's when they held some of the biggest campaign events. On a given day, we'd be traveling through four or five cities. I'd go through so many places in a week that I'd be running alongside the limo and I'd have to look down and read the sewer covers to see what city I was in. I only got back to Springfield for twenty-eight days. I wish I hadn't rented an apartment. It was just a waste of money."

After all the voting machines had been put into storage and after Arthur Bremer had been put behind bars, Marty let himself back into his apartment, sorted through weeks of "occupant" mail, ran the water to flush the rust out, picked up his phone and heard what he expected to hear: no dial tone. At least he'd built up a lot of overtime pay. He could afford the comforts of a young professional. He bought himself some better tailored suits for the various seasons. He moved into a nicer apartment on South Grand Way. He picked out a brand new dark brown convertible Corvette Stingray. Now and then, Marty would still plug in his old Fender Stratocaster guitar. He'd noodle around with some of those songs Soul Seekers used to play. But he had other things on his mind.

"Out on the road I'd noticed that so many agents who were bucking for promotions had advanced degrees. I needed something extra for my resume. So I started taking night classes in legal studies at Springfield's Sangamon State University. My classes looked at the philosophy of law and how judicial rulings rewove the social fabric."

The law enforcer found the subject fascinating and came home after work to write term papers that earned him straight A's.

During the day, Marty helped the other field office agents track counterfeiters and forgers. But mostly he plumbed the heartland for assassins. South and central Illinois boasted some of the nation's strongest prisons and asylums. And their inmates—as well as others who ran free—were forever applying for the job of killing the President. Empowered to commit them for twenty-four-hour psychiatric observation, Marty was supposed to rule out which of the threat-makers might be mad or bad enough to do it. The legal student had to make some tough calls.

"There were a lot of false alarms. Some drunk would mouth off in a bar, or some guy would get back at his neighbor by sending a crank letter to the White House and signing the neighbor's name. We'd sometimes have to remind them that even a verbal threat to the President carried a maximum fine of a thousand dollars and a five-year jail term."

In 1987 Hunter S. Thompson told students at Marquette University that George Bush was "the meanest yuppie who ever lived" and that he'd like to kill him. Thompson said he canceled a trip to D.C.

after a Secret Service agent paid him a visit. According to Thompson, "The agent said my life might become a series of terrible misunderstandings if I ever thought about going to Washington without consulting him first."

"When I trained in Washington I visited the 'Fantasy Factory,' a nickname for the Service's Intelligence Division. Specialists at the Factory pieced together plots and counterplots, hoping to beat an assassin to the punch. The Fantasists might hear wild rumors about a death squad of hopeful martyrs that had slipped into America to kill Henry Kissinger. It might just be another terrorist cock-and-bull story, but it couldn't go ignored. The Intelligence guys would read poisoned pen letters around the clock and tape phone calls passed along by the White House operators. Each month the White House got around 800 sinister calls and letters. The wacko communiques could range from a trite crayon drawing of Richard Nixon with a knife through his eye to an incoherent phone conversation that ended with the earsplitting sound of the caller blowing his brains out."

The Secret Service is capricious in releasing statistics to the press. Spokespeople claim that current figures on yearly threats are classified. But in 1978 the agency reported that its Protective Research section processed more than 14,000 cases, made 406 arrests and obtained 311 convictions or commitments. This compares with 1975, when Treasury Secretary William Simon reported that the Service screened 200,000 pieces of information, interviewed 4,000 people, and made about 60 arrests. Most of the Fantasy Factory's intelligence comes from the FBI, which, as the seventies wore on, had less intelligence to give. This was because of the national outcry against the Bureau's domestic surveillance of groups it considered "subversive." In 1976, Gerald Ford's Attorney General, Edward H. Levi, issued guidelines that sought to correct the FBI's history of illegal break-ins, unauthorized wiretaps and smear campaigns against leaders such as Martin Luther King Jr.

But the curbs on surveillance provoked Secret Service director H. Stuart Knight to complain that by hamstringing the FBI, the guidelines endangered the President's life. The Secret Service brass also claimed that the Freedom of Information Act made police, here and abroad, fearful of sharing intelligence with the agency. The Service grumbled further that the Privacy Act made every organization, from the mental hospitals to the telephone company, stubborn about divulging people's records without a subpoena.

"I didn't buy the conservative line that came out of headquarters. I was glad the FBI couldn't spy on people like it used to. The government should go through all sorts of shit to get what it wants. Besides, it was about time that the FBI stopped sending us reams of data that were garbage. Knight admitted he couldn't say the *quality* of the FBI intelligence was any worse. He couldn't describe to Congress what kind of information the Service was looking for if the guidelines were relaxed. He even contradicted a Congressman who claimed that better intelligence would've kept the attacks on the Presidents from happening. As for the Freedom of Information Act, everybody should be able to see what the government has on them. The F.O.I.A. and the Privacy Act are just like the Miranda law. People said the Miranda law was going to handcuff the cops. It didn't. They still got their confessions. If some other police agency really feels that somebody's a threat to the President, they'll get the information to the Secret Service. The other agencies sure don't want the President's death on their heads."

The Secret Service had its own version of the FBI's Ten Most Wanted list—only the Service's list was much longer and it was made up of people whom the Service never let out of its sight. No way you would find Tony Randall's name there. These were people who'd already tried to kill one of the Service's protectees or who'd made it clear that they'd like to. Their collective fantasies could drench the White House in blood. Before JFK's death there were about a hundred names on the list. But as the American mind grew more fevered, the total rose toward the end of the seventies to about four hundred, where it leveled off.

Four times a year, the central office sent agents out to question the 400 potential assassins, who were known informally as the "quarterlies." Whenever the President visited a city, agents checked up on the quarterlies who lived in the area. The agents also fed the names of hotel guests and conventioneers into the Service's computer to see if any of them might be, if not a quarterly, a member of the larger watch list.

The Service was always trying to get a better bead on whom it should call a quarterly. So it asked psychologists what patterns they saw among past assailants. The experts observed that many of America's assassins grew up in poverty; that they'd been nagged by sexual inadequacy; that at least one of their parents had died or deserted them. The fact that these assassins were often losers who couldn't hold a job only seemed to inflate their extraordinary ambition to become historic figures.

"I must have fame, fame!" declared John Wilkes Booth. According to early assessors, all the assassins were out-and-out psychopaths. Yet revisionist interpreters emphasized that bona fide political grievances rankled the men who'd attacked Abraham Lincoln, William McKinley, Harry Truman and Bobby Kennedy. America's assassins were different, though, from the foreign terrorists and craven generalissimos whose attacks were calculated to claim power. Many of our assassins were resolutely nonpartisan. Before he killed the liberal John Kennedy, Lee Harvey Oswald first shot at right-wing General Edwin Walker. Giuseppe Zangara, who fired at Franklin Roosevelt, said Herbert Hoover would have made just as good a target.

Almost all of America's assassins, the psychologists agreed, acted out of some private torment. Your run-of-the-mill murderer was often a violent youngster from a stormy home. But the assassins had deceptively mild manners. They were often milquetoast loners, terrified to ask someone out on a date. "Model prisoners" in their own homes, they choked down their urge to rebel against their parents. But when the assassin resolved to assert himself, he desired a victim far grander than the parent who'd belittled him. He set his sights on that magical dad who came home every night on the national news. Some who hoped to join the pantheon of assassins began a sort of home study course. Sirhan, already familiar with the assassinations of McKinley and Archduke Franz Ferdinand of Austria, started "mind-control exercises." Bremer read up on Sirhan, Oswald and Booth.

But these dark dreamers craved more than fame, according to some psychiatrists. What the assassins truly longed for was a permanent identity. What better way to find one than to share a page of history with America's President? Marching serenely to the electric chair, Zangara lost his cool only when he found out that there'd be no photographers to record his execution. Sirhan, who'd admired JFK, proclaimed, "They can gas me, but I am famous. I have achieved in one day what it took Robert Kennedy all his life to do."

The sketch that the experts drew of the typical assassin made enough sense. Trouble was, that sketch looked like hundreds of thousands of Americans pushing their shopping carts through the land's liquor barns and hunting stores. Who could say which of those Americans might take aim and fire? A 1984 panel of eleven mental health experts headed by Dr. W. Walter Menninger could agree on something: there was "no scientifically valid model to predict who will be assassins." One of the panelists said the judgment was best left to the Secret Service. So the bomb bounced back into the Service's court. It was up to Marty to take his best guess, to decide if a new threat-maker qualified as a quarterly, and if an old quarterly should stay on the list.

"We'd get these letters covered with hieroglyphic spaghetti writing. A lot of times there was no return address, unless you counted the enclosed map of the solar system. We'd have to find these people and talk to them. It helped that I'd taken that crash course in psychology at St. Elizabeth's. But the only way you really develop a feel for mentally ill people is to meet a lot of them. I started out following a senior agent around, and only after a couple of years did I start to get the hang of it. ·

"Of the 400-some quarterlies on the Service's list, about 125 were 'out of pocket,' that is, walking the street. The rest were locked in overcrowded penitentiaries and asylums, waiting for release. All of them had files tagged with a red sticker that advised the prison and hospital staff that should the inmate ever escape they were to call the Secret Service *immediately.*

"On business I would walk down the halls of high security mental wards where howls and shrieks clawed at my ears and the patients smooshed their faces against wire-reinforced glass that made their noses look like they'd melted.

"The person who wrote the letter to the White House would be waiting in 'the quiet room.' One of the staff psychiatrists would lead me there. He'd read from a manila folder, bringing me up to date on the patient's behavior. The doctor would run on about the patient's 'paranoid delusional system'—how the patient had 'acted out' or 'displayed diminished affect.'

"I'd say, 'Thank you. Could I speak to him alone for awhile?' That helped. Most of the patients I talked to didn't like their doctors. They'd usually open up more if there wasn't anybody in a white coat around.

"Unless one of these threat-makers had the ability to carry out his threat, we didn't bother with him. Most of the people couldn't focus on one topic longer than thirty seconds. They had an attention span like a strobe light. One minute they'd want to kill the President, the next minute they'd want to kill their landlord."

"One time my partner and I drove out to the return address on a letter. We rang the buzzer of this house for a couple of minutes before a young woman opened the door. She had on high heels, and she had a towel wrapped around her head, but other than that she was stark naked. Water was dripping off her breasts.

"We didn't even get a chance to tell her who we were before she said, 'Come in, come in, *come in!*' My partner and I looked at each other. She just started wobbling into her kitchen on those heels, toweling herself off. She said, 'You want some coffee?'

"So we followed her inside and I said, 'We're from the United States Secret Service. We'd like to talk to you about that letter you wrote to the White House.' It was like she didn't hear me. She just jumped into some other conversation where I didn't know what the hell she was talking about.

"And then I told Harry—'No, don't go to the store, go to the gas station!'

"I said, 'Miss, we need to talk to you for a minute.'

" 'Yeah, yeah, we'll get to it. What do you want in your coffee?'

"We sat down at the kitchen table and watched her get the coffee. She had a real good body. But honestly, there was nothing erotic about this for me. I kept biting my lip, trying not to laugh, and glancing at my partner, who was also trying to keep his composure. She sat down and crossed her legs and said, 'Now where did you boys say you were from? Oh yeah, the White House.'

"But then she looked over to her cat, which was sitting on the kitchen counter, and she said to the cat, 'No, I am not going to do that! Stay out of this!'

"I imagine if you were trying to have a conversation with a cat, it *could* drive you crazy. Those cats just don't react.

"I would usually tell a first-time threat-maker who had an attention span like this lady to watch it, that she could do time just for *saying* she wanted to kill the President. I'd tell her we'd be back if she said it again. But I wouldn't recommend her for quarterly observation. I'd tell my partner, 'Let's not plant the seed. If we start badgering her again, she might get it into her head that killing the President isn't just an interesting idea, it's her *destiny.*'

"These people only became dangerous when they started thinking that the President wasn't just the answer to their problem, but the *cause.* That's why you had to sort of bait them to make them act out their fantasies. I'd try to work them into a lather. A guy might believe that there was a nuclear warhead housed in his nose. And he might tell me to deliver some ultimatum to the President, like all the U.S. arms negotiators must undergo rhinoplasty. So I'd lock eyes with the guy and I'd say, 'I already gave your message to the President.'

"The patient would say, 'You *did?!*'

" 'Yeah. And the President doesn't agree with you.'

" 'He doesn't?'

" 'No. In fact, he said it was a stupid idea. One of the stupidest ideas he's ever heard. He said you must be crazy . . . So what're you gonna do about it?'

"The guy would start to sputter, and I'd watch his eyes. I'd wait to see if he was going to throw an ashtray or something. He might just blow his nose—you know, release some of the pressure on that warhead. I really wasn't trying to be cruel. You just had to see how far he'd go.

"Some of the quarterlies made no bones about their blood lust. Rafael Cancel-Miranda was twenty-five in 1954 when he and three other Puerto Rican Nationalists shot up the House of Representatives, wounding five Congressmen. When I met him, Cancel had served almost twenty years and his moustache had grown gray. He was doing time at the Federal Penitentiary in Marion, Illinois, the

country's highest security slammer. There wasn't much chance of
Cancel escaping. But I had to keep checking in on him because
Cancel, not wanting to lose his terrorist status, kept firing off threats.
I guess he didn't want Washington to forget him. He'd tell me point
blank, 'When I get out of here, I will go to a store, buy a gun, go
to the White House and start shooting.'

"I'd say, 'Rafael, do you know who the President is now?'

"He'd say, 'It don't make no difference to me. Same imperialist
scum.' "

Cancel, who'd been punched out countless times by convicts and
guards, turned down clemency because he wouldn't apologize for
what he did in 1954. In 1977, Jimmy Carter set him free anyway.
Even when he was out, Cancel, at forty-nine, told an American
audience, "If you want war, you're gonna get it."

"I had another quarterly who also didn't feel any remorse. He was
a slight kid in his early twenties. I don't want to use his real name.
His family has suffered enough. I'll call him Brad. A couple of years
before I met Brad, the police found him in this foul-smelling apartment grilling some kind of steak. It turned out to be human flesh.
Brad had killed an old man who lived in his building. He was eating
the man and drinking his blood. I got involved only because Brad
had been writing from his asylum, threatening to fix Nixon by the
same recipe. Brad had a simple reason for eating his neighbor: the
old man was one of the few people who'd been kind to him. So Brad
wanted to be just like the old man. He said he wanted to 'become
him.' A voice told him to do it.

"I asked another quarterly how he 'knew' that the Pope was a
homosexual. He said it was because everytime he'd seen him on TV,
the Pope formed his mouth into an O shape.

"Certain words and pictures would really set them off. I called it the Susquehanna Hat complex, after that Three Stooges episode about the guy who'd strangle people whenever anybody mentioned the Susquehanna Hat Factory.

"There was a teacher who'd just moved from Canada to a rural town in central Illinois. I'll call him Caspar Osgood. The Canadian Mounties had notified the Secret Service that they had some threatening letters that mentioned Nixon. My partner and I were supposed to check them out. So one night, after dark, we walked up to this real creepy old house where Osgood lived. Osgood opened the door. He was around forty, a little over six feet and he had short salt-and-pepper hair and thick glasses. After we said who we were, he let us in. There wasn't a lightbulb on in the house. Just candles. He had pamphlets and magazines stacked almost to the ceiling. I remember flipping through one comic book called 'The Gay Blade,' which told about a teenager who got wrapped up with Communist homosexuals. Osgood had actually arranged a lot of these books and pamphlets so they formed a kind of throne. That's where he was sitting when he started ranting to us about the Communist homosexual conspiracy.

"We soon found out that there was one word that was guaranteed to set Osgood off: 'Hutterites.' The Hutterites are a religious group that's been around for something like 350 years. They farm in Canada and the Midwest and they believe in common ownership of goods, which Osgood of course saw as a Commie conspiracy.

"Apparently he'd once taught some Hutterite kids in Canada. Then he got fired. He'd been a teacher at a half-dozen schools and at least one school had accused him of molesting boys. Anyway, he called the Hutterites 'a closed sect' and he said they were 'corrupters of little children.' I tell you, the more this guy kept blathering about 'the queers,' the more upset he got, getting all red, drumming his fingers, until finally I said to him matter of factly, 'Well, we understand that *you're* gay.'

" '*Whaaaat!*' he screamed. He jumped up. I thought he was going to attack us.

"It weighed on my conscience that night whether to tell the principal of Osgood's new school about his past. This was a real farm town and I guess they were happy to get a teacher. But I thought, maybe I should say something, he's dealing with children. Finally I went to the principal as part of the background check we were supposed to do. I didn't say exactly what the problem was. But the principal got the idea quickly enough and balled me out for not telling him sooner. The people in these little towns, they thought we were way too liberal. They wanted us to cart off these 'nuts' before they embarrassed the community."

Once headquarters asked Marty to check out a potential psycho who'd scrawled a crayon mash note.

"We drove a good four hours into the sticks to find a certain house. We rang the door bell. A man and woman answered. We asked if the person who sent the letter lived there. The woman said, 'Yes. He's our son.'

" 'Well, your son has written a letter to the White House, saying he wants to shoot the President.'

"The father took our copy of the letter and said, 'Let me see that! The teacher said there was something funny about what he wrote for his class assignment.'

"The parents invited us inside and they called their son down from upstairs. Their son turned out to be *eight years old*. I almost fell over.

"I sat him down and tried to explain the seriousness of his actions. I figured as long as they had sent us all the way out there, I'd fill out all the spaces on the report. I asked the kid, 'You ever been married?'

"He said, 'Nooo!' He started laughing. Another unremorseful threat-maker.

"I filled out every line on the form: 'Subject claims no sexual deviations . . . Major political affiliations: Cub Scouts of America . . . Military history: None . . . subject is EIGHT YEARS OLD!'

" 'What a waste of time,' I said, as we drove away from the kid's house. You could say that the Service had been scrupulous in finding out who had made those crayon squiggles. You could also say that the kid's note fell through the same bureaucratic hole as the request for a press pass that came from a convicted murderer. The convict, on a work-release job with a radio station, got the Service's okay to cover a 1976 visit by Swedish King Carl Gustaf. The killer had given his address as 128 Third Street, Trenton, New Jersey—which happened to be the location of Trenton State Prison.

"At least the kid's note broke the routine. So many of the quarterlies' stories were the same. The CIA was always reading their thoughts. Or someone was transmitting electrical messages into their brain through lightbulbs and appliances. It could get very tedious. But I felt sorry for these people. They were their own saboteurs. You'd keep seeing the same faces. A lot of them had a grievance, like most Americans. They tried to get it resolved through their families, through the police, through the institutions. Finally, they reached the Supreme Court of Mental Grievances—the White House."

Marty became something of a celebrity with the quarterlies. Whenever he walked into the locked ward of a psychiatric unit in Danville, Illinois, the inmates would start applauding.

"I think they had fun when I was there. I think I made them feel important. The President had sent his personal representative. My folder said right there: 'The White House.' Their letter had gotten results! After a while I started to wonder if these guys, who'd usually been abandoned by their families, if they were just telling me this stuff so I'd keep visiting them.

"Sometimes weirdos came to visit the Springfield office. They'd usually be babbling, again, about the rays that the CIA was zapping into their brains. One agent used to get them out of the office by lining their hats with tin foil and telling them, 'See—now the rays can't get through.' That seemed to satisfy them for a while.

"The field office was also a magnet for anybody who thought they were tougher than the Secret Service. In the entrance there'd be a couple of administrative aides sitting at desks behind a counter. When they buzzed us in back it meant that there was someone out front that they couldn't handle. For instance, one day we heard them buzz, and another agent and I went to see what the problem was. I looked through the window of the office door. There was a stocky guy out there with his hands stuck down his pants. He was rocking back and forth on the balls of his feet. I opened the door and we came out. It looked like the pupils of his eyes were vibrating. So I said to him, 'Can I help you?'

"He said, 'You know karate?'

"I said, 'A little bit.'

" 'Well, how fuckin' good are you at it, man? 'Cause I'm a fuckin' expert, man.'

"I just wanted to know if this guy had a gun, so I said, 'Why do you have your hands inside your pants?'

"He said, ' 'Cause I'm *ready,* that's why!'

"I could see the secretaries were starting to freak out. So I said, 'Well, we're ready too.' That's when the other agent and I leapt over the counter and wrestled the guy to the ground. He didn't have a gun but we carried him outside and told him that if he came around there again, we'd arrest him. I imagine we violated his constitutional rights. But sometimes you have to use your instinct and worry about the legal consequences later.

"I used to ask my superiors for a bullet-proof screening area, or at least a set-up where I wouldn't have to jump over a counter. They'd tell me not to be such a pussy. I could handle it.

"Then in 1980, a man who'd been committed to a mental hospital after he'd tried to break through the White House gate walked into the Denver field office and said that he was sick and tired of getting hassled by the Secret Service. The man took a .45-caliber pistol from under his coat and fired it twice into the stomach and chest of agent Stewart Watkins. Another agent shot and killed the gunman. Watkins died five hours later. After that, the Service strengthened its field office security."

Marty's most fatiguing tangle with the mentally unbalanced, and with his own government, started when Richard Nixon visited Pekin, Illinois, on June 15, 1973. On that day, an hour or so after Nixon touched down, a man we'll call "Daryl Luke Raeburn" drove into the Greater Peoria Airport. He rolled down the window of his car and asked the Peoria County sheriff's deputies if he could drive a little closer to the runway where Air Force One was waiting. Just as the deputies were waving Raeburn through, a cop in an airport tower looked through his binoculars and spotted a high-powered rifle in the backseat of Raeburn's car. The deputies ran after Raeburn, arrested him and called the Secret Service. Marty was in town, standing near the speechifying Nixon, when his boss told him to hot foot it over to the sheriff's office.

"I hurried over. The deputies showed me to the questioning room. There was this dark-haired guy in his thirties there. A lot of the quarterlies were short or frail. But this guy was muscular and about six-foot-two. It'd been so hectic that day that when I sat down to talk to the guy I didn't ask him his name. I just got to the point: 'I heard you were trying to get into the airport with a rifle.' Ninety-nine percent of the time, when someone is caught with a rifle, it's a mistake—a hunter who forgot to leave his gun at home.

"That's what Raeburn said. He said he'd been heading out on a hunting trip and he got lost. 'I got off at the wrong exit,' he said. But there was something cagey about him, and I couldn't quite buy that a guy who lived around there, who was headed for the woods, could get lost at an airport. Particularly after he admitted that he'd been to the airport once before that day.

"But it wasn't till I'd been talking with him for fifteen minutes that I said, 'Can I see your driver's license?'

"He threw his license across the table. When I looked at it and saw his name, my eyes lit up. Bing! Bing! The day before his name had come over the teletype. He'd been writing the White House, sending drawings that showed how easy it'd be to kill the President at, say, a rally, if such and such were done. He also outlined his theory on nuclear disarmament. The White House got these letters just as Nixon's trip was being planned, so Raeburn's name was a late add to our look-out list. Raeburn lived about thirty miles away from Peoria. Since there wasn't enough time to get there to interview him, I'd asked the local police chief to have his men watch this guy, day and night, till Nixon was out of town. Apparently they let him get out of their sight.

"I asked Raeburn, 'How come, if you were lost, you asked to get closer to the President? Why'd you have your gun already loaded? What about the man-sized target full of bullet holes in your trunk?'

"He said, 'I want to talk to a lawyer.'

"He was willing to talk some more, but he sidestepped anything that could incriminate him. Just to make sure he was the same guy who'd written the White House, I asked him for a handwriting sample. I asked him to write a letter to the President. He wrote something like, 'Dear Mr. President, I'm being held by one of your agents . . .' The whole while we were doing this, Raeburn had a smirk on his face—like he knew exactly what he could get away with. I'd never met anybody like this guy. He seemed like he really could bring off an assassination. He was one shrewd bastard.

"Four hours after Raeburn's arrest we had to let him go. We didn't have any grounds to hold him. Looking into his background, I found that Raeburn had received Marine marksman training and that he'd once shot himself in the stomach. I wrote in my report to Washington: 'Subject is definitely of protective interest.' They agreed. They put him on the watch list immediately."

Nine weeks after Marty grilled Raeburn, the Secret Service announced that it had uncovered a conspiracy to assassinate Nixon in New Orleans and that the White House was calling off its motorcade through the French Quarter. Never before had the Service publicly announced a possible conspiracy. New Orleans police wondered why in hell the Service had tipped off the conspirators, giving them time to get out of town.

Insiders said the reason was this: the President's men were up to their old tricks. They didn't want to miss a chance to give Nixon an image-boosting motorcade. The press announcement was reportedly the only way that the Secret Service could force the White House to scotch the motorcade and make Nixon speed to his speech on an unannounced route. Official spokesmen denied this. They said Nixon himself had nixed the motorcade. Later that day, however, reporters who saw the President arrive in San Clemente heard him fume to his secretary, Rose Mary Woods, "They called last night. They canceled. They'll never cancel another time."

Woods told him, "We prayed for you."

The day after the New Orleans speech, the Secret Service announced that it was pressing on with its investigation into a "very serious, very large" conspiracy by "nonmentals." A police informer had told the New Orleans cops that six black militants had met to talk about using rifles and possibly a hand grenade to do Nixon in. The police put the six under surveillance, but the cops turned down a Secret Service request to arrest the militants. The cops said there wasn't enough evidence for conviction.

Meanwhile, the Secret Service was hot on the trail of Edwin Gaudet, a former New Orleans cop who'd been arrested three years before when he tried to throw a burning flag on Nixon's car. Recently a woman claimed she'd heard the hot-tempered ex-prizefighter say in a drugstore, "Somebody ought to kill President Nixon. If no one has the guts, I'll do it."

Gaudet had fled to the Sangre de Christo Mountains in New Mexico, where he'd been living on a commune. The bearded twenty-nine-year old Gaudet was a wily outdoorsman, and he hid out in the mountains, watching the Secret Service posse and trading a few shots with them. When he finally gave up, he announced, "The Pope is head of the Mafia." Authorities, however, found no evidence linking Gaudet with the black militant conspiracy. And eventually the government dropped the Nixon-threat charge, after its sole witness refused to make a positive identification that it was definitely Gaudet who'd made the threat in the drugstore. Some of Nixon's harsher critics sniped that all this conspiracy talk was just Nixon's way of winning sympathy in the midst of the Watergate scandal.

Watergate was spilling over into Marty's life. Even as the Secret Service probed Gaudet and the militants, Marty continued to match wits with Daryl Luke Raeburn. Raeburn had sued him for false arrest. Charging that Marty had defamed him and caused him "mental anguish," Raeburn demanded $50,000 in damages. Raeburn also sued Peoria County. However, he promptly released the sheriff's office from liability when the county's insurance company made an out-of-court settlement with him. Not bad for a guy acting as his own attorney.

Marty had to post his own surety bond for $50,000. Then Assistant Attorney General Henry E. Petersen sent word to Illinois that he didn't want Assistant U.S. Attorney Max J. Lipkin to defend Marty.

*       *       *

"Antiwar protesters were filing all kinds of lawsuits charging that the Secret Service had abused their rights, so the Justice Department didn't want to hear about me. It didn't matter that the agents were taking the blame for Nixon's staff or that there were those serious threats in New Orleans. The Justice Department had enough on its hands with Watergate."

Editorialists like Harriet Van Horne had also been charging that the Secret Service had been turning asylums into "holding tanks" for "harmless loonies and zealous reformers." A former public defender quoted in a 1972 *Washington Monthly* article claimed that many so-called threat-makers "don't have the wherewithal to assassinate anyone. The [preventive detention] statute is just being used as a vacuum sweeper. Seldom do they [the government] take it to trial."

"In my case, Petersen phoned Lipkin to say that the Secret Service agent would have to get 'his own' lawyer. The federal government wasn't responsible for my actions. Petersen's message, however, arrived at Lipkin's office just as Lipkin was in a circuit courtroom asking that my case be moved to Federal Court. Given that he'd already done that, Lipkin pressed the Justice Department to let him follow through in my defense. Three months after I had met Raeburn, U.S. District Court Judge Robert D. Morgan dismissed Raeburn's suit, ruling that a federal employee couldn't be held personally liable for his official acts.

"It happened that eight months after I'd arrested Raeburn at the Peoria airport, a man named Samuel Byck walked into the Baltimore-Washington International Airport and shot three people in the course of hijacking a plane that he'd hoped to crash into the White House to kill Nixon. Secret Service agents had interviewed Byck two years earlier, after he allegedly said that someone ought to do Nixon in. In his interview, though, Byck denied that he'd ever said such a thing, and the agents reported that he was 'quite intelligent and well read.' The following month, Byck checked himself into a mental hospital, and by Christmas Eve of 1973 he was picketing the White House, dressed as Santa Claus and calling for Nixon's impeachment. Byck, who'd carried a bomb onto the plane, blew his brains out after being wounded by police snipers."

To Marty, the incident underlined the danger that Daryl Luke Rayburn could have posed. The Secret Service brass agreed that the Justice Department had given him a raw deal. The Secret Service's new director, H. Stuart Knight, wrote Marty a letter expressing his regret over the way the affair had been handled.

"I appreciated the gesture. It showed that the agency would stand behind its own. On the other hand, I saw how another part of the government would screw you over if it was politically expedient. Never mind that you'd been doing your job. It was a real eye-opener."

# CHAPTER SEVEN

# *Foreign Bodies*

GOING to the wall in the Raeburn case may have earned Marty some points at headquarters. A short while after the judge threw out the lawsuit, the Secret Service brass began to consider Marty, along with agents from around the country, for a promotion. By this time Marty had collected not only some solid evaluations but also his master's degree in Legal Studies. (He ranked among the top three students in his class.) H. Stuart Knight sent Marty a letter saying he was "exceedingly pleased" with his agent's 4.0 scholastic average and that he was "proud to have individuals of your caliber as members of the team."

In 1974 the Service picked Marty as one of a small number of agents it was sending to guard the President and foreign dignitaries during their trips to New York. Marty started out staying for several months at a time in that city's hotels. But tiring of room service, he finally found himself an apartment at 92nd and Third—on Manhattan's fashionable Upper East Side.

New York had the largest Secret Service office outside Washington, and it percolated with agents who might not have been tolerated in other cities. For example, the Service tells its agents to try to leave street crime to cops and not to draw a gun unless the life of a citizen is really in danger. In 1983 Houston police criticized two Secret Service agents after they reportedly saw a man pump several rifle shots into an unarmed doorman at a condominium. The agents, who were doing an advance for George Bush, allegedly made no attempt to arrest the suspect. By contrast, the New York field office agent tended to take a more vigorous approach to crime, wherever he found it. The year before Marty came to the Apple, cops had booked a Secret Service agent for trying to settle a traffic dispute with his revolver. Seems that a taxi driver cut off the agent at an intersection, so the agent—who guarded John and Carolyn Kennedy—chased the cabbie in his car and fired a shot over the taxi's hood.

Marty himself saw that the New York street guys just had no patience for impolite motorists.

"One day I was headed in a car to New Jersey with an agent named John. We were waiting in line at the Holland Tunnel, about five cars back from the toll booth, when this long luxury sedan cut in front of us. Inside this car there were four bad-looking brothers. They had on the big-brimmed Superfly hats—I mean, right out of Central Casting. Obviously, they didn't want to wait in line. But John, who was driving, saw this and said, 'Just a *minute!*' He put the car in park and said, 'I'll be right back.' He got out and walked up to the pimpmobile and knocked on the window.

"Now John was a big guy—I'd say, six-foot-four, 240 pounds. But I was still thinking, this is stupid. There are *four* guys in that car. But when they rolled down their window, John just wound up and— BANG!—knocked the driver unconscious. Then he walked back to our car and drove around them.

"John had a simple sense of right and wrong. He didn't screw around on his wife and he didn't like guys who screwed around on theirs. He'd give you the shirt off his back. But he also was a stick of dynamite. You'd step on his toes accidentally and his face would start getting red before he remembered you were on his side. He was always in trouble in the office, shouting at grade fifteen agents, 'I won't fuckin' do it!'

"They'd plead, 'John, calm down.' They didn't want to lose him. A little muscle comes in handy when you're dealing with New York City.

"Around this time I also got to know a mythic Secret Service rascal named Brooks Keller. Ever since I'd started in St. Louis, I'd been hearing about Keller's antics. The chief of the St. Louis field office was an uptight guy who wore a Panama hat. So Brooks scoured St. Louis for an identical hat till one day he was getting his shoes shined and he looked up and he saw a stack of these hats in a store window. Brooks went in and bought one hat a size too big and another hat a size too small. Then he had them engraved with the boss' name. The next hot day, when he was heading out to lunch, the boss suddenly found that his hat didn't fit. The other agents told him that when it gets humid, your head swells. Then a cool day would come, and the boss' hat slipped down over his ears. The agents told him people's heads shrank when things cooled off. After a couple of months of this, the boss checked into the Mayo Clinic to have his skull examined. By that time I think Brooks had left the field office.

"Time and again, an agent would meet a fetching woman in some far crevice of the globe and he would proudly unzip the news that he worked for the Secret Service, and she would ask the inevitable question: 'Oh! Do you know Brooks Keller?' Chances were that down at the end of the bar there'd be a photo of Keller's ruddy kisser, grinning down at them. Keller's idea of providing safe transport for an Arab sheik was to pull up in a speedboat armed with champagne. One of Keller's two curvaceous crew members would then help the sheik aboard. President Kennedy once summoned the agent to Air Force One and demanded to know when Keller was going to invite him to one of his parties.

"Keller's Secret Service bosses were less enchanted with him. He earned a record number of suspensions and disciplinary transfers. Still, probably because he had family wealth, Keller never seemed to sweat getting fired. To a by-the-book supervisor, Keller was *unnervingly* merry. One story had it, though, that he'd once gotten so pissed at Al Whitaker—an intimate of J. Edgar Hoover's who ruled the New York field office for decades—that Keller chased Whitaker around his desk with a gun."

Marty had met Keller before, but it was only in New York, working the foreign dignitaries with him and partying at his apartment, that Marty really came under Keller's influence.

"He was one of the few agents I'd bum around with after work. He had friends who were writers, theater people, artists. He had a mind of his own and a life outside the Secret Service. Brooks was sort of like the Service's roving minstrel show. He'd liven up one field office, then he'd get bored and have himself kicked somewhere else. The Secret Service was free airfare around the world. He said that his father and grandfather, all the men back in his family, all of them had only lived to be fifty. Brooks wanted to have some fun before he joined them.

"More peculiar tales than Keller's could only come from the foreign dignitaries themselves. Once I looked into the back seat of a limo and saw India's President Neelam Sanjiva Reddy urinating into a vial. The President then drank his urine, spiritually purifying himself, as that sainted assassin's victim, Mahatma Gandhi, had done. Customs like these surprised me less and less as I traveled . . . Seeing someone drink his urine wasn't as bizarre to me as seeing a guy beat his wife to make her carry a sack of grain. President Reddy made a more shocking sight in the operating room of the Memorial Sloan-Kettering Cancer Center, though. I was dressed in hospital scrubs, watching over the leader during the removal of a coin lesion from his left lung. The doctor said to me,

'You want to see what cancer looks like?' He held up this black, speckled blob. *That* frightened me more than any assassin who might be waiting outside.

"For out-and-out zaniness, nobody could hold a candle to a delegation from the West African nation of Gabon. In average height, the Gabonese guards stood about five feet; but in their resolve to enjoy the Western world, they were giants.

"The commercial jet they chartered should have had padded walls. When the stewardess came down the aisle with the cart full of little liquor bottles, these Gabonese guards would push her aside and pour every bottle—Scotch, gin, bourbon—into one bowl and start chugging it. Then they'd start playing with their guns, cranking them back, pointing them at each other, laughing. They'd handcuff people and store them in the overhead luggage rack.

"The women on the delegation wore traditional tribal dress, so the guards went wild when they walked through Kennedy Airport and saw copies of *Playboy* on the newsstand. They started rubbing the pictures. When we got them into the limos, they started puking and passing out.

"I *knew* this was going to be trouble, and I was right. Their President, Omar Bongo, kept President Ford waiting on the South Lawn for about twenty minutes. Then we flew with them to Pittsburgh, where the president of U.S. Steel bowed from the waist. You see, Gabon has some of the richest iron ore and manganese deposits in the world. It was hilarious. All these U.S. Steel executives in their Brooks Brothers suits, sitting across the board room table from these little guys in these outlandish outfits like I used to wear in college— big bellbottoms, four-inch heels, aquamarine jump suits. Naturally, endowed with such a sense of fashion, they loved to shop. One day, a tractor trailer pulled up to the Waldorf-Astoria and the delivery man brought all these boxes up to the twenty-fifth floor.

"We asked them, 'What's all this?'

"They said, 'TV sets. Sign here.' I don't know how many channels they get in Gabon. But everybody on the trip went down to Times Square and bought at least one TV.

"President Bongo himself was a nutty guy. One day he walked into our command post at the Waldorf, grabbed a gun off the bed and started pointing it around the room. Very calmly we asked him, 'Uh, could you please put that down?'

"At night Bongo's own guards would sit out in the hotel hallway, pull out those big knives and carve intricate designs into their flesh. Blood dripped all over the carpet. It was a nightmare for the maids, but the guards had wanted to commemorate their trip."

Marty also grew familiar with the hermetic rituals of American diplomacy. Sometimes a dignitary's bags had no sooner arrived at his hotel suite than a necromancer from the CIA or the State Department would show up with an additional piece of luggage.

"We'd ask him to open his briefcase, checking for weapons. Inside, you'd see rows and rows of hundred dollar bills. 'What's this?' I'd ask.

"The guy would just smile and say, 'Spending money.' "

Years before U.S. authorities fingered Bahamian Prime Minister Lynden Pindling and Panamanian General Manuel Noriega as being conduits for drug dealing, Marty believed that another Caribbean head of state was making a sham of diplomatic privilege.

"I'm sure this guy was dealing drugs. The people who'd visit him, the way we'd move him around in the middle of the night made it clear. We were giving him a legitimate shield. We kept away the press and the cops while he emptied and filled that diplomatic pouch."

Officially, the job of protecting visiting rulers had rested with the State Department since 1922. That changed in 1970, when two incidents made Nixon lose confidence in the State Department's guards.

First, there'd been a near-assassination in the lobby of New York's Plaza Hotel. A city cop managed to grab a gun away from a Cornell grad student aiming at Premier Chiang Ching-Kuo, son of Taiwan President Chiang Kai-Shek. Then there'd been the melee in Chicago, where pro-Israeli protesters so mercilessly heckled French President George Pompidou that Nixon made a trip to New York to apologize to him. Later that year, when the twenty-fifth anniversary of the United Nations came up, Nixon asked for a 1.65-million-dollar security appropriation and called in the Secret Service.

The following year Congress gave the Service the full-time job of protecting all visiting heads of state. Even Henry Kissinger, when he became Secretary of State, rejected his own department's security force and put in for Secret Service protection—at a reported yearly cost of one million dollars. In fact, one of Marty's first foreign details was escorting Kissinger on the first leg of his hush-hush peace shuttle to Communist China.

The Service was flattered that the White House and Capitol Hill thought its agents were the country's ablest bodyguards. But guarding the "foreign digs" also posed a new drain on the agency's manpower, a new budget fight in Congress, a new distraction from the counterfeiting work.

"What most concerned us was the word from on high that we were supposed to show the same dedication to these foreign potentates as to our own President. The same dedication, even though some of these yo-yo's came from nations that were about six months old, and some of the older potentates made you want to throw up.

"Imelda Marcos, strictly speaking, wasn't entitled to Secret Service protection when she came to America without her husband. Still, Washington knew nothing if not that Imelda was, to put it diplomatically, a special case. I'd studied the film that captured the 1972 attempt on her life—where this dark-suited engineer slashed

Imelda's right arm with a foot-long bolo knife. Now I had to set up security for the former beauty queen's assault on New York's most expensive boutiques. Imelda had adored Manhattan ever since she first visited the city for psychiatric treatment. She'd made a secret of her Manhattan doctors' diagnosis that she was manic-depressive— and of her mood-soothing regimen of tranquilizers and lithium. But anybody who'd ever dealt with a quarterly could see the frenzy in her shopping.

"As soon as she arrived at the Waldorf Towers, the jeweler from Harry Winston came up in the elevator carrying two suitcases and flanked by his own two bodyguards. The suitcases were filled with pearls, rubies, necklaces, you name it. She'd take them out and literally wallow in them. We also had to let in men bringing her cash from the New York branch of the Philippine National Bank. In a single trip, the couriers would bring her as much as $250,000 in crisp bills." (Between 1973 and 1986, they brought some $30 million in cash up to her suite.) "I used to tell friends, 'You can't believe the money this bitch is wasting.'

"I'd stopped in the Philippines one time when we were escorting the President of Fiji back home. Manila had ghettos like I'd never even seen in St. Louis or Harlem. But now here was Imelda gorging on the most expensive caviar they had on the menu. I saw a bill from her florist lying around. I couldn't believe my eyes: $17,000. I thought to myself, 'What the fuck is going on here?'

"Her whole attitude made my skin crawl. Right after she'd been slashed, Nixon heard that her knife wounds needed something like seventy-five stitches, so he'd arranged for her to be treated by a hand surgery specialist who also treated Van Cliburn. Van Cliburn became a regular at Imelda's suite at the Waldorf. He and his mother would come up and he'd play the piano while Imelda sang opera. You can be sure Van Cliburn was getting something out of it, but her singing—God, it was enough to make my ears fall off."

*     *     *

Imelda did remember her Secret Service agents, though. She gave them all chunky, engraved gold watches. Marty gave the one he received to his mother. On Thanksgiving, Imelda saw that her agents, away from their families, looked glum. So she called down to the Secret Service command post and told them that she was throwing them a Thanksgiving party. When the agents showed up at her suite, they found not just a catered feast—turkey and all the trimmings—but also a flock of gorgeous Filipino women.

"I remember all that. But it didn't endear her to me. It wasn't *her* money to spend. I would've rather had a sandwich."

Another detail found Marty "socializing" at the Waldorf with Anastasio Somoza, the portly Nicaraguan President whose estimated personal wealth of $500 million once prompted a State Department analyst to call Somoza's form of government a "kleptocracy."

"Up at Somoza's suite, Somoza would kiss his wife goodnight and say, 'I'm going downstairs to have a brandy.'
"She'd smile and say, 'You have a nice time, dear.' She knew exactly what he was going to do. It was one of those marriages.
"So we rode down to the lobby with him and walked into one of the Waldorf bars where the real expensive Mayflower Madam-type hookers hung out. These blond, WASPy girls saw this well-dressed character stroll in with two guys wearing lapel pins and you could just read their eyes: 'Oooh, a *big* fish just swam in!' Somoza sat down at the bar and all the girls found some reason to come over to talk with him. We sat at a table behind him for hours, sipping our club sodas while he got drunk with the hookers. Finally he picked one out and his aide booked him another room upstairs. Then we took him up and waited outside. One time I told Somoza, 'Look, you're going to leave your door ajar.' You'd hear him getting rough with her in there. I wasn't about to go back to my boss and say some hooker just

cut the throat of the guy I was supposed to protect. Tell you the truth, it was the perfect opportunity for some Sandanista rebel to become the heroine of her revolution.

"Somoza used to get shitfaced drunk. One night we brought him back to the Waldorf and he crawled on his hands and knees across the lobby, laughing. Another night he went hopping from one disco to another. Everybody was kissing his ass until we got to this one dive disco. Somoza staggered up to the door and demanded to be let in. The doorman, who was your regular guy from Brooklyn or Queens, hesitated about lifting the rope.

"Somoza said, 'Do you have any idea who I am?' We all winced. Honestly, we were embarrassed to be with him.

"I walked up to the doorman, like I was going to tell him who this big slob was, and I whispered, 'If he's an asshole, don't let him in.' So the doorman didn't.

"Somoza couldn't believe it. When he saw he wasn't getting anywhere acting like a king, he told the guy, 'Hey, I was born in New York. I grew up on the streets of New York!' The doorman still wouldn't budge. Somoza said to me, 'You mean, *you* can't get me in there?' Like if we were his *usual* bodyguards, we probably would've wrapped that rope around the doorman's neck.

"I just shrugged and told him, 'Sorry.' As we were talking back to the limo, I gave the doorman a wink."

Marty's mask hadn't slipped during that 1976 visit. After Somoza went home, a Merrill Lynch executive, who'd held a reception for "His Excellency," wrote Director Stuart Knight praising Marty and fellow agent Harry Horton for being "extraordinarily personable in their attitudes."

"What else could I be on duty? But in 1979, when I heard that he'd fled Nicaragua for Paraguay, I jumped up and down."

* * *

A year later Somoza was driving to his exercise class when ambushers ripped off the top of his white Mercedes Benz with a bazooka blast and then riddled the ex-dictator with machine gun bullets.

If ambushers had opened up on Somoza when he'd been riding around New York, the Secret Service detail would have been beholden to die for him.

Marty's former boss Jerry Parr reflects, "That's something to transcend. I had Somoza. I had Arafat. I had a lot of foreign leaders who, one might say, were politically odious. Would an agent be faulted if he refused to die for a foreign leader? I don't know. It hasn't happened that I know of. We have talked about it. Let's not beat around the bush. There are 140 some countries in the world, and we have to guard even the obscure ones. The only perspective you can have is that because someone's a leader, he's worthy of protection—I *guess.* It would be hard to predict how far an agent would go if a foreign dignitary was attacked. A lot of agents have a very nurturing instinct to shield and protect—like they were protecting a child."

Chuck Rochner, the dapper senior agent who supervised Marty on some of his diplomatic details adds, "Maybe you could influence history for the better if you could keep the President from being assassinated. Because, next week, he could go to the Soviet Union and work out an arms deal. He could do something great for the country that you weren't in a position to do. That's how I came to grips with the chance of dying. But with [Soviet Foreign Minister] Andrei Gromyko, or [Somoza's Marxist successor] Daniel Ortega— well, it's best not to think about it too long. It is something all agents have talked about. They've wondered, 'What are we doing here?' "

Marty: "Rochner and I asked ourselves that very question in September of 1977. Gromyko was in New York for a UN General Assembly session. Thousands of Russian expatriates were planning to use his visit to spotlight the Kremlin's treatment of political dissidents. As lead advance agent for the Gromyko detail, I'd spent weeks setting up security. I knew that Ukrainian demonstrators were planning a 'freedom parade' and a rally outside the Public Library. The advance word was that it'd be peaceful. But I had my doubts, and that day I was getting sketchy intelligence about how big the crowd would be. I had to put in my order for agents and cops, so I made a judgment call. I asked for support that at the time, for a foreign dignitary, was unprecedented.

"The other agents weren't thrilled to be working back-to-back shifts, and nobody wanted to think about what the tab would be for the police overtime. But that afternoon a bunch of the younger demonstrators—they were all wearing these scout uniforms—broke away from the rally and started marching up Madison Avenue. The other demonstrators started following them. So suddenly you had about three thousand people headed uptown toward the Soviet Mission, where they knew Gromyko was.

"Up at Sixty-sixth Street some cops had set up barricades. The cops thought they could turn them east and hold them in that one block, on Sixty-sixth Street. But these Ukrainians just charged through those barricades—actually started hurling these wooden saw-horses at the cops. So now the Ukrainians were marching up Lexington, against traffic, and they wanted to come down Sixty-seventh Street, between Lex and Third, where the Soviets have their mission. This was getting serious. I was standing with the other agents in front of the mission, and up at the corner of Sixty-seventh and Lex I could see the cops trying to hold them off. Never have I seen a riot like that. The cops arrested a woman because they said she threw a piece of wood at them. When that mob heard the cops had her, they went berserk. They were throwing bottles and cans of red paint. Some tough Ukrainian women were punching the police horses in the snout and setting their tails on fire. The horses were rearing up and the cops were just trying to hang on.

"Down in Washington, agents could always get a laugh by standing outside the Soviet Embassy and talking into their wristwatches. The Soviet guards would run out in a huff, as if some spy would really stand right outside their door and talk over a microphone. But that afternoon, in front of the mission, we weren't laughing. I thought I'd asked for enough support. The damn Nineteenth Precinct was right across the street from the mission, but it still wasn't enough. Some of the agents and cops were getting panicky. We were the last line of defense.

"Somebody said, 'Let's move the limo in front of the fence so they can't get through.'

" 'Absolutely not,' I said. Everybody started screaming at me.

"I said, 'No. It'll be like a step ladder to get over the fence.' So they left the limo where it was.

"I guarantee you, inside that mission those Russians had machine guns pointed in our direction. They're very paranoid and they don't fool around. Gromyko was inside. If they shot off a few rounds, they'd say they were protecting their sovereign territory. Finally, reinforcements arrived. There were almost a hundred cops on the scene. Barry Farber, the Conservative candidate for mayor, jumped up on the police barricades with a bullhorn and tried to calm down the Ukrainians. Even when they stopped their charge, though, the Ukrainians said they were going to block Lexington Avenue until the cops let that woman go. The cops finally did release her, and two hours after all this started everybody went home with blood on their shirts. About ten cops and an unknown number of demonstrators were injured.

"Gromyko kindled one more crisis before he winged out of New York. A motorcade was trundling the Kremlin's eminence toward Kennedy Airport when I heard a message come over the radio. I was riding in the lead car. Somebody had been spotted with a rifle near the Soviets' Aeroflot runway. I tried to get a handle on what was happening out there, but there was a lot of static on the radio and the agent I was talking to sounded confused. Soon we were almost at the airport, but I wasn't going any farther till I understood the situation. So I stopped the motorcade on the airport access road and I said to the agent on the radio, 'All right, slow down. Speak in short sentences. What is going on?' We didn't move till they moved Gromyko's plane to another runway. Gromyko's plane looked wonderful taking off."

In a letter to Bob Taylor, who was then head of the Dignitary Protection Division, Chuck Rochner lauded Marty's foresight in ordering up extra cops for the Soviet Mission. "If the demonstrators had reached the Mission, the Secret Service would have undoubtedly suffered casualties, destruction of automobiles, and professional embarrassment."

"The cops deserved the credit for holding off the crowd at the Soviet Mission. But those Ukrainians came close enough to overrunning us to start me thinking. I was all for keeping the peace on East Sixty-seventh Street, or wherever. But just a couple of years before, a KGB defector told how the Kremlin had a contingency plan to kill Nixon. And that isn't such a big thing when you consider that the Kremlin has a contingency plan to kill us all.

"Yet there I was, ready to take some lumps—maybe even a bullet—all in the defense of Andrei Gromyko. Not only that. The people who were doing the attacking were *human rights* activists. They were, I would say, on our side. That's what got me wondering, 'How did I get into this situation?'

"Diplomacy had already left me with a limp. In February of 1976 I'd been working the motorcade of Pakistan's Prime Minister Zulfikar Ali Bhutto. Bhutto's motorcade was leaving Kurt Waldheim's house on Sutton Place. I was running along, trying to climb into the follow-up car when suddenly the car sped up. I had my hand on the door, but I lost my footing. A Pakistani guy saw me getting dragged underneath and pulled me into the back seat. The accident left me with a four-inch scar, torn ligaments and tendonitis. I was out of work for a month.

"Bhutto went back to Pakistan, where his election-rigging pro-voked street riots and ultimately a military coup. His successor, Mohammed Zia ul-Haq, who would later win a five-year U.S. aid package of $3.2 billion, had Bhutto arrested and sentenced to death. In 1979, I read about Bhutto's hanging and said to another agent, 'Three years ago I was supposed to *die* for that guy. Now his own country's executed him.' "

Bhutto.
Gromyko.
Somoza.
Marcos.
The shady Caribbean head of state.

"All of them formed a gang that crept up on me. First I had to surrender my opinions about American politicians. Now it was dicta-tors. *'Frisk him, Sam, he might be packing a conscience!'* It was as if indifference was the better part of valor.

"It was all getting confusing. I mean, the Church Committee had just come out with its findings about the 'Executive Action capabil-ity' of the CIA, regarding the CIA's plots to kill Fidel Castro and Rafael Trujillo and Patrice Lumumba; also the part the CIA played in assassinations in Vietnam and Chile.

"Just for fun, I wondered, what was the policy when those 'digni-taries' came to New York? Were Secret Service agents still expected to die for them—even though another part of the government was trying to off them? What if the people on the CIA's current hit list came to New York? I thought somebody ought to let us know. Post a memo or something. Of course Congress told the CIA it couldn't have any more hit lists. But who really knew? Maybe they'd decide that New York was the best place to get the job done. Lots of local mob action. The Company could control the Executive Action better. It wouldn't have to get anybody across any Bay of Pigs. But what if a Secret Service agent got caught in the crossfire? Gee, that would be regrettable. Except, on the upside, people would say, 'The government *couldn't* have been connected.' All that may sound screwy. But these were the sort of things you wondered about then. It was in the air."

# CHAPTER EIGHT

## *A Ford, not a Lincoln*

AS one of the senior members of the New York protection squad, Marty, at twenty-eight, had been learning to call more of the shots.

"I wasn't just working the foreign gigs. New York was one of the few cities where Washington let field office agents do much of the advance work for the President's trips. Since Gerald Ford, more so than Richard Nixon, liked to get out and press the flesh, I was on the phone with a lot with W–16, the Secret Service's office at the White House.

"Even within the confines of New York you never knew where a Presidential visit would take you. One hot summer day I went to the tenement apartment of a woman who'd threatened Ford. She was sitting in front of a fan that blew air off a big block of ice. And while she was talking to me she was heating up an ice pick on an electric stove. The ice pick would turn bright orange, and she'd wrap a piece of her hair around it and give herself a do.

"Talk about changes in scenery. That night, I was at a state dinner with Ford. But all during the speeches, I kept staring at the women with their hairdos by Kenneth or Norbert or whoever. And every time some lady touched her curls I'd see that woman with that glowing ice pick.

"I started to see what a mighty spell the Presidency cast upon people. Both august and anonymous citizens forgot themselves when the most powerful man in America came near. Even Senators. If they could sit closer to him, or squeeze into a picture with him, it made them feel more important. You wouldn't believe how testy a Senator could get if we had to hold him at a door while he saw a photo opportunity getting away.

"When the President came out in public, working the ropeline, you'd see a ceremony of patriotic rapture you could only compare with the evangelical laying-on of hands. The Secret Service used to tell the President—just like we told every candidate—that he shouldn't actually shake people's hands. He should just touch the hands, quickly, and move on. But a lot of times he didn't do that, or he wasn't quick enough, and the people in the crowd would clamp down on his hand with their two hands, and they wouldn't let go. They want to preserve that feeling of their flesh and the President's.

"The way we were taught to make a guy let go was to reach low and give him a tap in the balls. You don't tap him hard, just a little wrist flick—*bing!* Just to break his concentration, so the President can get his hand back. The camera and everybody's eyes are on the President's face, so it isn't really noticed. Even the guy doesn't completely realize why he let go, he's so excited. With women, there's a pressure point just above the breast. Sometimes ladies would wait for hours for him. They'd be standing on that ropeline, drinking coffee from big styrofoam cups to keep warm. Damned if they were going to give up *their* spot. And then the President would finally arrive and get to them, and it would be just too much for them. They'd be squeezing his flesh like it was the parchment of the Declaration of Independence, and suddenly these ladies would lose control of their bladders. Right then and there.

"The President always came with a special set of crowd problems.

For instance, we brought with the President the cars with the big running boards. People would surge out onto the street so they could get a closer look at the motorcade, and sometimes they'd be so distracted after just seeing the President that they didn't see these running boards headed straight for their legs. At the last second you'd have to reach out and shove the people away from the car, or their legs would be broken. Of course some people thought we just did it for kicks. As we'd speed ahead, I'd hear them screaming, 'Assholes! Shitheads!'

"That sort of misunderstanding really bothered me. We didn't have time to explain that we were trying to keep them from getting hurt, and so we left behind these people who'd tell their friends the Secret Service was a bunch of fascist storm troopers.

"Some people would get offended when we'd ask them to take their hands out of their pockets. We might take away the flowers they gave the First Lady, or we'd step in front of them if they were running too fast. If it's any consolation, we also used to throw little body blocks in front of Ford—run interference—so he wouldn't wander off into the crowd again."

There was no getting around it, though. The Secret Service gave former University of Michigan MVP center exalted defense. Working on Ford's advances, Marty saw that the protection meted out to Presidential candidates looked like a team of school crossing guards next to the Roman legion that shielded the man himself.

Just one of Ford's multi-city trips would call for up to a hundred agents. Days before Ford traveled down the street of a distant city, specialists from the Technical Security Division would search for time bombs. They'd crawl under bridges, cart away mail boxes and look under manhole covers before caulking them shut. They'd order helicopters and boats. The advance agents would put together a fifty-page report. They'd time how long the motorcade took to cover its route, marking the points where a traffic jam might give a sniper a few extra seconds to take aim. They'd make sure a local hospital had plenty of the President's blood type. They'd have hotel elevators inspected. They'd feed the "watch list" computer the names of hotel guests, chefs, waiters, maids, doormen, busboys, bellhops. They'd fax ahead photos of threatening "look-outs" who lived in the area.

A few days before the President's arrival, two hulking military cargo planes would deliver the President's bubbletop limousine, three or four other armored limos, metal detectors, and hundreds of thousands of dollars worth of electronics. The agents would bring all their blinking, beeping divining rods up to the floor where the President would sleep, sweeping for bombs and bugs. They'd x-ray the walls with a fluoroscope, peering through its radiant green dust for anything larger than a cockroach. They'd take off doors, roll out beds and roll in a battery of teletype machines from the State Department, the CIA, the FBI, the NSA and, of course, the Secret Service. They'd wheel in an electronic scrambler the size of a Frigidaire to make sure the President had a "secure phone."

And finally the President would hit town—waving and smiling and surrounded by the expectation of his own death and the world's destruction. Bringing up the rear of his motorcade was a stretch Cadillac convertible, customized with a tilted, reversed seat that gave a Secret Service machine gunner a better angle on any air attack.

Up ahead, in the press van, the "death watch" camera rolled. The networks were dead set on never again having to depend on a Zapruder home movie. So they taped every second of the motorcade. "If he didn't get killed by the end of the day," Marty said, "they erased the tape." Following the President's armored car was "Halfback," the limo that held the President's two constant companions: the doctor with his black bag and the military aide with *his* "black box"—the conduit to the President's nuclear arsenal.

In seconds, the aide could open his briefcase, consult his codebook and punch in the phone number for Armageddon. Meanwhile, back at the airport, near Air Force One, there waited one of the four modified Boeing 747s that made up the National Emergency Airborne Command Post, otherwise known as the "Doomsday" fleet. Freighted with communications equipment, one of those flying war rooms was always close to the President and the Joint Chiefs of Staff, so that, when hell broke loose, the commanders could fly above the radioactive wasteland—or so they hoped.

But given that he always had these deathly downers lurking around him, Gerald Ford was, of the Presidents Marty guarded, singularly good-humored.

"He was a real agent's man. When agents were shivering outside at Camp David, Ford would sneak them an egg sandwich when the boss wasn't looking. He'd wink and say, 'Boy, it's cold out here. I'll get you a cup of coffee.'

"That's the kind of thing you never forget. The fact that 'Passkey'—Ford's code name—inserted himself into crowds did make him harder to defend than the standoffish Nixon. But how much more amiable could a President be toward his bodyguards than to have a face that was the spitting image of one of our own? The head of the White House detail was a stocky, balding agent named Dick Keiser. Keiser's face was enough of a Xerox of Ford's that crowds used to applaud Keiser when he'd step off Air Force One before Ford. Asked if he thought he might be shot by mistake, Keiser said, 'I hope so.'

"The agents also got on well with Ford's family. Jack Ford found that when he waltzed into a Georgetown bar and his studly musclemen scoped out the place for danger, they usually came back with some cute girls. Those agents were just purebred bird dogs. Of course, agent Chuck Vance didn't have to leave Ford's Palm Springs retreat to find a date. On the sly, he started seeing a flirty blonde in cutoffs named Susan Ford. Vance would leave her secret messages like, 'Just say Trouble called.' Susan, who'd made the number three spot on the Symbionese Liberation Army's hit list, liked Vance. She said that he made her feel safe and that he opened car doors for her, 'like my father.' Naturally a daughter could grow close to men who'd three times saved her dad from dying.

"Back in 1970, when I was working in Los Angeles, I used to climb the steps of the Federal Building and pass a woman who'd carved X's into her forehead. She was holding a vigil for Charles Manson, who was standing trial inside for the murder of actress Sharon Tate and eight others. Even before the murders, Manson's hatred of Richard Nixon had earned him a Secret Service interrogation. The woman on the steps was Lynette 'Squeaky' Fromme. Squeaky and I developed a relationship. She called me a pig and I'd tell her to stick it up her ass. Five years later, when I heard on a car radio that she had pulled a .45-caliber automatic on President Ford in Sacramento, I said to the agent sitting next to me, 'I never thought she had the guts to do it.' "

Ford had just come out of the Senator Hotel and was shaking hands and grinning when a teenage girl who was standing nearby noticed that "the color went out of his face." Ford had just offered his left hand to a tiny red-robed woman who'd emerged from some magnolia trees. She was now pointing a pistol at Ford's genitals.

Larry Buendorf, thirty-seven, model agent, Navy pilot, expert skier, Marty's pal from the Shriver days, shouted, "Gun!" He dove into Squeaky Fromme. His palm swallowed her. Luzania leaned into Ford, buckling the President's knees to make him a smaller target. Other agents formed their wigwam around Ford. "Everyone get out of the way, get out of here!" called an agent.

One of the Secret Service men grabbed the collar of Ford's blue suit and they piloted him away in a flying wedge formation. Larry Buendorf pushed Squeaky up against a tree and handcuffed her. "Don't get excited," Squeaky said. "It didn't go off. It didn't go off. Can you believe it?" Some witnesses said they'd heard the sound of a trigger click. But Squeaky's lawyers later insisted she never pulled the trigger. Her gun had four bullets, but its firing chamber was empty.

"Seven days after Squeaky Fromme's attack, the President was in my hometown, St. Louis. Ford was scheduled to speak to the National Baptist Convention at Kiel Auditorium, where Benny Sharp had played to a crowd of 16,000 people. On the day Ford was to appear, several bomb threats had been called into the auditorium. Thirty minutes before Ford got to the event, cops spotted a man crouching in a catwalk high above the stage. The man had a .45-caliber automatic pistol.

"I was standing at one of the auditorium exits, waiting for Ford to get there, when I heard the description of the gunman come over a cop's radio: suspect was Caucasian, about six feet tall, about 170 pounds, wearing a white shirt, dark pants and a black wig. As the cops were chasing this guy through the auditorium, the whole drama was being broadcast over the police radio. All the people standing around could hear it. Everybody was listening closely to the radio and getting sort of nervous. Then they heard that the guy with the gun was heading for our exit. Well, everybody panicked. And for some reason, the mounted police decided to gallop on their horses right into the crowd, swinging nightsticks. The cops created a stampede, and in the ensuing confusion, we lost the guy with the gun."

Then, seventeen days after the Squeaky Fromme attack, Ford was in San Francisco. He walked out of the St. Francis Hotel, stopped at his limo and waved to the crowd across the street. A gunshot perforated the cheering. The President blanched and clutched his chest. A second before, in the crowd, a Vietnam vet whose combat experience had left him with mental problems, had spotted the chrome barrel of Sara Jane Moore's .38 and he had yelled, "Gun!" When several people grabbed for her arm, her pistol expelled a bullet that ricocheted off the St. Francis Hotel and down the street, expiring just as it thumped a cabdriver in the groin. One San Francisco cop wrenched the gun from Moore's hand; another cop grabbed her hair; yet another pounded on her back and cried, "Goddamit! Goddamit!" Some Secret Service men hustled her into custody while other agents, who'd pushed Ford into his limo, raced the President to safety.

For eighteen months, Moore, a dowdy forty-five-year-old veteran of five failed marriages, had been working as an informant for the FBI and the Bureau of Alcohol, Tobacco and Firearms. She had agreed to spy on her fellow radicals, and then feeling guilty, had confessed to them about her espionage. Soon she was getting telephoned death threats. The FBI didn't want to protect an informant who'd blown her cover, so Moore tried to get arrested.

Two days before her attack on Ford, on a Saturday, Moore called San Francisco Police Inspector Jack O'Shea, whom she knew, and told him, "I'm going to see if the system works equally for the left as well as for the right. I'm going to Stanford to test it." Stanford University was where Ford would be speaking the next day.

O'Shea recalled that she had asked, "Would you arrest me if I asked you to?"

He had replied, "Well, I'd have to have a charge. Do you want me to arrest you?"

She laughed, "No, I was only kidding."

O'Shea phoned the Secret Service and asked if they wanted Moore picked up. An agent told him it "might be a good idea."

The following morning, Moore met up with an undercover ATF agent and drove to the home of a right-wing gun dealer to see if the John Bircher was breaking any gun laws. When Moore came back home, she found two cops waiting for her. They took away her .44-caliber pistol and charged her with concealing a weapon. Then they called the Secret Service agents to ask if they wanted Moore kept at the police station. The Service said no, because it would be sending agents to question her. The cops then released Moore at a time when it was too late for her to make Ford's speech at Stanford.

That night, Secret Service agents brought Moore into their field office and interviewed her for ninety minutes. They decided not to take her into custody and ruled that "she was not of sufficient protective importance to warrant surveillance."

The morning of the attack, Moore called the Secret Service field office, trying to reach the agents who'd interviewed her. An answering service took her message. She made two more calls to the Service, then one to the FBI and another to the cops. Completely ignored, she pulled on a pair of yellow polka-dot slacks and cowboy boots and dropped her son off at school. Then she drove back to the home of her right-wing gun dealer and bought herself the .44. And still trying to get arrested, she drove at breakneck speed, loading her gun in the front seat. Finally, she reached the St. Francis Hotel. "The security was so stupid," she said later. "It was like an invitation."

"The Secret Service took a lot of heat when all this came out. At a hearing into Presidential protection, Senators squawked that it was bad enough that the Service didn't have the names of Oswald, Sirhan, Ray, Bremer, Fromme, and Moore on its watch list. Now the agency didn't even seem willing to give surveillance to a would-be assassin who had begged for it."

But Secret Service officials testified that not till after the shooting did anyone relay Moore's phone messages to the agents who'd questioned her. One of the cops who'd interrogated her testified that he'd told those agents that Moore "might be another Squeaky Fromme."

The agents, Martin W. Haskell and Gary Yauger, insisted that the cop had said no such thing and that when they'd asked him, "Do we have a problem?" he replied, "No." Agent Yauger, whom Marty knew from the McGovern campaign, said that he'd conducted over five hundred interviews with potential assassins. He testified that he'd asked Moore, "Are you going to try to shoot the President?"

He said she calmly answered, "No." She'd said she bought a gun because her life had been threatened. Yauger reported, "No animosity to the President or the Ford Administration"—in fact, she'd called it a "noncontroversial administration."

"I agreed with Yauger's decision. The Secret Service had acted like I'd hoped it would, this being America. They couldn't get a threat out of her. So what grounds did they have to hold her? They might have put her under surveillance. But she didn't have a history of violence. And when a person has spent a year and a half *doing* surveillance for the FBI, you tend to make allowances. The agents guarding Ford that day had the right instinct. Ford had been talking about crossing the street to shake some hands. The agents advised him against it."

Ford praised the Secret Service for the way it handled the affair and he pledged that he wouldn't capitulate to attackers by curbing his glad-handing. "The American people are good people," Ford declared. But why did they keep pulling guns on him?

Ford gave himself a backhanded answer when he fumed that if a President couldn't walk among the American people, then "something has gone wrong with our society."

"It *was* odd that all this mayhem should hail down upon easygoing Jerry Ford, when his more widely reviled predecessors, Nixon and Johnson, had stayed out of harm's way. Of course Johnson knew enough not to stick his hand into a nest of sidewinders; and Nixon was just lucky.

"Still, after Squeaky and Sara Jane, we walked on cat's paws. One night a bunch of us were walking down a hall with Ford when a fold-up table fell on the floor. *Bam!* We all thought it was another gunshot. We pushed him down and piled on top of him."

*     *     *

Ford survived to see his chance to be elected to the office he'd won by default. For the Secret Service, though, the 1976 election promised only another complete disruption of its organization. Counterfeiters loved campaigns. In nonelection years, the agency allotted sixty percent of its manpower to the investigation of counterfeiting and forgery, and forty percent to protection. Now those proportions would have to be reversed. Even then, the Service would have to borrow hundreds of Treasury and Customs agents.

(In the 1976 campaign, the Service once again bestowed authentic Presidential-style bodyguards on any candidate who squeezed at least $5,000 out of at least twenty states.) Strapped with a campaign budget of $16 million, agents said the Service was overextended in guarding nineteen Presidential and Vice Presidential candidates and their spouses.

Among Ford's challengers was a rebellious Republican named Ronald Reagan.

"I hooked up with the Reagan campaign out in California, where Reagan's Pacific Palisades neighbors came to dread us. They griped about agents closing off the streets and nosing into their party guest lists. One neighbor even claimed that an agent told her not to turn on her sprinklers. When she asked why, she said he replied, 'Because we have agents hiding in your bushes.' But Reagan had great support with us. Maybe it was because he'd made four Warner Brothers movies based on the life of William Henry Moran."

Moran had served fifty-five years in the Secret Service, eighteen of them (1918–37) as director. In flicks like *Code of the Secret Service*, Reagan played ace agent Brass Bancroft. And when Reagan galloped out onto the campaign trail, the Service saddled him with the code name "Rawhide." Rawhide liked to ride horses around his property, and when he did, Marty joined up with his posse.

\*  \*  \*

"He and I would collect wood, and he'd tell me macho stories about when he was governor. How he really kicked ass when those hippies were storming the campus buildings. Then when 2:00 P.M. arrived, no matter how busy his staff was, Reagan would lie down at the pool with his sun reflector. That might seem like a vain, sissy thing to do, but Reagan had this cowboy way of describing it. He said he was getting 'a coat of tan.' Like it was some kind of leather treatment—which I suppose it was.

"I got a feel real fast for what Hollywood-on-the Potomac would look like. Once, on a campaign plane, Reagan encouraged his chum Jimmy Stewart to relive his days as an Air Force pilot in World War II. Now God bless Jimmy Stewart, but the man is *old*. They sat him down in the pilot's seat and he started talking about the Big War and saying this Boeing 727 was 'just like the ole B–29.'

"Well, I'm sorry, it's *not* just like the old B–29. He was groping around for different switches while the co-pilot was saying, 'No, no, don't touch that!' I was a little worried.

"Maybe others just acclimated to the Reagan style easier than I did. One L.A. field office agent, Robert Powis, got on famously with Reagan. We'd be working a rally and Powis would point Reagan over to someone whose hand he'd forgotten to shake. Other agents would look at each other and ask, 'What's Powis *doing?* Is he running Reagan's campaign now?' Four years later, when Reagan would at last move into the White House, Powis would become deputy Assistant Secretary of the Treasury, outranking the director of the Secret Service.

"That agents on the campaign might come across each other in a tavern was beyond question. You'd always be hearing about some hijinks. Agents driving around drunk at a hundred miles an hour on an airport runway. They didn't have to worry about getting arrested. The chief of police was usually in the car with them. Sometimes, if agents couldn't get a seat on Air Force One, or if they didn't want to ride on the commercial jet, they'd get on the C141 cargo plane and go to sleep in the back seat of a limo.)They weren't supposed to, but they did. One time a limo got loose and started rolling backwards. Somebody hit the brake, but if one of those big armored cars started moving, it might've rolled right out the back of the plane.

"We developed these warped ways of keeping the humor up on the campaign. Like when we were checking in at a hotel for the midnight shift. We'd inevitably end up standing at the front desk behind some rich fat lady who'd go on and on about her wake-up call—how the desk better not forget to call her at such and such a time. So we'd write down her name and room number and the time she wanted to get up. We had to make wake-up calls to the other agents anyway. All night long we'd look forward to dialing that lady's room number. Five minutes before she wanted to get up, we'd ring her and say, 'Hello, Mrs. So and So? GET-YOUR-FAT-ASS-OUT-OF-BED!' When we'd leave the hotel, we'd see her at the front desk complaining.

"After Rawhide lost his party's nomination, his aide Michael Deaver sent me a bracing thank-you note: 'Someday, like Shakespeare's old soldier who survived the battle of St. Crispin's Day, you will be able to come across a comrade of yours in a tavern and pull back your shirt and proudly display the scars of battle, honorably won . . .' Or, at least, sporting a coat of tan.

"As the candidates closed in on November, I had no plans to vote for any of them. By this time, I'd pretty much stopped listening to their speeches. You can't concentrate on the crowd if you're searching for meaning in what a politician is saying. What's to hear? It was like they were all shuffling the same deck of three-by-five cards. 'A future for our children.' 'Peace in our time,' 'Time for a change.' Every once in a while you had to turn around and check the podium to see if it wasn't the candidate from last week."

Yet every so often a truly rare human moment broke through to Marty.

* * *

"The Secret Service was the first to know that Ford was picking Bob Dole as his running mate. Another agent and I were supposed to track down Dole so he could find out. We found him in the Senate barbershop. He was getting his hair cut when I told him, 'The President will be calling you.' You could see the shock, the thrill, in his face while he sat there with hair on his shoulders. His life was changing!

"Then the White House operator put the call through. The operators always say, 'Stand by for the President.' It's so funny. Whenever people hear that they stand up at attention, as if the President could see them. Sure enough, Dole stood up from his barber chair. History was happening to him!

"Unfortunately, not enough history. After they lost, Dole returned to the Senate. And Ford was set free to travel around the country, less harassed by loopy women and mad men. Susan Ford married her secret lover from the Secret Service. She called Chuck Vance her Superman and he called her his Princess. Her pipe-puffing dad fetched himself a princely sum by sitting on corporate boards and by appearing as a sage commentator on television. Shortly after he'd left office, he was in New York, having just signed an exclusive deal with NBC. One night he was staying—statesmanly—at the UN when he told Marty that he wanted to take his usual swim.

"So I set it up with the hotel manager, who said, 'The pool closes at eleven P.M. The President could go up after that.'

"I told him, 'I want to keep this between you and me.'

" 'Sure,' he said. 'I won't say a word.' A little after eleven I came around to Ford's room and took him up to the pool. Nobody was in the pool, so he dove in and started doing his laps. I walked around the edge and went into the men's locker room. There was this one middle-aged business-type in there getting dressed. He was dawdling: powdering himself, splashing on after-shave, putting his socks on snugly. I sat down on a bench aways from him. He wasn't paying attention to me. Well, I wasn't in there more than five minutes before Ford came through the door, stripped off his trunks and walked past the guy naked. This guy did a double-take. He started blinking and wiping his face with his hand.

"He looked at me and said, 'I think I'm going crazy. I could swear I just saw President Ford walk past me naked.'

"I said, 'Really?'

" 'Yeah. My wife won't believe this.'

" 'That's funny, I didn't see anyone.'

" 'It was President Ford, naked! You didn't see him?'

" 'No. I didn't see anything.'

"I let the guy dangle for a minute. He started looking really worried. Finally I said, 'Hey, it was him. You're not cracking up.'

Water was one place where Ford stood little chance of hurting himself. Even when he didn't have the runway stairs of Air Force One to contend with, the former Chief Executive still faced danger in mounting the stage steps of New York's Shubert Theater.

In August of 1977, Ford's assistant, Gregory D. Willard, wrote to H. Stuart Knight "to commend the actions of a Special Agent . . . which I understand were never officially reported to the Secret Service." .

"At the conclusion of the performance [of 'A Chorus Line'],"  President and Mrs. Ford began to proceed backstage to meet the cast. To reach the stage it was necessary to step onto a small step. Directly to the right of the first step was the orchestra pit, which was covered with a black cloth making it appear as part of the step itself. The orchestra pit was approximately seven feet below the level of the step.

"President Ford stepped onto the step and paused to regain his balance. As he began to move to the stage, he placed his foot squarely on a portion of the cloth and attempted to step up. As President Ford began to fall, Agent Venker reacted instantly, grabbing him by the hip and by his belt. He literally lifted President Ford to the stage. In the process Agent Venker ripped his suit coat and dress shirt from the force of lifting President Ford.

"Without question, had Special Agent Venker not responded as quickly and professionally, President Ford most certainly would have suffered very serious injuries from the resulting fall."

"The Fords were very nice," Marty recalled. "They had me up to their suite afterward. He said I'd saved his life. I don't know about that. Well . . . I suppose he could've been impaled on a clarinet."

# CHAPTER NINE

# *The Presidential Complex*

"ONE day during the '76 campaign, I was sitting in the cockpit of Ronald Reagan's plane and, just as the plane was lifting off, I happened to turn around and see Reagan jump up from his seat and start gasping. A peanut had gotten caught in his throat. I think it was Mike Deaver who wrapped his arms around Reagan's diaphragm and gave him the Heimlich maneuver. Reagan was okay after that. He went back to shuffling his three-by-five cards and everybody on the plane breathed easier. But I'm sure they all saw the omen in what happened. It was like somebody was saying, 'Beware the peanut farmer from Georgia.'

"First time I heard I'd be guarding a guy named Jimmy Carter, I said what everybody said, 'Jimmy who?' He sounded like some country-western singer. But once I was on his detail I could see this guy wasn't going to be overlooked. For one thing, he wouldn't let the voters forget about Watergate. He'd also thought up all these media gimmicks. He wanted to get next to the people and show them how cost-conscious he was. So he'd stay in people's homes instead of hotels. One night he'd been out stumping all over New Hampshire in a blizzard, and when we finally got him to the house where he was supposed to stay, he'd fallen asleep in the back seat of the car. To get him inside, another agent and I had to carry him over the ice. That was typical Jimmy Carter. He'd pinch pennies on a hotel and ignore the extra trouble of guarding a private home. So what if he put the whole neighborhood into an uproar?—that got people talking about him. Yeah, he was one slick hick politician. Carter's homespun politicking carried him into the White House."

After spending another year in New York, Marty met up again with Jimmy Who. Seven years had passed since Marty had become an agent. At last he'd made it to "Crown," the throne of the Secret Service. Marty had visited the White House before, but now, *look,* he had a reserved parking space in the driveway. He strolled past the uniformed guards with a wink and a nod. His office was the Oval Office. He was, as the agents there were always saying, a heartbeat away from the President. *Bum-bump, bum-bump.* The last line of defense. Bum-bump. The difference between life and death. And it was in this emergency-room atmosphere that Marty and Carter got reacquainted.

"I hadn't been at the White House long, but I knew the sound of the panic buttons. The Secret Service put them in all around the place so that if the President was ever attacked or he had a heart attack or something, he could call for help. All the agents had been told that if we ever heard him press one of those panic buttons, we were to get into that room *immediately,* no knocking, hand on our guns.

"So one day I heard the alarm go off in a bathroom near the Oval Office. Hand on my gun, I rushed to the bathroom door, practically knocking it down. Inside I found Carter, zipping up his pants. Apparently, he'd pressed the panic button, thinking that it flushed the toilet.

"Carter was pretty chilly to me after that. I might have taken it personally, but the other agents told me that was just the way Carter was. He didn't have time for a lot of chit-chat—all that hail-fellow-well-met that Ford dished out. Carter was going to have a stripped-down Presidency. Cut the pomp and circumstance. He wanted to hunker down with the voters, show 'em he was accessible. It started on Day One. Carter told us that, after his swearing-in, he wanted to *walk* down Pennsylvania Avenue from the Capitol to the White House, as Thomas Jefferson had done in 1801. It would be a show of humility, a protest march against the insider politics of the past.

"Still, this wasn't 1801, and to the agents, checking thousands of eyes, looking for glints of steel, it was like walking a gauntlet. On that freezing day, even Rosalynn Carter wore three crucifixes under her coat.

"Most of America's Presidents had tugged at their Secret Service leash. Wilson, Harding, Truman, Eisenhower, Johnson, Kennedy, Nixon—all of them had griped about the way the agents cramped their style whenever they tried to get away for poker, golf, sex, whatever. But Carter's inaugural walk idea set some kind of record for starting up with the Secret Service. He had other ideas, too. He told the Secret Service that he wanted them to replace the big limousines with smaller town cars. He told the military bands to forget 'Hail to the Chief.'

"The way I saw it, he was getting bogged down in minutiae. He'd get personally involved in arguments about who would use the White House tennis courts. He wanted to know why he was riding in this car versus *that* car. You just wanted to turn around to him in the back seat and say, 'What *difference* does it make? You're in a car. You're safe. Relax.'

"Carter told the agents he never wanted to hear any police sirens. But one morning we were taking him to church and we got into a traffic jam and so, very briefly, the cops turned on their sirens. Carter took [White House detail head] Dick Keiser aside and read him the riot act.

"For all his campaign folksiness, Carter, once he was in the Oval

Office, showed all the charm of his mentor, cantankerous Admiral
Hyman Rickover."

Former White House aide Paul Costello remembered, "The agents
really did not like the way Carter dealt with them. Ford was very
personable to agents, and Carter was not. But Carter was that way
with all of us. He could make people feel warm in a small group—he
could touch them. But one on one, he could be brutally cold and
dismissive. I don't think he gave the agents a lot of thought. He
thought of them as bodywatchers, pure and simple. They had their
role like everybody else in the White House."

"The times when Carter did notice you," Marty said, "made you
wish he'd go back to ignoring you. One day I was standing post on
his house in Plains [code name "Driftwood"]. Carter walked past me
on his way to go fishing. When he came back a couple of hours later,
he said to me, 'Oh, still awake, huh?' Another time, we were with
him in Panama, where was signing the canal treaty. We were running
alongside his motorcade when a tropical storm broke out. Man, we
had to jog for miles while that rain came down in sheets. Our shoes
squished, and our suits shrank so much it looked as if somebody
stretched our arms on a rack. Anyway, Carter got out of his dry car
and he looked at us standing there soaking wet. Then he said, 'You
guys don't have enough sense to come out of the rain.'
"I grant you, he had an impossible job. But he also had this
complex. Whenever he felt insecure, he showed it by getting petty.
He was an unbelievably sore loser when the Secret Service beat his
team in softball. He also had this one-sided rivalry with an agent
named Jack Smith. Jack was the nicest guy in the world, and he was
really into long-distance running. He subscribed to all the magazines.
Jack and Carter would jog, and Carter would get absurdly competitive. Anytime Jack set a new time, or broke some barrier, Carter

seemed to take it personally. He'd say, 'Well, let's see how good he is when *he's* fifty-four years old.'

"Then there was that time Carter entered that marathon. It was a hot, muggy day, and he ran at a pace he couldn't possibly maintain. Jack Smith was jogging next to him, and he tried to get him to slow down. But Carter had to push it. And so he passed out. We thought it was all over. We laid him down in the back of a car. He could barely breathe. His eyes rolled back up into his head. We got his doctor and gave him oxygen and, thank God, he came around. But we thought we'd lost him. An agent kept asking him, 'Mr. President, do you know where you are?' The networks almost broke into their programming with a national alert.

"Maybe it was because he didn't come as close to getting shot as Ford did, but in Carter's mind, I think, the Secret Service was always blowing the danger out of proportion. Carter used to command a submarine, so he probably thought, 'Why shouldn't I be able to navigate my way through a little crowd?' Sometimes we'd be working him through some people, and he'd tell us to back off a bit. 'Give me some room.' Sometimes, instead of just ignoring him, we would. Within fifteen seconds the crowd would have grabbed hold of him and he'd be looking back at us with this terrified face, sort of apologizing.

"I remember one other time when it seemed to dawn on him that maybe his job was riskier than he thought. Carter was coming to New York to sign a big federal bail-out package for the city. So a couple of weeks before, I went up there to hold meetings with about fifty people from the military, the cops, everybody who was going to help with security.

"Well, the night came when Carter was to land at the Thirtieth Street heliport on the East River, and you wouldn't believe the army that turned out. Every police, fire, Air Force, Marine, and emergency rescue unit in creation was there to show off their hardware to the

President. I guess they wanted to let him know where his federal money was going.

"You had the cops lined up next to their bomb truck. The firemen had their Halo gas extinguishers strapped to their backs. They had their 'Jaws of Life' saws for cutting people out of wrecks. Frogmen were treading water around the pier. And then everybody heard the President's helicopter coming, and they all looked up in the sky as he descended on this pier that was lit up bright as day with klieg lights. I tell you, it was like something out of *Close Encounters of the Third Kind.*

"Carter climbed out of the helicopter and he looked around and saw all these people in asbestos suits and masks—everybody was wearing a different kind of mask. I went over to escort Carter to his car. As we were walking across the helipad, we came up to this state-of-the-art mobile operating room. Carter was curious, so he peaked in the back and saw a team of surgeons standing around an operating table with water dripping off their elbows. They were bathed in this eerie antibacterial light. And of course they also had on *masks.* The surgeons waved to Carter with their rubber gloves, as if to say, 'Hi! We're here just in case your head flies open. Until then, have a nice day.'

"Carter looked at them and then he looked at me, and a visible shiver came over him. Like he'd just seen himself on that operating table. Like all these people knew about something that was going to happen that night that he didn't know.

"I shivered too. I'd often get this weird feeling of dread in situations where you were supposed to feel the safest—where the security was completely overdone. I mean, one of our biggest chores was keeping all the lifesavers from hurting each other. Once I was waiting for Carter to come out of a building in Hannibal, Missouri. Just to pass the time, I counted the number of people who I knew were carrying guns. Besides the Secret Service, you had sheriffs, state troopers, detectives, SWAT teams. They'd come from all over the state. I counted about two hundred and fifty armed people. I knew that a lot of them didn't know who the others were. There had to be a few wild cops who saw conspirators behind every bush. I thought, God, nobody light a firecracker, we'll all get killed in the crossfire.

"You'd run into problems communicating when you got that many law people together. We had a close call when Carter came to New York to speak at the United Nations. I was out on First Avenue, waiting to move him into the U.N. from the U.S. Mission. Carter was in the Mission, riding down on the elevator. Suddenly, we got a radio call. Somebody had spotted a rifle in the window of an apartment building overlooking the street.

"Up on the roofs, police marksmen had the window in their crosshairs. They couldn't take any chances. If the President stepped onto the street, they were ready to take that sniper out. So some agents ran to the apartment building, but when they got there, they found that the elevator wasn't working. They had to climb the fire stairs—up something like seventeen floors. Finally they got to the right apartment and as soon as they knocked on the door, they heard on their radio that a police helicopter had just seen somebody pull the rifle inside and hide it under a sofa.

"The door of the apartment opened. This real middle-class-looking couple was standing there. They said they didn't know anything about a rifle. The agents said, 'What about the one under your sofa?' That's when the couple broke down and said their son had been using a toy rifle with a telescope, just so he could see the President. Of course, by that time we'd stopped Carter in the lobby of the U.S. Mission. Once again, the Secret Service was making him late. But at least that couple's son was alive to watch him cross the street."

Back in 1976, when President Ford dropped into New York, the Secret Service told the cops that it would be putting its own marksmen on certain rooftops. "If anybody does that," Police Commissioner Michael Codd told the Service, "he'll be arrested. That's basically a job for us."

When Carter was in office New York City police sounded off to the New York *Times* about Secret Service hauteur. Patrick Vecchio, a twenty-year vet of the NYPD, claimed that the agents "treat local police as if they were Keystone Kops."

The NYPD told the *Times* that, during the 1976 campaign, almost every time a candidate visited the city, news reporters and photographers had complained about Secret Service agents. Newspeople said that even when they'd had the right security-clearance tags around their necks, agents had pushed them around. One of the city's top cops told his Secret Service counterpart to tell his agents to cut out the strong-arm stuff.

"When I had advanced in New York, I had no trouble with the police. A lot of agents, though, didn't see what you had to *bend* to make things work in New York. You can't *do* everything you'd do in Omaha, Nebraska. New York has more problems in one day than other cities have in a year. Some of the agents would try to show off their college education to these street-smart cops from Brooklyn. That didn't fly. Cops have egos as fragile as eggs. If you start out saying, 'You're going to do this and this,' the cops may actually sabotage your trip. I'd always ask, 'I wonder if you guys could help me with this?' Say that, and they'll bend over backwards for you."

It wasn't just the cops in New York complaining. In 1979, officials of the International Association of Machinists and Aerospace Workers charged that Secret Service agents had intimidated and harassed union demonstrators at every stop made by the Delta Queen, a riverboat carrying Carter down the Mississippi. Specifically, they harassed the media trying to get to the protesters; they acted as Carter's political agents to keep the protesters out of sight. After an investigation, Secret Service director H. Stuart Knight had to admit that agents had "erroneously" shunted off protesters to a separate, roped-off section in Davenport, Iowa. But he said he found no evidence of intentional harassment or wrongdoing by agents in Davenport or any other city. He said the agents' actions hadn't been politically motivated. Still, he shot off a directive to every field office in the country, reminding his agents to honor citizens' Constitutional rights.

The same year, a militant San Francisco union leader named Jane Margolis sued the Service for false arrest. She claimed that an agent and a cop had dragged her from a Detroit union convention where Carter was speaking, handcuffed her and held her for forty minutes. The agency made an out-of-court settlement with Margolis for $3,500. It also sent her a rare letter of apology.

All these complaints hurled at Carter's agents suggested that maybe the Secret Service wasn't completely blameless during the Nixon years, when the agency had claimed that White House staffers had kept protesters out of sight.

There'd been criticism during the Ford years, too. During Ford's trip to Europe in July 1975, West German government officials complained that U.S. Secret Service agents wouldn't let them into their own offices without looking at the proper ID. A high-ranking West German police official reported that Ford's bodyguards were "arrogant and overbearing" and "constantly tried to impose their views." He added: "What they did here recalls the Occupation period of the first postwar years."

"I took the charges of Secret Service bluster with a grain of salt. Cops, protesters, reporters and politicians could also be pushy, surly and curt, too. You have to keep in mind that a lot of Europeans don't even like American tourists, much less guards from the imperial White House. They find our whole country arrogant and overbearing. All the other world leaders ride in the cars that the host country provides. The Americans have to ship in this monster armored Cadillac. The Europeans think, 'What's this? Our cars aren't good enough?' Naturally, the Germans, get really touchy about that.

"But West Berlin is the one city in Europe where they do defer to the Secret Service, because the U.S. is one of the four nations that watch over the city. In every other place, the host government has the final word. England is always a problem. The police there don't carry guns, so they make the Service strip down its firepower. We had a battle royal with Canada. Carter was going to Ottawa for a summit and the Canadians wanted all the agents to turn over their weapons at the airport. Well, our experience showed that the security the Canadian Mounties give hasn't advanced a lot since the days of Rin Tin Tin. There've been some slip-ups. So Carter cancelled the trip. We had to give him credit for that.

"I was on that trip that Carter took down the Mississippi, and I don't remember any trouble. I'm not saying there wasn't any. I'm not saying that no agent ever got rough or rude. But people file formal complaints after almost every trip. You try to keep the number down, but you know there'll never be a political event where somebody's toes don't get stepped on. I tried to shut out problems I wasn't personally involved in. I'd just concentrate on what I projected as an agent. That was the way I dealt with all the craziness on the street. When everybody around me was jumping up and down, I'd move a little slower. When everybody was screaming, I'd think about exactly what I wanted to say, and then I'd say it. You had to lower the energy a few degrees. I wouldn't chant exactly, but I'd hum some old song."

It was plain to see, though, how a White House agent could grow cavalier, could pig out on power. Never in his life had Marty consumed so many calories of authority. Because the President always had the right of way, Marty found himself holding the throttle for all sorts of transportation. He could stop a train. "It's dangerous to have the President stalled at a railroad crossing for too long." If the

President needed to be overseas tomorrow, Marty could order up an Air Force F–14, or commandeer a commercial 707—whatever it took to get overseas ahead of the Chief.

"The commercial jet often wound up being cheaper than the F–14, and sometimes an agent just wasn't near an Air Force base. So the agent would go to an airport, and hand an airline rep a government I.O.U. The airline rep might say that they weren't scheduled to take off for another five hours. But the agent would say, 'I'm sorry, we're taking off *now.*' Flight crew of six. Passengers: one.

"If it involved the President, money was no object. The Service doesn't have to make public the specific costs of Presidential protection, because, according to the Service, that would compromise security. A friend of mine had to fly across South America. He wrote out a check for $30,000. Once I was working with an FBI agent. He couldn't believe I was just going to sign for a Lear jet.

"He said, 'You're going to do *what!?*'

"I said, 'We got it covered. Nooo problem.'

"So he said, 'Don't you have to *ask* somebody?' Hey, nooo problem. He could never spend money like that without getting authorization from thirteen people. But that's the Secret Service. It's a much smaller organization and it leaves much more up to the discretion of the individual agent. *Whatever it takes.*

"If America's Chief Executive wanted to shake some hands on an assembly line, I would set it up. I'd walk into a *Fortune* 500 company and the CEO would drop what he was doing, hold all calls and listen, one by one, as I laid out the game plan. I had been dealing with captains of industry ever since Carter started picking his Cabinet.

"I once had to do a background check on a guy Carter was considering for Deputy Secretary of the Treasury. One of the people I had to interview was the guy's boss, who was one of the managing directors of a major Wall Street investment firm. It was all very confidential, so when I called the boss's office, I only explained to his secretary that I'd like to ask him a few questions regarding a Treasury nomination.

"I got to his firm—wood paneling, portraits of the partners everywhere—and I met his secretary. I could see that she was very excited about something. The boss came right out of his office with a big smile and a handshake. Then he closed the door of his office and sat down behind his desk with this look of anticipation. So I started in.

" 'President Carter is considering John So-and-So for the post of Deputy Secretary of the Treasury. I wonder if you could tell me something about him.'

"Well, the boss's jaw hit the floor. He said, 'John *So and So?* I thought . . .' He sort of laughed it off. 'I thought you might be telling me, uh, that I was nominated for Secretary or something.'

"He laughed and I laughed, and then I went on asking him, 'How has Mr. So-and-So performed? What's his current salary? Would you have any misgivings about his loyalty to the government?'

"The boss paid the guy a lot of compliments. But I could see that he was deflated. I guess he really did think I'd come by to announce the crowning achievement of his career. He thought he was going to work shoulder to shoulder with the President, turn the economy around, then come back to Wall Street with more power than he had now. But *nooo,* it was some young turk under him who was heading for D.C. I felt bad for the guy, like I'd ruined his day.

"You had power out of all proportion to your age. I went back to arrange something at Fort Leonard Wood, the same Army base where I'd trained as a private. Now three-star generals who used to strike fear into my heart were calling me 'Sir.' After just a few years. I couldn't quite believe it.

"Of course there were countless times when I felt like a glorified doorman. Boredom found me sometimes even standing outside the Oval Office. We'd kill time by pitching pennies up onto the little ledge just beneath the ceiling. There's probably a small mountain of pennies still up there. But there were distractions. People would come in and wait. People who, though they were some of the world's most rich and famous nabobs, bit their nails, cracked their knuckles, tightened their ties, smoothed their hair. They were jittery about their audience with America's biggest celebrity.

"Paul Newman kept pacing the floor. He said, 'I'm so nervous.'

"I said, 'Listen, the next shift'll be here in a couple of minutes. Come on down, have a cup of coffee. I'll give you the mini-tour.'

"After we had some coffee, he said, 'Thanks. That helped.'

" 'Don't worry, *he's* probably more nervous than you are. People heard of you before they heard of him.'

"Sophia Loren sat down in a chair. There were two chairs in the anteroom and almost no one sat in either of them. She just sat down and crossed her legs and read something. She was so naturally cool that even the most unflappable White House people were totally mesmerized by her.

"Muhammad Ali was nervous at first. So I kind of narrowed my eyes at him and said, 'Hey, you don't look that tough.' We did a little verbal sparring, joking around.

"He looked over at this high-tech phone and he said, 'What would you do if I made a mad dash for that phone?'

"I replied, 'You couldn't outrun this,' and I lifted open my jacket.

"Finally, he went in with this yuppie who'd brought him to see Carter. When they came out, the yuppie was all flustered. I think there'd been a mix-up about how much support Ali was willing to give Carter. Ali was saying, 'I never promised you *nothing.*' I laughed.

Hourly installments of the Carter drama were revealed in that anteroom. Walter Mondale, Cyrus Vance, Zbigniew Brzezinski, Griffin Bell, Harold Brown, Michael Blumenthal, James Schlesinger, Joseph Califano, Benjamin Civiletti, Stansfield Turner, Robert Strauss, Stuart Eizenstat, Hamilton Jordan, Jody Powell, Bert Lance and others, charged, trudged, slinked, swaggered and staggered past the credenza, under the chandelier, in and out Carter's egg-shaped office.

"There'd be heavy days and boring days. The White House is an artificially relaxed place, with gardens, grandfather clocks and fireplaces. But you could count on at least one world crisis a week. You knew when something heavy was up. One after another, they'd all run in there and shut the door.

"On a given day, the White House reporters would give anything just to know who'd been in, how fast they'd been moving and what they'd been mumbling when they walked out. But reporters were still snitches. An agent who drank a beer on a Presidential trip always risked having some reporter make a big deal out of it. At the same time, the press could have all-night orgies of destruction at hotels. They'd be breaking furniture, pushing kegs of beer into the pool, cracking the diving board. But that never came out. Because if the press can't hush up a story, who can? It was always a cat-and-mouse game.

"I once stopped into a CBS camera truck to ask for a drink of water. While I was there, I got a call and had to radio back through my wrist mike. I started getting all this feedback, meaning the guys on the truck were monitoring the Secret Service frequency. One of the guys with headphones started turning red. We knew they were doing it. That's why anything important would have to be said in person.

"But the press was usually more fun to party with than other agents. I figured the reporters were a little more liberal and open-minded. You'd still have to be careful, though. One time I was at a party, sitting around on the floor with a bunch of reporters, and somebody said, 'You're coming to our party next week, right?' I answered, 'Can't. I have to go overseas.'

"Well, they all started in on me: 'Where? Where? Where're you going?'

"At that time, only a few people knew that Carter was making a spur-of-the-moment shuttle trip, trying to shore up the peace talks between Egypt and Israel. So all these reporters kept grilling me, saying, 'Come on, we're your friends. This'll be off-the-record.'

"So finally I said, 'Okay. We're going to Egypt.'

"Well, next thing, this anchorwoman who was giving the party got up, and tiptoed over to a telephone and called her newsroom. Right in front of me. I said to her, 'Hang up the phone. How fuckin' *dare* you?' I was livid. To the credit of everyone else there, they backed me up.

"After that she'd leave messages on my phone machine everyday: 'Are you still mad at me?' I never called her back.

"If a reporter didn't screw me, I'd give him a tidbit. And anytime the press corps was standing outside in the rain, waiting for Carter, I'd tell them if he wasn't coming out again. No point in wasting people's time."

One of Marty's closest friendships was with NBC correspondent Jessica Savitch.

"She'd just been assigned to the White House. So I'd tell her little things that I thought might help her catch up with the newshounds who'd been there for years. She was a hard charger, and, of course, a real stunner. I knew she was going places."

Marty also became friendly with the UPI's sassy veteran correspondent Helen Thomas.

"One time a woman with a knife broke into Ted Kennedy's senate office. Fortunately, Carter had given Kennedy Secret Service protection even before Kennedy announced he was running. So an agent was there to get the knife away from the woman. But the woman had managed to stab the agent. I was over at the White House trying to find out how he was doing. We weren't getting any information from the hospital. So I broke the story to Helen Thomas. I figured she could find out what was going on if anyone could.

"Most times, though, Carter's family was easier to deal with than Carter. I got a real kick out of his mom. Miz Lillian always made such a big deal out of meeting you. She'd squeeze my hands and say, 'Oh, your hands are so warm.' You could see how this was a woman who'd go and join the Peace Corps in India when she was sixty-eight. Later on, she admitted she thought the White House was boring. No wonder she was always trying to liven the place up. One time there was a big state dinner for the Prime Minister of Ireland. Apparently Miz Lillian liked his speech because she started shouting, 'You *tell* 'em, Prime!' Jimmy was giving her this smile like, 'Shut up now, mother.'

"I had been at the White House almost a year when I was made one of Rosalynn Carter's principal agents. I was flattered to be chosen, and Rosalynn [code name: 'Dancer'] and I hit it off fast. I liked her enormously. Here she was, one of the most active First Ladies since Eleanor Roosevelt, sitting in on Cabinet meetings, going to twenty-seven cities and eighteen countries in her first year, knocking the socks off these macho South American leaders who didn't want to talk to her at first, and still I'd see how she was like any mother. She worried about whether her son's jaw would straighten out. I'd take her and Amy out to the suburbs for Amy's violin lessons. Rosalynn and I would sit on the washer and dryer while Amy practiced in the other room. Rosalynn would ask me if I thought Amy was getting any better. I'd say I thought so. I mean, Amy still sounded like she was strangling cats, but at least she played better than Imelda Marcos sang.

"Rosalynn, naturally, went to teas and ribbon-cuttings and all that. But one of the most tense moments I remember happened on her detail. We were in Chicago. Rosalynn was coming out of a hotel where she'd been talking with Mayor Jane Byrne. It was freezing, but out on the street there were about fifty to a hundred people waiting.

"I was checking out the people, and in the glare of the klieg lights I saw this one guy about three rows back in the crowd. Now I've seen hundreds of thousands of people, but this guy's face chilled me to the bone. He was right out of *Taxi Driver.* Shaved head. Perspiring profusely in the cold. I knew this guy was having some kind of psychotic episode. But I didn't know if he had a gun, and I didn't have time to get on the radio. So I just locked eyes with him and I started talking to him telepathically. I gave him a look that said, I know you're having trouble, but whatever's going on in your life tonight, please, just hold on a few more minutes and we'll be gone. The cameras were rolling, and I didn't want to get too rough because that could have provoked him. But if he had made a quick move, I would have jumped him. I was committed that far. I kept visually pleading with him: Neither one of us wants to die. Think this out. I'll never forget when the car came and I put Rosalynn inside. I saw him still standing there with that look.

"Rosalynn and Jimmy got to relax a bit at Camp David. Out in Maryland's Catoctin Mountains, on 134 acres of forest patrolled by Marines and surrounded by a high-voltage electrical fence trimmed with barbed wire, the Carters could imagine that they were back home, walking through the Georgia pines. They were still prisoners of the Presidency, but at Camp David we tried to give them a little more breathing space.

"The danger was that you could get too relaxed. One time Carter almost escaped. One of Carter's aides called him at the family's cabin and Carter didn't answer. So the aide called the agents and asked, 'Where's the President?' Back at the White House we had the Presidential locator computer that told anybody on his staff where the President was at any minute of the day—whether he was taking a nap in his bedroom or signing a treaty in France.

"But out at Camp David that day, nobody knew where he was.

Absolute panic broke out. Fortunately, we got a call from the sentry
at the front gate. He said the President just showed up at his post
and told him, 'Open the gate. I want to go out.' Somehow Carter had
wandered out of his house and none of us saw him leave. We ran to
the gate. I don't think Carter even knew we weren't behind him. I
think he just got to the point where he assumed we were watching
him even if he couldn't see us.

"On moon-bleached autumn nights, I would walk through the
woods behind Rosalynn and Jimmy while they held hands. One thing
I have to give to his Administration—the two of them really did love
each other. I have some beautiful mental images of them in the worst
of times.

"I remember one of those nights when the three of us were walking
down a perimeter road. It was close to midnight. You could hear all
the sounds in the forest. The crickets. A twig snapping. Suddenly I
heard this metallic rattle up ahead. I knew immediately it was an
M–16 rifle. Then somebody yelled, 'HALT!' In the moonlight, I
could see this young Marine private. He was brand new and he'd
been told that *no one* came down that road at night. I'd already
radioed the command post to tell them where we were, but I guess
the message hadn't reached the Marines yet. So Rosalynn and Jimmy
froze, and I stepped in front them.

"In a real quiet voice, I told the Marine, 'I'm with the President.
I'm going to take my flashlight, and I'm going to put it on my face.'
Real slowly, I walked up to him and showed him my ID. He was
scared shitless. He thought he was going to be court-martialed. I told
him he'd done the right thing, that it could've happened to anyone."

But how could that scare compare with the eye-popping, hair-
raising *hare-torpedo* that nearly sunk Jimmy Carter, former sub
commander? Newspapers across the country called it the "Killer
Bunny" attack and carried sketchy third-hand accounts. The White
House denied that it ever happened. But Marty saw the rabbit.

* * *

"Hey, I *saw* it happen. We were down on the farm in Georgia. Carter and an agent were fishing in a boat on a pond. I was on shore with another agent. Suddenly, I heard some rustling in the woods behind us. I couldn't tell what it was at first, but soon enough I saw it was a rabbit—I mean, a *big* rabbit—running away from a fox. The rabbit ran to the edge of the pond, looked back at the fox and then jumped into the water. It started swimming toward Carter's boat. The agent in the boat saw this torpedo-like thing shooting toward him and he got on the radio. He said, 'What is that?'

"I said, 'It's a rabbit.'

"He said, 'A robot?'

" 'No, a *rabbit.* As in Bugs Bunny.'

"Well, Carter saw this projectile coming, and he picked up an oar and started rocking the boat, trying to hit the rabbit with the oar. Water was splashing up on to the agent. Between the President and the fox, the rabbit didn't know what to do. Finally, it started paddling away from the boat."

After that rabbit, whenever a cat got into the White House, the agents would say, "Kill it! It's got to be a robot!"

The agents could use a laugh. There were real threats, real human weirdos, who tried to invade the White House on a daily basis. Every day deranged people showed up at the front gate. Many of them, over the years, had insisted they *were* the President, or the First Lady or the Son of God.

One "Jesus Christ" drove a hundred miles to reveal to the President the "Third Secret of Fatima." Another Jesus came to collect two million dollars. One visitor asked for a million for breaking up an imaginary drug ring. Another wanted the President to remove the radio transmitter that the CIA had implanted in his brain.

Psychiatrists said these voice-activated people suffered from— what else? —"the Presidential complex": the delusion that only the

Commander-in-Chief could solve a problem or be entrusted with some information. In 1964, it was reported that about fifty disturbed visitors a year were taken from the White House into custody. Come 1973, the Secret Service reported 411 people had shown up behaving very strangely. Of those, 129 were sent off for observation. A total of 328 people tried to get into the Nixon White House between January 1971 and July 1974. According to Dr. David Shore of the National Institute of Mental Health, about ninety percent were diagnosed as schizophrenic. The three-quarters who were paranoid-schizophrenic were true oddballs, Shore noted, because schizophrenics with delusions seldom act upon their fantasies. Many of these people had come from great distances. Only fifteen percent lived around Washington. Though many felt persecuted, only twenty-two percent actually made verbal threats.

The visitors who the Secret Service thought warranted a closer look found themselves headed for St. Elizabeth's Hospital, the 320-acre facility where Marty had been trained. "St. E's," the country's largest federal mental hospital for civilians, was founded in 1855. From 1946 to 1958 the hospital was the home of poet Ezra Pound, who got himself a lovely room there after pleading insanity to the government's charge of wartime treason. One of St. E's first inmates was Richard Lawrence, who shot at Andrew Jackson because Lawrence—who believed he was King Richard III—thought Jackson was keeping him from his land in England.

The modern White House had a direct line to St. E's. When the Secret Service sent a guy over there, the doctors would talk to him and either release him with a warning or accept him for observation of at least twenty-four hours. Some critics said the White House guards were trigger happy when it came to dialing the funny farm. In 1976, a Philadelphia man filed a $300,000 damage suit against the government for sending him to St. E's. The man claimed he'd simply asked a guard to pass along a letter to Gerald Ford.

*         *         *

"Washington is full of certifiable people, and some of them are quite powerful. It's a wonder they don't send some Congressmen to St. E's who say they have appointments with the President. Mistakes happen. But most of the people the Service called in weren't just trying to deliver a letter, or were mumbling to themselves. They hadn't come for the Easter egg roll. They were aggressively trying to get inside the White House.

"A certain number were regulars. Some had just been released from a hospital and they were supposed to be on medication, but they'd forgotten to take it. After they'd gotten themselves under control again, some of them would thank us. We tended to send more people over when it got really cold. At least they'd get food and shelter for a night. That was the least the White House could do for them."

Each administration faced its intruders as it saw fit. A deranged man once threatened to kill President John Adams, so Adams invited his would-be assassin up to his office to talk it over. The man never came back. President Monroe was less hospitable. He erected an iron fence around the house in 1818 and had sharpshooters nesting in the trees. President Tyler set up the Metropolitan Police in 1844, and, fearful of "the infernal machine" (a bomb), Tyler once had his guards gingerly open a suspicious package that turned out to conceal ... a cake. During World War II, Franklin Roosevelt agreed to close off West Executive Avenue, but he drew the line when advisors urged him to paint the White House black so as to ward off an air attack.

Harry Truman, who thought the Secret Service slowed him down on his six A.M. walks, was happy his guards were around on November 1, 1950. At the time Truman and his family were living at Blair House, across the street from the White House, which was then being renovated. Truman was taking his afternoon nap in a bedroom right above an unlatched screen door when two Puerto Rican nationalists named Griselio Torresola and Oscar Collazo stormed the yellow-brick mansion. Firing a Walther P–38 automatic, Torresola plugged two uniformed guards with three bullets each. One of the guards, Leslie Coffelt, just before he died managed to get off a shot that killed Torresola. The weak-eyed Collazo shot a guard in the knee, then missed his next eight shots as he dodged bullets that cut his nose and ear and tore a hole through his hat. A Secret Service agent finally stopped Collazo with a blast to the chest. In less than three minutes twenty-seven shots had been fired. Later, Truman commuted Collazo's death sentence and Jimmy Carter gave him clemency.

In 1963, a North Carolina plumber named Doyle Allen Hicks drove his pick-up truck 446 miles nonstop to the White House gates. There he told guards that he wanted to warn President Kennedy that Communists were conquering the Tarheel State. Turned away, Hicks came back an hour later and rammed his truck through the wrought-iron gates. The guards stopped him twenty-five feet from the front door.

Almost ten years after that, the Nixons were down in Florida when a twenty-year-old Army private named Robert Preston stole a helicopter in the middle of the night and headed toward 1600 Pennsylvania Avenue. The White House was notified, and when Preston flew over the fence at around 2:00 A.M., on a Sunday, agents and guards rained shotgun fire on his chopper. Preston nevertheless landed on the South Lawn and climbed out of the aircraft alive. The Florida soldier, who'd washed out of flight school, served two months of a one-year sentence in Fort Riley, Kansas.

Ten months after Preston's invasion a twenty-five-year-old ex-taxi driver named Marshall H. Fields crashed his brown Chevrolet sedan through the northwest entrance. Fields plowed up the driveway and parked his car about twenty feet from the door. Fields then climbed out of his dented Chevy. He was wearing an Arab headdress. A gas mask dangled from his waist. His black-gloved hands gripped detonators and he told the Secret Service agents that the railroad flares strapped to his legs were sticks of dynamite.

The Service had a file on Fields. Recently he'd sent letters to the Washington media proclaiming, "I am the Messiah to those who wish to believe." Talking to the agents in Arabic and in English, he asked to speak with the Pakistani ambassador. Four hours after he arrived, Fields gave himself up. He'd been showing erratic behavior ever since his father, a retired American diplomat, had died the spring before. During the assault, the Ford family had been off skiing in Vail. "Had the President or any of his family been here, we would have taken more authoritative action," said Secret Service spokesman George Cosper. Marksmen had had Fields in their cross-hairs the whole time. "We are compassionate," added Cosper. "We don't want to take a human life if he's penetrating an empty house."

One pleasant summer night in 1976, some women who were demonstrating for the equal rights amendment noticed thirty-year-old Chester M. Plummer pacing nervously outside the White House fence. The women watched the black taxi driver, who was carrying a three-foot length of pipe, cross the street, come back, hang onto the fence, look in, and then sit down. Finally, Plummer climbed over the eight-foot spiked fence. Almost instantly he tripped seismic sensors that flooded the lawn with light. A twenty-five-year-old guard named Charles Garland ran out and told Plummer three times to halt. With his pipe raised above his head, Plummer kept coming. When Plummer was sixty feet inside the fence, Garland shot him in the chest. Plummer crumpled onto the grass. About ninety minutes later he died at George Washington University Hospital.

The Secret Service said its guards had followed an undisclosed established procedure. Gerald Ford, who'd been reading in his private quarters, believed Garland had done "his duty in accordance with his best judgment." Described as quiet and nice, Plummer had no history of grievance against Ford. But one of the few things that was known about Plummer was that he'd had a falling out with his father, a District of Columbia security guard.

Each intruder pushed the Secret Service toward fortifying the

White House better. Technical Security hid video cameras in the
bushes, in lanterns and under ground. The Service saw to it that
guards opened all briefcases and fluoroscoped all packages. Crash-
proof gates were installed at a cost of $550,000. The agency outfitted
the house with radar and gave agents a Redeye anti-aircraft missile
launcher.

"All the same, I felt the White House could be safer. Carter had
the tightest security of any President up till then. But I was still
surprised how vulnerable the White House seemed. During the
Carter years, guards stopped all fence jumpers without killing them.
Several people who crashed their cars into the reinforced gates never
made it up the driveway.

"But there were more casual breaches of 'the second perimeter'
that worried us. In 1977, a freelance writer who had an appointment
with a Presidential aide opened the veranda door to the Oval Office
to ask a startled Carter for directions. The writer said he'd gotten
lost. And in 1979, Carter was in the East Room giving a briefing on
the U.S.-Soviet strategic arms treaty. Suddenly, a man jumped up.
Just a few feet away from Carter, he opened up a plastic bag and
started sprinkling ashes. The man then denounced the treaty. A
Secret Service agent quickly ushered the man out."

All the President's food comes from sources carefully monitored
by the Secret Service. But in the first months of Carter's term, the
Service received reports that assassins who planned to poison the
President had infiltrated the Navy stewards in the White House
mess. It was never disclosed what came out of the Service's look into
the reports.

In 1977, however, a former Pentagon researcher revealed what
could have been the most disturbing "attack" on the White House.
Lowell Ponte, who worked for the International Research and Technology Corporation, a think tank, said that in 1969 and 1970 a team

from the U.S. Army Chemical and Biological Warfare Research Center found its way to the air conditioning systems of the White House and the Capitol and released "chemicals that could have been deadly germs or nerve gas." Ponte reported that "neither the Secret Service nor the FBI nor Capitol Hill police knew [about the mock attacks]. Had the Army teams been real terrorists the President and the entire Congress would have died."

"On a daily basis," Marty said, "the best the agents could do was to keep Carter and his family from making targets of themselves. Carter, for instance, liked to sit on the Truman balcony. As far as I know, he was one of the few Presidents who did—other than Truman. But one day there was a demonstration at the Washington Monument. Protesters were dropping banners out the windows. And it occurred to us that with the right rifle, a sniper could hit Carter on the balcony. So I went up to the residence to tell Carter we'd like him to come indoors.

"He said, 'Whaaaat!'

"I said, 'They're right over there.'

"He looked up at the Monument and he came inside. But he was steamed. You couldn't blame him. Sometimes I'm sure it seemed to him like he was the only one in America who *wasn't* guaranteed any personal freedoms."

It was ironic that Carter should be on the Truman balcony. It was almost as if Truman was calling from his eternal nap to remind Carter, "Watch where you nod off." Marty was attuned to little historical resonances like that.

"I'd get these weird sensations of history all the time. At the Ford Theater, where Lincoln was shot. And at the White House at night. Strange things happened when the daytime staff cleared out. At night the uniformed guards watch the Oval Office and the agents watch the residence. One night, though, an agent stopped by the guard post outside the Oval Office, and there was no guard there. This was unheard of. I mean, your first thought would be, 'My God, somebody's *inside* the White House!' So the agent got very concerned and he radioed for support. Everybody started looking around for the missing guard. Finally, they found him. He was up in the branches of the big tree in the Rose Garden. He was pointing at the planes flying in and out of National Airport and muttering something about Soviet spy planes. The guy had flipped out. It was incredible. The White House had to send one of its own guards over to St. Elizabeth's.

"But I can sort of see how he'd be drawn to that tree. When I was on the midnight shift, I used to stare at it. At the end of a day, when you knew some history had been made, the White House could feel almost electrically charged. The Rose Garden would almost seem biblical, like Eden, with the tree of Good and Evil in the middle. The President would be sleeping upstairs. And I'd be underneath him, sitting in one of those first-floor rooms, in the dark. And I'd look out the windows—you know, through that old imperfect glass—and I'd think about what somebody was thinking one hundred years ago in that room. I'd look and look at the whole scene until I had everything memorized, so I'd never forget how it felt to be there, so that moment would always be safe."

# CHAPTER TEN

# *Company, Man*

WHEN dawn came to the White House, and Carter's Georgia mafia started working the phones again, history's ghosts got spooked, and split. It was another day on the job.

On the go again, Marty was apt to forget even that Jimmy Carter was President. "I could stand there in the Oval Office and watch him address the nation. But I'd have to go home and turn on the TV and see the speech replayed to get that feeling you were supposed to feel—you know, where everybody in the room quiets down because 'the President is speaking.' "

Television also had a way of investing Marty with extra stature. Every night, his family and friends would look for a video post card from him.

Marty's boyhood pal George Sarantakis remembered, "I'd watch a newscast, and *there* was Marty. He'd get off Air Force One and Jimmy Carter would be right behind him. One time I was in Washington and Marty gave me a tour that was pretty amazing. He showed me the Oval Office and Amy Carter's tree house. It was a real heart-stopper for someone off the street."

"I never expected to have lunch at the White House," said Viola Venker, "but I did. I went to the White House and had lunch. We met Mrs. Carter and she was lovely to us. Of course, I used to worry about Marty. When I heard President Ford had been attacked, it was like somebody had stabbed me or had hit me real hard in the stomach. But Marty is very thoughtful and he would try as soon as he could to call me and let me know he was all right. I was real proud of him. I liked going around saying, 'My son's in the Secret Service.' Did he tell you he met Queen Elizabeth? He did. And I still have the vodka Andrei Gromyko gave him, and the engraved watch from Imelda Marcos. I thought it was real nice, Marty hobnobbing with the rulers of other countries."

"Freezing your balls off at Camp David isn't glamorous," Marty admits, "but I tried to keep my eyes open and drink it all in. The President's day is your day, and no matter what anybody says, nobody sees the President the way an agent does. The Secretary of State gets maybe half an hour with him. We were there all the time. And we saw the guy when his head was hanging the lowest. It made me remember that, for all my bitching about Jimmy, his job was a lot toughter than mine.

"But where Jimmy went, I went. We landed one time in the Azores. Do you know how many times Air Force One has landed on those desolate little islands in the Atlantic? Not many. So the whole island turned out to greet us.

"A woman came up to me and said, 'Are you somebody?'

"I shook my head and said, 'No, I'm nobody.'

"She replied, 'I don't care. You came off that plane. Please touch my daughter.'

"What could I do? I touched her daughter. Other people asked me for autographs. I signed, Cary Grant. Why disappoint them?

"You travel with the President and you get to see things very few people see. Once I was doing the advance for Carter's visit to the Berlin Wall and I had to take aerial photos of his motorcade route. I got friendly with a helicopter pilot, who said, 'If you can keep it to yourself, we can pull something that you might find interesting.'

"He knew the exact time that Rudolph Hess, the last Nazi in Spandau prison, went for his walk. A couple of days later I met the pilot and we flew down into the prison's courtyard. There were a couple of guards around Hess. They looked up as if they thought we were swooping in to shoot him. Hess was in these prison pajamas, thin as a skeleton, but he still looked right at me with these two defiant eyes. It was eerie.

"I went to the funerals of two Popes. I accompanied Rosalynn to the service for Pope Paul VI, and then a month later, Pope John Paul I died and we headed back. At that time I went through the private catacombs under the American Ambassador's residence in Rome. Being raised as a Catholic, I was fascinated with Vatican politics. The cardinals would argue about which limo they'd get. They were stricter about their pecking order than the characters in Washington. It was strange going to those two funerals after listening to all those crazy people in America who wanted to kill the Pope. To think that three years later some guy would get his wish—he'd shoot the new Pope on the same streets we rode down.

"One of the most intense experiences in my life was going before Christmas to the birthplace of Christ—touching the spot in Bethlehem where Christ supposedly came out of Mary's womb. I said to this Israeli guy, 'How do you know *this* is the spot? How do you know He didn't come out right over *there?*' The guy said Christ's disciples had marked the spot. Who knows? I just know the feeling I got standing there, in this little cave under the Church of the Nativity, as Israel and Egypt were close to declaring peace. All these people started singing 'Silent Night' in a half dozen different languages. It wasn't planned, everybody just started. I was over in a corner, getting chills.

"I was at Camp David with Menachem Begin and Anwar Sadat—they hadn't been there long when I was heading up one of the asphalt walkways toward my post. I passed Sadat, walking with his cane and smoking his pipe. Then when I got to my post, I saw, coming from the other direction, hands in his pockets, Begin. I'd been hoping that the two of them would have a chance to get away from their negotiating teams and just *talk,* one-on-one. So here they were, heading toward this juncture where I was standing. It's silly, but I could feel myself coaxing them toward me with little hand movements, like a traffic cop. Finally, right in front of me, they met. And they went off by themselves in the woods. Begin picked up a leaf and rolled it in his hands. Just by their body language, I felt something good was going to happen. That was a precious moment.

"One night I was in Israel at a gathering of Holocaust survivors and I was the only person allowed to sit, for security reasons, at a table of death camp survivors. There was a little resentment about that at first, but then I got into long talks with these old people. Since my family was German, we talked about the German mind. Then Menachem Begin made this impassioned speech. I don't think I've ever been so moved by a politician—by this former terrorist who was ready to put his hatred behind him.

"Another time I was in Hamburg, Germany, and the only room I could find close to the President was in the house of an old woman. She invited me up to her room. While we were watching TV and drinking beer, she kept asking me what was this Secret Service I was a part of. Was it like the SS? Then I saw a death camp number tatooed on her arm. Jeez. She told me her whole story. It almost made tears come to my eyes.

"It's hard to communicate the overload of sensations—these alternating currents of war and peace. We'd go on drills to the underground shelter where we'd take the President in the event of a nuclear war. They've got dozens of these shelters under the mountains outside Washington. One of the big ones is under Raven Rock

Mountain in Maryland. Eisenhower ran the country from there for three days during an evacuation drill. Another big command post is called Mount Weather. It's carved out of a mountain in Virginia, underneath this innocuous-looking weather station. That's where the Cabinet, all the Supreme Court Justices, and something like two thousand government officials are supposed to go. Lucky for them. I guess.

"They put these places underneath rusty little feed stations. You'd never know what was down there. But once you walked through these big, bank-vault doors, and rode down hundreds of feet in an elevator, you stepped into a self-contained world. War rooms with banks of communication equipment. Dining rooms. Big storage pantries for food. An underground reservoir with water-purifying equipment. Beds. The most frightening part, I thought, was the homey way it was all decorated. Curtains over false windows. Children's rooms with dolls and toys. All these little touches to remind the survivors what it used to look like on earth."

Marty savored all these moments. And yet his travel, above and below ground, was becoming all too breathtaking. The years spent ricocheting from state to state and continent to continent, they were wearing on him. Seniority didn't exempt him from spending a third of his duty on the midnight-to-eight shift.

"Every three weeks, you're supposed to change your sleep pattern. When your shift's done, you often end up collapsing at Camp David rather than driving home. So even when you're off, you can't get away from the guy.

"The hardest part is skipping across time zones. Say you're on a midnight shift in L.A., standing outside the President's door when he's sleeping. As soon as you're off, you board a plane to Boston. You try to get some sleep on the plane, but somebody's always laughing and waking you up. Three time zones later, you land in Boston near

7:00 P.M. You've only got a couple of hours before you're on duty again at midnight. After a while clocks just become decorative objects.

"There were many nights when I used to wake up in some dark hotel room and not know where in the world I was. I'd look at my watch and it'd say seven o'clock. Great. A.M. or P.M.? And by the way, what day is it? I'd get up and search around for a pack of matches: Oh, Geneva, Switzerland. Then clunk, back to bed. Sometimes we'd have to hammer on an agent's door, practically break it down, and the guy still wouldn't get up. On the plane guys who'd never had a nose bleed would suddenly find blood gushing out of their noses—from not getting enough rest."

"The burn-out factor was a problem for a lot of us," admits Chuck Rochner. "Just when you got some kind of a reprieve in a field office, you found yourself back on a detail."

Chuck Vance, who ended sixteen years in the Secret Service shortly after he married Susan Ford, called the job "tremendously stressful. Every year, [the agents] have a physical examination and monitor their vital signs. Every year, those signs begin to deteriorate: high blood pressure, things like that . . . I [still] find it hard to relax."

Donald Bendickson said he'd spent twenty years "basically living at the whim of somebody else maybe three years—with my family during Christmas . . . Stress is an individual thing. Some people handle it and some people can't, but it all takes its toll . . . inwardly or outwardly."

An agent for nineteen years, Jim Kalafatis said, "We had two agents die within a month, of sudden heart attacks. They were athletic guys, in good shape. The first thing you do is call down to the office and ask, was there any history of angina? You think, maybe the guy abused himself: drinking, rich food; maybe he didn't listen to his doctor. But when a guy dies suddenly, it kind of scares everybody. You say, I'm healthy. I don't have heart problems. I don't think the medical guys know completely what stress does to you. You have other weird things. We've had several guys die of brain tumors. Maybe it was related, maybe not. You don't know."

In 1978 the Secret Service commissioned a study of the effects of stress on agents. It was the first check that the agency had done on itself in its 114 years. And fittingly, it had its bodyguards questioned by the same psychiatrist who helped profile past assassins. With his researchers, Dr. Frank Ochberg, an associate director of the National Institute of Mental Health, spent a year interviewing agents around the country. When the study was finished, Secret Service spokesman Robert Snow said, the agency had presented a "pretty general" portion of it before Congress in the course of seeking appropriations. The Service let the agents themselves read selected pages of the report so long as they didn't take them out of the office.

"First chance I got," says Marty, "I stopped by W–16 at the White House and took a look. The report said that, roughly speaking, in terms of tension faced by an average person, an agent aged two years for every year he guarded the President."

Ochberg was reluctant to talk to reporters about the specific findings of his study. But in an interview he did say, "Law enforcement agencies across the country have all recognized that there is a need to understand how officers deal with and tolerate stress. The Federal Government has at last recognized it should do the same. The idea that the Secret Service is supposed to be beyond stress is not true." More unnerving than the danger of being shot, Ochberg said, were the long stretches when the highly trained agents had to stand post in hallways, fighting off boredom. The Service interviews spouses and family members before it hires an agent. Even so, Ochberg found, an agent's family still winds up resenting the drubbing his job gives to his home life. "It gets so that they can never invite people for dinner, because they might have to leave at the last moment. The daughter of one agent told him sarcastically that she didn't expect him to be at her wedding."

Ochberg and his researchers also interviewed some of the wives of agents. "There are many, many lonely hours," said a woman married to an agent for twenty-nine years. "When his responsibilities on the job increase, so do the tensions at home. You just force yourself to cope with all the problems. But since you don't know any other life, you get used to it."

Another wife didn't want to be interviewed: "I have nothing good to say about what it's like being married to a Secret Service agent, so I'd rather not say anything at all."

"Maybe it was just as well, then, that I never touched down long enough for any romance to take root," Marty admits. "In those ten years, I could count my relationships on one hand. That's how often I'd meet someone with the will and the means to keep up with me. I met one woman in Paris. I was walking out of the American Embassy toward my car and she saw me. She was standing at the fence, so I walked up to her and we started talking. She came from a real rich family in Chicago. She was gorgeous and great fun and she spoke French better than the French. She'd fly around the world to meet me. That was the only way we could keep it up.

"By this time I was making enough money to buy a townhouse in Reston, Virginia, outside Washington. But I still wanted to keep my apartment in New York. So I was looking for someone to split the rent. A stewardess I knew introduced me to a girl named Debby Johnson. She was coming to New York from Kansas because Eileen Ford encouraged her to model. That's how beautiful she was. We spoke on the phone, met and before we knew it, had something like a relationship."

"It was only supposed to be a temporary arrangement," Debby recalled. "But it ended up being four years. In the beginning I found Marty very intimidating. He was extremely intelligent. And yet he wasn't pretentious. He had a bizarre sense of humor. I did too. I surprised him a couple of times. I wasn't making enough as a model, so I started working as a stewardess. If I could find out what city Marty was in, I'd fly there. I'd call the various hotels till I tracked him down. One time I'd just been in Central America and I caught up with him in Tokyo. When he was in Washington I'd take the shuttle down there on the weekends. Ninety percent of the time he'd be with Carter at Camp David. I'd hang out at Marty's townhouse. I'd tell Marty, 'I love sitting in front of a fireplace by myself.' Even when we were together I got frustrated walking down the street with him. He'd walk *behind* me, like he was guarding me. I told him, 'You're off work, *get up here!*'

"Force of habit," Marty confesses, "The Secret Service always seemed to be just a few steps behind me. I was never off duty too long before someone at W–16 would track me down, tell me some detail was short a few men and ask me if I could put off vacation for a bit. Off I'd go to Andrews Air Force Base. Truth told, I got antsy if I stayed anchored too long. Admittedly, I was relieved when Rosalynn Carter unpacked her idea of seeing the South Pole. But there weren't many other places I wasn't game for visiting. My eye sockets may have looked like two black railroad tunnels, but nothing lit them up like a glittering new city viewed from the air.

"The protection division tends to attract a speedfreak who's always hungry for excitement. At Grade Thirteen, I could've angled for an administrative job. I could've asked to join a field office. I didn't want to. I knew guys who'd only been in a couple of years and already they were talking about their retirement. They sounded like they were serving a jail sentence. There were a lot of guys who did their tour of the White House, soaked up the prestige, made their contacts and then settled down at a desk job. They went home at five every day in their new government town car. Their careers were on schedule.

"But that wasn't my mind-set. I liked going to strange places. The reason I joined was to be out there in the crowd. I still wanted to get that gun before it went off. I still remembered how deeply it hurt the country when John F. Kennedy was killed."

He remembered. As cynical as he'd become about politics, still he believed in the theology of Dallas, the sanctity of the last President whom the Secret Service had out-and-out loved. As numb as he felt listening to the candidates drone on while reading from three-by-five cards, he could still picture JFK's vigorous doodles hanging in Sargent Shriver's home. And sure, he detested the dictators he'd been forced to protect.

"But it wasn't like I thought they were fair game for anybody to take a shot at. I just wanted our country to stop supporting them, and that included subsidizing them with the lives of Secret Service agents. I didn't blame the Secret Service for inviting Marcos and Somoza here, giving them the red carpet treatment. In fact, I have to think that, as conservative as a lot of the agents were about law and order, they might've been as skeptical as I was about foreign policy. I mean, they saw the behavior of these scumbags, just like I did. I suspected that, in their guts, they may also have recoiled at the covert plots of the government's *truly secret* service, the CIA. When you're out there every day trying to prevent an assassination, it gets ingrained in you that assassination is wrong. No matter what the justification is. It's just not what America is about.

"I was proud of what I was doing. I believed that most agents did their best to uphold the Service's ideals. When somebody in the newspaper claimed that a Secret Service agent had leaned on a reporter or a protester, I gave the agent the benefit of the doubt. I knew what it was like to be sued for false arrest. When some Congressman started getting snide about the Service's skill at spotting assassins, I wanted to testify: 'Yeah, you try to do this job.' "

The Secret Service brass may have given into Haldeman and fired Bob Taylor, but Marty still relished the fight Taylor had put up and the rumor that Bob Woodward and Carl Bernstein's 'Deep Throat' was a Secret Service official.

"It made sense. We installed Nixon's secret tapes, and took care of them. The agents may not have wanted to see Nixon impeached, but after what happened to Taylor, they owed one to Haldeman. I hope it was the Secret Service that nailed him."

Marty saw his fellow agents as sharing his dark sense of humor, epitomized in some T-shirts that a few agents had printed up. The T-shirts were emblazoned with a bullet-riddled Presidential seal and the motto: 'YOU ELECT THEM, WE PROTECT THEM.' Marty may have read more sarcasm into the message than other agents, but probably no more than did Jimmy Carter. When the agents wore their shirts to a softball game, Carter fumed, and shortly afterward a Secret Service memo forbade the improper depiction of the Presidential seal.

Always ready to hit the road, Marty could be counted as a guy you could slap on the back and call a team player.

"He was a free spirit," says Chuck Rochner, "but he was also extremely efficient. I have very fond memories of him. I always thought he was a very unique character, very upbeat. I liked his style. I would've worked with him anytime."

Marty could help the team loosen up. On a weekend at Camp David, when Carter was in for the night, the agents would retire to their log cabins, slip into flannel shirts or turtlenecks, kick back around the fireplace and pop open some beers. And they'd watch Marty impersonate several of the "Saturday Night Live" crew in a spoof of Jimmy Carter.

Paul Costello, who handled the press for Rosalynn Carter says, "Marty was great to travel with, because the pressure and stress was intense day after day. The schedule was constantly changing. Just when you were ready to jump out of the plane at 37,000 feet, you could turn to Marty and he'd bring you back to the fact that this was just a job. He was great fun. If you were in a hot town, you knew you wanted to have dinner or a drink with Marty."

"I always let people know where I was coming from. I didn't slap them in the face with it, but I just didn't see the point in standing on a lot of formality. I wasn't interested in becoming assistant director of the Secret Service, I was satisfied with the money I was making. I felt that I was good enough at what I did that I could be myself, or something close to it. Maybe I'm wrong, but I think I got along with the Presidents, except for Carter, because I was down-to-earth.

"I tried to keep the bluster of high office from bending my sense of civil behavior. One time I was on duty on the first floor of the White House when this big guy came blasting down the stairs. He screamed at me, *'Which way outta this damn place?!'*

"I stood up and said, 'Well, which way do you want to get out? Are you walking, or are you . . .?'

"He said, 'I'm getting picked up! I want to get outta here as fast as I can.'

"I told him, 'You have to go back up the stairs and out the North Portico.'

"He said, 'Get off your lazy ass and escort me out.'

"I said, 'I'm sorry, I can't leave my post. But if you follow my directions, you'll be right there.'

'You don't think I know who you are? I know you're with the Secret Service. I'll have you know I'm United States Senator John Culver [Democrat from Iowa].'

"I said, 'I'm glad to meet you. I'm Marty Venker.'

"He didn't like that. He said, 'I know your director personally. I can get him on the phone right now and have your job.'

"I pointed to the phone. 'There's the phone. Pick it up and dial it. I'll give you the number.'

"He started sputtering. He said, 'I can have your budget slashed. I can have everybody from headquarters in my office tomorrow to explain your behavior.'

'Fine. Do it.'

"The more nonchalant I was, the more angry he got. By this time he was really getting red and spit was forming on his lips and I started to doubt that he *was a Senator.* I mean, you dealt with angry politicians all day long, but this guy was as bad as a CO–2 case. I started to wonder if he might be some nut who got into the White House.

"I didn't think I could handle him by myself. He was six-foot-two and weighed a good 250 pounds. So I pushed the panic button. He started to move toward me and I said, 'Stay on *your* side of the hallway and we won't have any problem.'

"Everybody from W–16 was there in seconds. A uniformed guard took him by the elbow to show him to the North Portico and he broke away from him. The President's military aide, with all his medals on, came down and tried to chill him out. Thank God, somebody finally escorted him out of there."

John Culver, who's now an attorney in private practice, recalled in an interview that he did have breakfast one morning with President Carter and some other members of Congress. "It was an eight o'clock meeting," said Culver, "and I told the President that unfortunately I had to leave at 8:45, because I had a large group of constituents meeting me at the Capitol at nine o'clock." When he climbed the stairs from the breakfast room, Culver recalled "There was someone sitting at the desk, saying, 'You can't go out this way.' I said, 'Fine, how do I get out of here?' He said you have to go down the hall and to the left or right. So I did. When I got down there, they said, 'You can't go out this way!' I understood them to be not the least bit helpful or interested in assisting me . . . They pointed me to yet a third station. And it was at the third station where I said, 'Look, I was invited here to a breakfast with the President. I need to get out of here. Will somebody show me the way out of here?' . . . And I said, 'I would like *you* to come with me and show me the way out. There must be a way out. Would you be good enough to show me the way? We're going to get out of here some way. I'm perfectly happy to abide by anybody's directions, and I want to do that. But I've been to three stations and nobody really seems too interested in helping me.' So that's what happened, and that's all that happened."

Culver, an All-American fullback who was a 1954 NFL draft choice, does have a well-known temper. In April 1965, as a Congressman, he got into a scuffle with five D.C. cops after a cab driver said he couldn't get Culver out of his taxi. Culver explained that, after dinner and drinks with a constituent, "I apparently dozed off. The next thing I knew I was being pulled out of the back seat of the taxicab. My first instinct on being awakened was 'I am being attacked,' and I resisted." Police booked the Congressman, then dropped charges after he showed his I.D. At an October 1980 campaign appearance in Iowa, Culver got into a brawl with an independent senatorial candidate who'd been heckling him. When the other candidate reportedly jumped onto the speaker's stage and pushed a college professor, Culver wrestled his rival to the floor.

But on the day he met Marty, Culver abided. "I made no threats about jobs, no threats about budgets . . . I never remember anyone coming on the scene at all." He did, however, remember a military aide being present—"I think it was an Air Force officer."

"Later on, the bosses at headquarters told me Culver was always making complaints about the 'attitude' of agents. [Culver denied this.] The funny thing was, when I looked into his voting record, I found out Culver took the kind of stands I'd agreed with. He started out working for Ted Kennedy and he was a defender of social programs and the environment and civil rights laws. That's what showed me that a liberal politician can be as big of a pain as a conservative one. I think anyone can develop a power-mad savior complex. I can't say I was sorry when Culver lost his Senate seat in 1980."

There was no doubt, though, that Marty, the agent who never liked wearing an earphone, could create static of his own.

"Certain orders you just had to ignore. They wanted us to seize novelty items, like giant three-dollar bills and porno bills, because they said they were counterfeit currency. I wouldn't do it. I told them, 'Get serious.' I resisted anything that smacked of boosterism or Big Brother.

"One time an inspector from Washington stopped by the Springfield office. He told me the director was sorry about that nut suing me for false arrest. Then he said, 'The director also told me he wants you to join the bond drive.'

"I had to laugh. I said, 'Oh, right, as you were leaving the office, the director said, Hey, ask Marty to join the bond drive!'

"I didn't want to join the bond drive. The inspector complained to my supervisor that I was a smart-ass. But my supervisor stood up for me. Another inspector got on my case because I wouldn't submit to what they called a 'privileged interview.' They wanted to know if I liked my boss . . . who was drinking too much . . . who was breaking the rules. If I thought someone was creating a problem, I'd approach him directly.

"But the interviewer assured me, 'Your response will be kept confidential.'

"I asked him, 'What do you think I am, stupid? That's what we tell the inmates at the mental hospitals.' "

Nor did Marty fall into line with headquarters' displeasure with the curbs on FBI domestic surveillance.

"It isn't the *quantity* of information you get; it's how you look at it. It's making sure that the information gets to the Secret Service. The FBI suppressed information it had about Oswald and Ray. J. Edgar Hoover was more interested in bugging Martin Luther King's bedroom."

A longtime agent encapsulated Marty's strength and handicap: "He was the type of guy who asks *'why'* a lot. *'Why* do it this way?' That probably started the day he came on the job."

Agent Jim Kalafalis, adds "I think a lot of guys would've liked to be like [Marty], but they were worried about their security and career path. If a guy has a $100,000 mortgage and three kids, he'll think twice about mouthing off. But Marty wasn't too concerned about that. He was very confident. He knew that, should he ever leave the Service, he'd make out. He knew he had what it took to get out and do something else. Marty wasn't the type of guy you'd call a *company man*. Some people might have considered him a trouble-maker. But we need a mix of people—people who aren't afraid to be critical."

If the Secret Service looked on Marty as a borderline blasphemer, it also saw that he made a natural spokesman to people who previously had overlooked the Service, or whom the Service had overlooked. Out went Marty to the colleges to recruit women and minorities.

"People would come up to me after I'd made my spiel. They'd say, 'I'm interested in joining, but I've done drugs in the past.' I told them to just keep their mouth shut. Don't tell any of the other agents what you told me. I laid the job out truthfully—the good and the bad points. Maybe that's why I didn't get many recruits.

"More and more, I started to feel like I was part of a minority in the Secret Service. The few guys I used to go out with after work were gone. One was an agent named Jim Ryan. He lived in the apartment above me in New York. One night we were on our way home from the World Trade Center, where the field office is. Jim was in his car and I was in mine, and he got hit broadside by someone going about ninety miles per hour. The rescue unit finally got his car door open, but I knew he was going to die when I saw him inside the car.

"Four months later, that infamous gadabout Brooks Keller—he of the shrinking Panama hat and the parties that JFK wanted in on—carried on the tradition of his male forebears by dying before he was fifty. He was forty-nine. He sat up in his bed in the middle of the night and had a massive coronary. He'd just gotten married and he'd started to settle down a bit. I'd been to his apartment just a couple of nights before he died. I went to his funeral. People from all over the world showed up. Headquarters may have been mad at him a lot of the time, but when Brooks died, the Secret Service lost an icon.

"It wasn't that the Service didn't still have wild, funny guys. Some of the biggest cut-ups I knew were closest to the White House detail. One time the advance agents were in Japan staying in a hotel in Shimoda. One of the agents got drunk and went on a rampage with the fire extinguishers. He went knocking on the doors, screaming at women in their rooms. The hotel called the U.S. Embassy. I didn't have much of a taste for 'Animal House' antics."

Paul Costello elaborates, "A lot of the guys crack jokes. It's not to say that many of the guys aren't funny, decent human beings. There are a lot of terrific agents and I think their belief in the protection of the President goes deep. But many of them come from a cookie cutter mold. They're fraternity jocks. High school football stars. They went into the Secret Service because it's the quintessential macho role. Some of these guys, well, their heros are Clint Eastwood and Ed Meese. That's why Marty was like polished glass amidst the rocks. Marty was much less rigid. There was a lot of depth there. He could talk about a whole range of issues. And he dealt with you like a human being."

Of course Costello was an outsider, a White House staff liberal who got on better with an agent closer to his political stripe. Yet even Steve Garmon, from his position as one of the Service's top dogs, acknowledged that most agents lost little sleep over the issues that bugged Marty. "Most of our agents are caught up in their own lives. They go to work, and they don't have all these weighty thoughts about whether the course of human existence relies on what they have to do today. When they sit around the bar at night, I'm sure some of the agents are given to philosophize about the legitimacy of it all. We preach the gospel that you can have your political views but don't bring them to work . . . You're pretty well indoctrinated when you come into the organization about what you have to do: uphold the law. Laws don't always make tremendous sense when they're taken out of context, but most of the people are fairly adept at rationalizing them to themselves. If it's necessary to do that . . . you could easily justify protection for Imelda Marcos. Poor morale, as far as I'm aware, is not a condition that tugs at the fiber of the organization."

An agent who watched Marty over the years said, "Marty was—I won't say he was a loner—but he always did his own thing. He was a free spirit."

"Yet I didn't always feel so spirited or free," Marty reflects. "I didn't have a lot of friends in the Secret Service. My boss in the New York field office didn't like to go home to his wife, so he'd come around to my desk when I was cleaning up some paperwork. He'd say, 'Hey, Marty, come on, we're going out for some brews.'

"I'd say, 'No thanks.'

"After a couple of weeks of my saying no thanks, he leaned down and said, 'What? You think you're too good to drink with us?' I just ignored him. But I really wasn't trying to be a snob. I admired the dedication of the other guys. But they weren't people I'd hang out with. The truth is, I was very lonely."

# CHAPTER ELEVEN

## *Sunglasses After Dark*

AND so his double life began.

"You'd have to say it started overseas. Foreign countries herded many agents on a Secret Service detail into a tighter flock: Americans huddling together in a downpour of slippery words and customs. A strange nation tended to remind me of how remote I was . . . When we'd land in a city, the other guys would want to go sightseeing, or go out drinking at some touristy bistro. They'd invite me to go with them. I'd tell them I was tired. Then, once I was sure most of them had left the hotel, I'd head out on my own.

"It was in London that things really started to change. Ever since 1976, I'd been hearing about this punk music scene and I'd wanted to check it out. So I went to one of the clubs, down in a basement. I couldn't believe the hysteria in the place. People were pogoing up and down like kangaroos. Slamming into each other. Getting all bloody and laughing about it. They had on the full regalia—the safety pins, the razor blades, little skulls dangling from their ears. Up on the stage, there was this band slashing away at their guitars, drumming as fast as they could. The music was so loud, even at the

168

back of the club, that I had to put my fingers in my ears. But I saw a couple of girls passed out on the floor with their heads stuck right *in* the speakers. Their heads were shaved, like the Manson family girls I used to see in L.A. Up on the stage, the singer was diving into the audience, and the audience was spitting at the band. That's how they showed they liked them. They called it gobbing. It was like applause—and, like every schizo quarterly I had ever interviewed had teamed up with those Ukrainian babes outside the Soviet embassy. And I *loved* it.

"I was absolutely electrified. For most of the years that I'd been in the Secret Service—the early Seventies—I'd stopped listening to music. I'd stopped playing my guitar. All you'd hear on the radio was that commercialized arena rock. But punk—man, it was floor-to-the-floor music! It was the first passion *I'd* heard in years. It was a revolt against the corporate record business—with its marketing MBAs and its slick producers who turned out rock that sounded like Henri Mancini. It was a revolt against the highest youth unemployment in Britain's history, and against the good manners of middle class people who wished they were upper class. Mostly, it was a revolt against complacency."

Even on Marty's part. Punk's cynical idealism was made for Marty. The punks told the politicians to sod off. And yet, gagging on rock's age-old themes of love and good times, the punks' songs were implicitly political. They might hail nihilism and "anARchy in thE u.K.," but like it or not, the original punks constituted a coalition against joblessness and racism. The punks would listen to reggae native to London's West Indian ghettos. Punk bands headlined the Rock Against Racism concerts that fought the sway of Britain's National Front in working-class neighborhoods.

"I relished the jolt that the punks put into Britain's legislators, businessmen, and editorialists. Minister of Parliament Marcus Lip-

ton huffed, 'If pop music is going to be used to destroy our established institutions, then it ought to be destroyed first.'

"Cancelling concerts, however, only seemed to make the music
fester and spread. The Sex Pistols, invented by a veteran of the 1968
Paris riots, recorded their sarcastic 'God Save the Queen' just as
Queen Elizabeth was toasting her Silver Jubilee. Banned from gov-
ernment-run radio, the song still clawed its way to number one on
the charts. The disaffected son of a diplomat started punk's most
enduring band, the Clash, which could always rip up a concert hall
with its anti-racist song, 'White Riot.'

" 'White riot, I wanna riot,' the mob shouted together, 'white riot,
a riot of my own.'
"I knew the feeling. All those years when I was working demonstrations, part of me wanted to join the protesters. Inside, I was
rooting for the dissidents. Bouncing up and down with a pack of
strangers stricken with St. Vitus' dance was the release I'd been
craving. It'd been years since I twisted and squirmed and sweated
buckets in those bronzeville dives in St. Louis. I'd finally found a way
to totally forget that straight life where I had to submerge part of my
personality.
"That was what punk was all about: re-inventing yourself. Any
working-class kid on the dole could snatch up a guitar and bang out
this music. And any of them could strut as defiantly as an aristocrat
by applying a little hair dye and makeup.
"The punks found metaphors for their mental and economic depression in precisely tattered clothes and shock-therapy coiffure,
meticulously tended. To convey the ideas of bondage and oppression,
they borrowed the paraphernalia of S&M sex shops: straps and
chains, stiletto heels, fishnet stockings, rubber pants, leather everything.
"Punk's ethos of disguise appealed to me. Just a glimpse of the

underground made me want to become a regular at any club likely to turn away Anastasio Somoza at the door. Of course I couldn't very well wear my suit to these places. At night, I'd rummage through the foul weather gear that the Secret Service brought along. Different details would pick up these odd camouflage and fatigue outfits in different countries. I'd put a couple of things together, I'd pull on some black steel-toe boots, slick back my hair with some Brylcream, and I'd fit right in. The punks were into battle dress. To them it was always foul weather. Just like the Secret Service agents, they'd wear sunglasses all the time, even on rainy days.

"It felt good to get out of that itchy suit. That suit and tie—my real camouflage. Whatever city I visited, I began to look for the secret passage to the lower depths. I always tried to develop friends in other cities. They didn't know what I did. I'd just call them and they'd say, 'Great, you're back in town.'

"If I was flying back to the States, I'd arrange to get a couple of days off and I'd stop in Paris to see my friend Suzanne, or she'd meet me in London. I'd send my gun on to the U.S. with my detail; they'd lock it in the gun box. What a relief to be rid of that thing! I could unwind. Suzanne knew the clubs I'd like in Paris.

"When I was doing that advance in West Berlin, I went exploring at night. The Germans were just getting into punk, but they were old hands at decadence. Berlin was a much more sombre angst-ridden scene, with junkies nodding out to this electronic music, no melody, just *blip, klinka, blip, klinka* . . . I really didn't get into it. It was as much of a mental ward as London, but most of the inmates were sedated."

Marty lived in Tokyo for more than a month when he worked on the advance for the 1979 economic summit there.

"Other agents would say, 'Come on, we're going over to the Marine base. They're having a four-dollar steak cookout.' I usually replied that You could get a steak at home. I had a decent driver, so I told him what I was looking for. I wanted to go to a place where only Japanese go. He'd say it was a long way. And I'd say that it didn't matter.

"The people there were just picking up on new wave music, but I found some acts that sounded pretty good, like the Sadistic Mica Band. My driver also took me into the Ginza district. There was this one theater where you went down some stairs. It held about 150 people. I was the only Caucasian. There was a play. It had long stretches of dialogue, but at various points they'd have sex on stage. Various techniques. At the end, the actors and actresses bowed and took questions from the audience.

"It wasn't your typical Western porn house audience. There was almost an equal number of men and women. They'd ask questions about the dildo the actors used, and the actors would pass it around the audience. The people would examine it, very scientifically. Then volunteers from the audience would come up on stage. They'd have sex with the cast, learn some new position and then sit down again. It was quite a demonstration. But I missed out on those four-dollar steaks."

Of course the netherworld were Marty felt most at home was in New York. America's own new wave was cresting in that city. Acts like the Ramones, Talking Heads, Patti Smith and Blondie were playing Max's Kansas City, Hurrah and CBGB's.

"I had a favorite place—an artists' hang-out that became the regular sound stage for droll party-as-theater concepts like the 'Yvonne De Carlo Polynesian Fantasy' and a Sunday funeral for sixties rockers like Hendrix, Joplin and Morrison. The place was the Mudd Club, named after Dr. Samuel Mudd, who'd gone to jail for honoring his Hippocratic oath by setting the broken leg of Abraham Lincoln's assassin, John Wilkes Booth.

\* \* \*

Steve Mass, the club's impresario says, "I created a fictional character, Dr. Mudd, who had a paternalistic presence over the teenage derelicts and revolutionaries running wild in the streets."

"I ran with that crowd," Marty recalls, "but musically I was drawn to the trashy, seductive stepchild of the rhythm and blues: *disco!*"

Like punk, disco was the creation of outsiders sour on mainstream white rock. It came thumping and humping out of the black, Hispanic and gay subcultures that danced till dawn in discriminating discotheques. Disc jockeys were the entertainment at these places. And to keep the patrons moving, the DJs looked for records that grooved you with a heavy bass and drum for at least five minutes. The sultry jams of black and latin groups coming out of Miami and Philadelphia worked well, and so did the Cameroon funk of Manu Dibango's "Soul Makossa." But there weren't many records that fit the bill till 1975, when acts like Shirley and Company and KC and the Sunshine Band began recording "extended mix" songs like "Shame, Shame, Shame" and "Get Down Tonight." At first, the major radio stations treated disco like punk: they wanted no part of it. So the only place to hear the music was where it was meant to be heard, at a *dance* club.

"After a few years," Marty admits, "disco—the word alone— became a joke. You had comedy acts like the Village People singing about macho men at the Y.M.C.A. You had John Travolta hustling in his white suit at every movie theater in a shopping mall. You had a mob of teenagers holding a Klan-style burning of disco records at a Chicago White Sox game. A lot of disco did suck. But at its best, disco was as good as the soul music of the sixties, which is why people like Diana Ross and James Brown had no trouble taking to it.

"Underneath that heavier beat, disco had all the same soul messages of freedom and heartache. A song like 'There But For the Grace of God' actually hits a lot harder at prejudice than Motown's more syrupy stuff. And besides that, the song literally *moves* you—it just pulls you out of your seat. Disco was actually closer to what I'd been into in St. Louis than punk was. I liked the punks' attitude, but my ear went out more naturally to the black sound. It was the same bloodline.

"The discos I'd go to were just as intense as the punk clubs. I'm not talking about Studio 54. I mean, I went to Studio 54, and at its height Studio was like nothing else, before or since. Its main DJ, Richie Kaczor, made investment bankers do things on the dance floor that they're still regretting. But Studio catered to that whole jet set Eurotrash crowd—Halston and Liza and Bianca and the rest of them.

"I was trying to get away from celebrities. So I went down into the bowels of Manhattan, to the private dance clubs. The Crisco Disco. The Paradise Garage. The disco they played there was rawer, funkier, more arcane. These were places that didn't get going till after midnight and they'd run till noon. Most of the crowd was gay—the leather boys, the drag queens. You saw some marvelous ensembles. The music meant more to the gays. Songs like 'I'm Coming Out,' 'I Will Survive'—those were national anthems to them. These places also attracted much more exotic women. You didn't always get their name, but you never forgot them, what they felt like.

"What I liked about those clubs was the anonymity. No one asked you what you did. Everybody had his own little secret and nobody was trying to pry it out of you. You were there to dance, to undress, to lose yourself. The rhythm just melted away whatever was bothering you. A place like the Garage served no liquor. Of course a lot of people were snorting coke and sniffing poppers—amyl nitrate. But the principal drug was the music. Those were wild nights. Totally tribal. Guys in jock straps dancing in cages. This whole ocean of sweaty bodies. Nobody caring if it was day or night outside.

"It became standard procedure for me to walk out of a club when the sun was up and take a cab up to my apartment. I'd change into my suit there, then I'd take a cab to JFK, where I'd catch the shuttle to Washington. Dulles Airport was right near my house, so I could make the trip, door-to-door, in an hour and forty minutes. I'd get into my car at my house and head to the White House for the four-to-midnight shift. I'd do this once or twice a week. Planes were like taxis to me. I ran on a continuous clock. I mean, a nine-to-fiver sees it's eleven o'clock and says, 'It's past my bedtime.' But in the Secret Service, you didn't have a regular bedtime. You were already spending two-thirds of your life awake at night."

Marty's new double life had its heritage in the evasions he'd always gone through to avoid telling strangers that he worked for the Secret Service. By this time Marty and Debby Johnson had cooled their romance and were living in different New York apartments.

"The one thing he hated most," Debby remembered, "was for anyone to know what he did for a living. The minute they found out, the questions would start. I'd tell one of my friends before she met Marty, 'This is what he does, so don't ask him about it.' But the first thing that would come out of her mouth would be, 'What's Jackie O *really* like?' "

"You couldn't tell someone at a party what you did because, next thing, half a dozen people would surround you and start firing questions," Marty remembers. "They'd ask about the President and start giving you their favorite conspiracy theory, on and on—it'd become like a seminar. So after awhile I'd just make up a different job every week. I'd tell them I was a pearl diver or a cow inseminator or some weird job I'd read about in a magazine. I liked seeing their reaction.

"But I found an underground even in sleepy old Washington, where the bars close at one-thirty. In a suburb in Maryland, there was this row of townhouses and in one of them there was an after-hours bar where you had to be buzzed in. You walked in and it looked like an ordinary suburban saloon—people sitting around, drinking, talking, listening to the jukebox. But if you knew the bartender, he'd buzz you upstairs. Up there was a disco where everything went on. Dancing, drugs, sex—a real group grope. Outside, limos would pull up to this townhouse, drop off some people and then drive away. All night long. In a way, Washington people have a more lurid nightlife than New Yorkers, because they have to stay hidden. The city was full of people who had to maintain appearances. They ran the parties like they ran the government—behind closed doors."

More than ever, Marty, the civil libertine, was opposed to the government's prying into the personal lives of citizens. Sources and Methods—"S&M"—was the Secret Service term for technical intelligence; the disclosure of which was a treasonable offense. More and more, Marty viewed his after-work activity as being subject to similar penalties.

"The funny thing was, on the job, a couple of times I came right in and said what was up. I'd be standing in front of the Oval Office and another agent would ask me, 'What'd you do over the weekend?'

"I'd tell him, and he'd go, 'Sure, Marty,' and he'd walk away laughing. They just seemed to think, 'That Marty, always making up wild stories.'

"The press corps was always looking for dirt on other people, so I used to throw some back at the reporters. Bettina Gregory, who'd just started covering the White House for ABC, asked me what Carter had done the night before. I'd joke, 'I'll tell you that, Bettina, if you'll tell me what you were doing in that leather collar the other night.' She'd turn ten shades of red and lose her train of thought.

"Later on, at a press conference, I caught her staring at me. It almost looked like she was thinking, 'How did *he* know about my leather collar?' I'm sure it was imagination. But that face of hers—it does look awfully severe."

Janet Paist, former Executive Producer of WNBC's "Eyewitness News," recalled the first time she met Marty. "It was a relatively staid party—news people are such bores—but off in a corner was this guy dancing like a whirling dervish. Somebody told me that the guy was a Secret Service agent, and I remember my boyfriend and me laughing, saying that we didn't know how comfortable we felt knowing that this kind of person was protecting the President of the United States. The guy looked kind of woolly. But the party wore on and I ended up dancing with Marty. Afterward we talked and he didn't seem crazy. He seemed very bright. He would talk about things that showed a wealth knowledge. About what 'news' was, for instance—he was fascinated with that. I like people who say what they think, and Marty did that. He was a great story teller. There was no pretence about him. He seemed not to be what I imagined a Secret Service agent to be. He was not dispassionate or cold or icy. I immediately trusted him. But I always harbored this sense that he really wasn't a Secret Service agent. Because it was just so hard to believe."

Agent Jim Kalafatis recalls, "One thing about Marty, he really had a way of making friends. He probably had a lot of friends in different walks of life . . . He always amazed me. He has a personality that could blend in with just about anybody . . . Some guys fraternize mostly with other agents. In Washington, there's no escaping the military and the government. But after a while you have to get away from that, and into the real world."

\*   \*   \*

Not all the agents were so open-minded toward Marty.

Paul Costello explained, "I think he was resented by some guys because he was viewed as aberrant. He was tolerated to some extent because the others said, 'Oh, he's one of the New Yorkers.' The guys out of New York were more idiosyncratic. There were the tough Brooklynites, and then there were the stylish guys who would pick up the models, and Marty fit into the latter group, sort of. But I think some of those guys felt he didn't represent the Secret Service in all its machismo. I think some guys scratched their heads and wondered, 'Why did they take this guy? How is he staying in? *Why* is he staying in?' "

"I'm sure there were people who thought I was a flake," Marty said, "but it didn't bother me. I was doing my job. And anyway, I liked that tingle you get when you have a big secret—when people think they've got you pegged, but they don't know *half* your story.

"I remember one night when I was in Washington, coming home at four A.M. from some club. I was in a car with a bunch of rowdy, freaky people. We were driving down Pennsylvania Avenue and we came to a stoplight right in front of the White House. While we were waiting for the light to change, I turned and looked at the White House—at this one window where I could see the agent on night duty. It was so eerie, sitting there in that car, in some leather get-up, surrounded by these wild people who didn't know what I did for a living, and watching that agent leaning back in his chair with the TV shining up on his face. It was like I'd stepped out of my body and I was watching myself."

# CHAPTER TWELVE
# *"And on Piano, . . ."*

"NOVEMBER 4th, 1979: I was working the midnight shift at Camp David when the Intelligence Division called. The agent on the other end asked me, 'Is the President awake?' I said that I didn't think so. The agent said, 'Well, if he's not up, he will be.' Then he told me that Iranian revolutionaries had taken over the embassy in Tehran. He said they'd taken a lot of American hostages. I later found that Carter had just picked up another phone. He was getting briefed. The first Day of Captivity had begun."

With every passing month, the kidnappers grew more aloof than Allah. And America came to feel like a country that had been buried alive. While citizens around commemorated each day with a hopeful yellow ribbon, Marty's underground life yielded a clue as to how restive one hostage family might be getting.

"One night I was at that after-hours club, the place where the bartender buzzed you up to the swingers' disco—where the people got dressed up in bondage attire. A couple of the regulars there pointed out this one woman who they said was the wife of one of the hostages. They said she used to come there with her husband.

"I was getting fed up with the situation myself. Like a lot of people, I began to blame Carter for not acting more decisively. Every day I'd see him lugging these big briefing books down the halls—he was studying up on Iran. I wanted to say, 'Hey, it's too late for that! You should've sent a strike force in right away. You shouldn't have been clinking glasses with the Shah on New Year's—telling him Iran was an *island of stability.*' "

"Of course everybody has twenty-twenty hindsight. And to look at Carter, you could see how this whole thing was wearing him down as much as anybody. He was all hunched over. He couldn't even rag on the agents like he used to. There's no question Carter was a hard worker, and deeply moral. When it came to bringing peace to the Middle East, he wouldn't let up. He smoothed out relations with the Chinese. He put the screws on Somoza. He put human rights at the head of his foreign policy. But I still don't think he was ready for the Presidency. I mean, how many crises did he go through as a one-term governor of *Georgia*? Wisdom doesn't come out of briefing books.

"It was too bad. Toward the end of the crisis he was getting better at being President. Maybe the best speech he ever made was the one he caught the most flak for, when he said America was suffering from a 'malaise.' You can say it's a sad day when America's leader tells his people they have a malaise, and maybe that was the wrong word. But the speech as a whole was on the mark. He captured how the country was letting itself be paralyzed, and how it had to rethink its role in the world, starting with Carter's own party, and himself. For once, he wasn't wearing that painful smile where he didn't move his eyes. He was speaking from his heart. He hit on some home truths. But a lot of people didn't want to hear things like that about their country or themselves. It only made them more depressed."

The time would come, after the hostages had paraded down Wall Street, when Secret Service agents would covet an assignment to former President Jimmy Carter. In his status as elder statesman, Carter would grow chummier with his bodyguards and let them hunt and fish on his Georgia farm. But during Carter's last months in office, the White House bodyguards took fewer pains to hide their disdain for the Chief.

"Privately, when I'd hang out with the agents on Air Force One, I'd find out they couldn't stand Carter," remembers Paul Costello. "They're basically very strong law and order people, and they saw Carter as soft on that. They loved Reagan. He was the quintessential agent's man."

By November 1980, UPI correspondent Helen Thomas reported that Rosalynn Carter's bodyguards were so disenchanted with the President that they all boasted about voting for Reagan. Months before that, though, the Associated Press had carried an item about one young agent who'd asked for a transfer out of the White House. That agent was Marty Venker.

"I still had an apartment in New York, and when I heard that Richard Nixon was moving to Manhattan from San Clemente, I grabbed the assignment. I was into the nightlife. I was tired of Carter. And, the truth was, I wanted to get to know Nixon. By this time I was way beyond any political allegiances. I was just curious about this guy who embodied half a century of history. For better or worse, Nixon is America. Five years before, in disgrace he'd flown off the South Lawn. And now, here he was, over his phlebitis, flying back to the East Coast. Everybody wondered what he was up to. I wondered.

"On February 14, 1980, I met Richard and Pat Nixon at the TWA terminal at Kennedy Airport. Flanked by five security cars, we drove the Nixons to 142 East 65th Street, between Lexington and Third. Well-wishers, reporters and some diehard Yippies were waiting when the waving Nixon stepped out of his limo, over a pile of garbage, and into his $750,000-four-story townhouse."

Nixon's new neighborhood held plenty of ties to his past. Within a few blocks stood the Soviet Mission and the headquarters of the PLO. Over on Park lived the Shah's twin sister. Right behind Nixon lived Kennedy-chronicler and enemies list member Arthur Schlesinger. Across the street resided Theodore H. White, whose *Making of a President* books had examined Nixon's campaign travails. Right next door, in a much grander townhouse, lived the personification of the Eastern establishment that Nixon detested—David Rockefeller. The Chase Bank chairman tried to be friendly. Not long after the Nixons moved in, he invited them over for a welcome-wagon cocktail. Nixon went; but that cocktail pretty much started and finished the neighborly bit.

"Every time I saw Nixon and Rockefeller cross paths on the sidewalk, they barely gave each other a nod."

No, now that he was gearing up for his comeback, Nixon couldn't dally in the enemy camp. Even the current President was kept at arm's length. Back in 1978, right after the U.S. and China agreed to full diplomatic relations, Jimmy Carter called San Clemente to thank Nixon for a piece of advice. Nixon had taken the call. But now that he'd landed in New York, Nixon was playing hard to get.

"The White House communications people called the Secret Service command post to ask for Nixon's private number. I asked who wanted it? They said, 'The old man wants it.' I told them I'd get back to them and I walked upstairs to ask Nixon about it.

"I told him, 'The President wants your private number.' He practically jumped out of his seat.

"He said, 'You didn't give it to them, did ya? You tell them that if he wants to get in touch with me, he can write.' "

All the same, Nixon had planted himself so close to the public that any of New York's colorful citizens could walk right up and knock on his door. That meant that any time the agents wanted to buy a coffee or a hero, they had to swivel their video joystick and sweep the street with their camera. Otherwise they might suddenly find themselves smothered by a fat lady babbling about the Pope and Cambodia.

Nixon's most immediate threat, though, was the press. In those first days after "Searchlight" hit town, a whooping tribe of reporters, photographers and cameramen camped outside his door, desperate to scalp a photo and scavenge a quote.

"Many times Nixon would call me on the in-house telephone and ask, 'Are they still there?'

"I'd look at the video monitor and see the press and say, 'Yep, still there.' For a week Nixon called with that same question. Then one day I looked outside and said, 'They're gone.'

"Half an hour later, Nixon called again and said, 'I want to go to the post office.' I said to myself, Oh no. Just for some letter we'll have to get into a big production. We'll have to call for the back-up car and the limo.

"So I said, 'Mr. President, do you want something *mailed?* I can have one of your staff members come by and pick it up.'

"But he said, 'No. I want to go to the post office myself.'

"I guess he'd decided the time had come. I mean, he'd been outside before. He'd been ducking the press by taking his morning walk at six A.M.—before they showed up at his door. But this was going to be his first trip out in the middle of the day. It may have been his first trip to a U.S. post office in over decade. His staff always took care of the mail. Anyway, we found the closest post office, Lenox Hill, and we called for the cars. Then, after we scoped out the street, Nixon came out of the house with this brown package under his arm.

"I figured that, since it was a weekday afternoon, the post office wouldn't have many customers. No luck. The station was jammed. And when Nixon walked in, the place just erupted. People weren't even subtle about it. They just screamed, 'Jesus, it's *him*! It's *Nixon!*' Ladies started whipping Instamatics out of their purses and snapping pictures. People were asking for autographs. Nixon was obviously eating up this reception, you know, like he always thought—'let the people decide.' So we were working our way up this line and I could see we were being watched by the Station Master and all his clerks. All of them, that is, except for this one clerk who seemed oblivious to the commotion. And that's the one who called out to Nixon, 'Next.'

"When I stepped up to the woman, I could see she was the ultimate bored civil servant—slow, real attitude, overweight. Suddenly, the most famous face in the world was standing at her window and, so help me, she acted like she didn't know who he was. She was in her own bureaucratic fog. Nixon pushed his package across the counter toward her. The package said: 'To: Former President Richard M. Nixon, San Clemente, Ca. From: Richard M. Nixon, New York, N.Y.' He was mailing a package to himself. Make of that what you will.

"The woman took one look at the package and said, 'What's the zip code?'

"Nixon said, 'What?' He turned to me and whispered, 'Zip code?'

"I stepped up and said to her, 'Can you look it up under San Clemente?' She got out her zip code book but she couldn't find it. I said, 'Well, look under San Diego. It's near there.' She still couldn't find it. Finally she handed me the book and I found it.

"She put the package on the scale. Then she said, 'That'll be $7.49.'

"Suddenly, Nixon got this look like he'd been caught doing something illegal. He lowered those eyes. He started fishing in his pockets. What do you think? He didn't bring money. Fortunately, the Station Master, who'd been sweating bullets watching all this, tapped this woman on the shoulder and said, 'No, no, no. *He* doesn't have to pay postage.'

"The woman got real indignant and screeched, 'Why not?'

"The Station Master said, 'He used to be President of the United States.'

"So I swear to God, she said, 'I don't give a damn *what* he was, the *scale* says $7.49!'

"Who knows? Maybe she was one of those people who thought Nixon should never have been pardoned, much less given franking privileges. In any case, all the other customers were watching this side show, so Nixon said, 'Well, I'll be glad to pay!' He started motioning for me to spot him a ten dollar bill.

"They didn't make him pay. But you could tell this wasn't the public appearance he'd had in mind. When he got back in the car, he fumed, 'That's what I've always said about government workers—they don't know what the hell they're doing.'

To Marty, Nixon differed from Carter in one immediate way: "Carter treated you like a maggot. Nixon treated you like a human being. He always asked about your mother, and when somebody in your family was sick, Nixon was the first to send a card or flowers."

Of course, Nixon had reason to be grateful to the Secret Service. Back in 1958, when he was Vice President, he was down in Lima, Peru, and a heckler threw a rock that grazed his throat and hit an agent, Jack Sherwood, in the face, breaking a tooth. The Nixons then went to Caracas, Venezuela, where protesters showered their motorcade with so much spit that the drivers had to turn on the windshield wipers. The mob attacked Nixon's motorcade with stones, pipes and baseball bats. The Venezuelan motorcycle cops stood motionless.

But twelve Secret Service agents formed a human fence around the car.

Nixon remembered the valor of those agents. And yet it sometimes seemed that he went out of his way to take his place as a martyr beside Jack Kennedy. (In his first term, Nixon's favorite limo was said to be SS 100X—the restored midnight blue, 8,000-pound 1961 Lincoln Continental that Kennedy had been shot in.) In Lima, and again in San Jose, California, in 1970, Nixon had insisted on jumping onto cars and taunting rock-throwing hecklers.

In June 1974, the Watergate-besieged President visited the Middle East. The Secret Service had received grave reports of Palestinian terrorist threats. But against the Service's wishes, Nixon stood waving with Anwar Sadat in an open-sided railroad car as it rolled past hundreds of thousands of Egyptians. In Cairo, he'd wandered blithely into a mob. His startled agents barely managed to pluck him from the throng and return him to his car.

Nixon had further terrorized his agents on the trip: in Saudi Arabia, by riding in a car without a Secret Service driver, and in revolutionary Syria, by ordering that the roof of his limo be opened so he could stand up and wave. Standing, walking, climbing, he was also defying his doctors who'd just diagnosed a lethal blood-clot in his leg. According to Bob Woodward and Carl Bernstein's *The Final Days,* Nixon's personal physician, Major General Walter Tkach, told agent Dick Keiser he was astonished by Nixon's recklessness. Keiser reportedly responded, "You can't protect a President who wants to kill himself."

Back in Washington, Woodward and Bernstein also claimed that when impeachment loomed the closest, Nixon's son-in-law, Ed Cox, worried that the "President might take his own life." Worried, too, about Pat Nixon's depression, Cox allegedly asked that the Secret Service stand watch in the White House's family quarters.

\* \* \*

"Nixon always felt he was overprotected," says Marty. "He resented that he couldn't pick his nose without some agent taking note. In 1973, he tried to cut his detail by a third. 'I don't like it and my family doesn't like it,' he said.

"I'd been warned of the lengths Nixon might go to elude us. One time he snuck out of the San Clemente compound. His valet, Manolo Sanchez, drove past the agents in a car with Nixon stretched out in the back seat under a blanket. Nixon just wanted to go to a restaurant. But some reporters saw him and phoned the house. They wanted to know what Nixon was up to. The Secret Service told them, he's not at any restaurant, he's here at home. But then the agents found he was gone and they chased him down. I guess he promised he'd never do it again."

Now that he'd come to New York, Nixon kept thinking about giving up his guards. The agents did, however, have their advantages. Nixon knew that he still had a few enemies out there; and surely, as he crept back into the public eye, he didn't mind having some Secret Service around to remind everybody what job he used to hold.

"He was getting older, too. He may have wanted the agents gone, but over the years he'd gotten so dependent on them that he'd sometimes space out. He didn't even open doors for himself anymore. One night we were walking home with him and he stopped in front of a townhouse three doors down from his house. He just stood there, staring at the door-knocker. People on the sidewalk started to recognize him. So as politely as I could, I whispered to him, 'Mr. President, this *isn't* your house.'

"You never knew what to expect from him. He'd wreak havoc at his doctor's office. He used to put the examination gown on backwards and tramp down the hall with the front flying open. The nurses would stop in their tracks.

"Sometimes he overestimated his mechanical skill. We were down in Key Biscayne once and he was trying to move a baby crib from one room to another. The doorway was clearly a lot narrower than the crib, but that didn't stop him. He kept ramming it from different angles. I tried to tell him it wouldn't fit. But he kept ramming it and saying, 'It'll go! It'll go!'

"One time the roof alarm at the townhouse went off. That alarm never malfunctioned, so when we heard it, we said, 'This is *it*— terrorist attack. We ran up the stairs with our shotguns and Uzis. When we got to the roof, we found Nixon poking a screwdriver into the air conditioning unit. Sparks were flying everywhere. He had almost electrocuted himself. But he kept saying, 'I can get it to go!'

"But putting all that klutziness aside, Nixon's political mind was still ticking. He was standing in front of Tricia's building one day, watching a parade from a distance, trying to figure out who was marching: 'It's not the Greeks. It's not the Jews. Not the Puerto Ricans—dressed too well.' So he said, 'Marty, see if you can find out what kind of parade that is.'

"I checked it out. When I came back, he asked, 'Did you find out?'

"I said, 'Yeah. It was the Gay Pride parade.'

"His eyes bugged out: '*Gay Pride?* Gay . . . PRIDE! Pr-*ide?* Funniest damn thing, I've . . . I mean, we had gays when I was younger, but they didn't march around about it.' Then he lowered his voice, and said, *sotto voce,* 'You know, they say Ed Koch is homosexual.' But Nixon'd never stick his neck out without covering his ass. So quickly, he added ' . . . but they say Koch is the best goddam mayor New York's ever had.' "

Morning was when the Fighting Quaker hit his stride. Charged up, back on what he called "the fast track," Nixon set out from his house at six in the morning, for his constitutional.

\* \* \*

"One agent would follow him in a car. Two more agents would follow on foot half a block behind. I'd walk at his side. We trooped down the nearly deserted streets. He inspected Korean grocers as they arranged their kiwi fruit. He reviewed the Sanitation Department's panzer division as it rearranged its street trash. Sometimes a cab driver would roll down his window and say, 'All right, Mr. President!' and give Nixon the thumbs-up.

"I remember one couple storming by him, mumbling, 'He ruined the country.' But most people were respectful.

"Once Nixon stopped to squint at a dumpster plastered with a poster 'exposing' the Trilateral Commission and its diabolical czar, neighbor David Rockefeller. Another time the oenologist who'd shipped his 200-bottle wine cellar three thousand miles would stoop and peer at a still-sleeping wino, as though dimly recognizing himself in some past or future life.

"Once we passed an abandoned car over by the Armory. It was completely stripped and burnt. Nixon was fascinated with it. He stuck his head inside and said, 'I'll bet somebody really got hurt in this one.' He was always curious about auto wrecks on the highway. I think he had a morbid curiosity about blood and damage.

"He almost always walked east to Lexington or Fifth and down toward the Plaza. He liked to stop and look up to the thirty-ninth floor of the Hotel Pierre. That's where he had his campaign headquarters when he first won the Presidency. The West Side was like bohemia for him. He'd only go over to the West Side when Julie wanted a cheesecake from Miss Grimble's. Almost never would he walk east of Third Avenue.

"One time he let a reporter follow him on a 'typical' morning walk. They went over to First Avenue. Nixon chatted with various immigrants, and bought a cross-section of newspapers. It was a telling glimpse into his mind, because he usually didn't do any of the things he did with that reporter. He had all his papers delivered to his house. Obviously, he didn't want anybody reading some article and tailing him on his real routine.

"I remember one time he wandered into a head shop that advertised 'smoker's supplies.' I think he was looking for cigars. But when he walked inside he found the walls of this place were lined with hardcore porn. There was a display case full of drug and sex paraphernalia. Pipes, coke spoons, bongs with nipples. Nixon was taking it all in, asking questions. He pointed to some two-headed vibrators and said, 'Now what's *that* for?'

"Behind the counter was this hippie. I mean, a real refugee from the sixties—long hair, the Grateful Dead coming out of the speakers. This hippie was speechless. You could just imagine him screaming inside his brain: *'Richard Nixon is in my head shop!'* He probably thought he'd dropped too much acid.

"A bunch of people outside had their noses pressed against the front window, steaming it up. I couldn't get over the scene. It was like some kind of time warp. The other agents were just cooling their heels on the street, having a cigarette. I couldn't believe they weren't picking up on this. Meanwhile, Nixon kept asking, 'And what's *that* for?'

On these walks with Nixon, all along the way he'd be talking. He liked to think out loud. Sometimes he'd throw out a test line to figure out where you were coming from—you know, to pinpoint your slur groups. He'd say, 'Somebody told me these people *ruined* this neighborhood.' I wouldn't bite, so he'd equivocate, '. . . on the other hand, it's all part of the immigrant cycle.'

"Most of the time, I'd just let him ramble—you got more out of Nixon that way. He'd have the most fascinating geopolitical debates with himself. That's when you couldn't believe he was the same guy who put his hospital gown on backwards. Naturally, he was heated up over Iran. He hated Carter for making a carpetbagger out of the Shah when he had cancer. He'd reel off all the options that the

President had for freeing the hostages. Then he'd pause, and he'd tick off all the drawbacks."

When the Iranians first took the Americans captive, Nixon told an interviewer that his gut reaction was, Why don't we go in there and knock these people over? After some more thought, though, Nixon conceded that a raid would be "too dangerous perhaps." In later public comments, he stood behind Carter's posture of peaceful negotiation. Yet as America's shame compounded daily, Nixon felt the urge to make a muscle. In April 1980, when he was in Europe pushing his book, *The Real War,* he told a questioner that it was time for Carter to "stop giving warnings and take action." A week later Nixon was in Germany when, in the early morning, Marty heard that Carter had tried to rescue the hostages and that the mission had left eight commandos dead.

"I knew Nixon would want to know. So I went to his hotel room. He was getting dressed. His first words were, 'How many helicopters did they use?'

"I said, 'Eight.'

"He screamed back, 'Eight? Goddam it! Go with *eighty!* It's not like we don't have them!'

Nixon's European book tour made a good warmup for a bout that he faced back home.

"Two weeks after we were in Germany, he did a live, hour-long interview with Barbara Walters. I remember when we took him over to the studio. He was ready for her, really psyched up. Right before he jumped into his car he did a kind of Muhammad Ali two-step.

In his interview, Nixon rated the 1980's crop of Presidential candidates. He praised Carter as "very intelligent" but called him "sadly

... an ineffective President." He also declared that "while I've retired from politics, I haven't retired from life."

Nixon knew he'd come off well. That night at the townhouse Marty's "walking companion" couldn't sit still.

"He paced the floor right above me till six a.m. Pacing, pacing. It gave me the creeps. I was wondering, What's he planning now? I tell you, the guy's an immortal creature. You can't kill him. You have to drive a stake through his heart.

Of course, Pat Nixon, who'd been begging her husband to get out of politics ever since he'd been a Congressman, slept through all the pacing.

"I liked Pat (code name 'Starlight'). Even after she'd suffered a stroke, Pat still did her own laundry. The washing machine was right next to the command post. I'd sit on the dryer and tell her about the time Miz Lillian called the Irish Prime Minister 'Prime.' Pat laughed like it was an episode of 'Hee Haw.'

"Julie Nixon was easy to get along with, too. She'd been my first assignment, back in 1971 when she came to Illinois to turn on the power at a water plant. I thought she had a real warm, honest face.

"Tricia Nixon Cox got on less well with the agents. One time she left on a trip and told the agents to be sure to water her plants every day. I don't know how she said it, but you know how the agents watered the plants? They pissed on them. Every day. She came home and found her plants dead. You could hear her scream from the street. That was a bit much—killing her plants—but I think even Tricia's dad thought she could tone down her attitude. One time Nixon said to me, 'How the hell Tricia developed that British accent is beyond me.' "

But Tricia's attitude was a frail petunia next to the thorny Vegas cactus that was the ego of Nixon's friend Frank Sinatra. That Nixon and the "Chairman of the Board" could be called friends was at one time unthinkable. In 1960, the then-liberal Sinatra had been such a zealous supporter of John Kennedy that he hired a private eye to tail Nixon during the campaign. Sinatra offered the Kennedy campaign evidence that Nixon had received psychotherapy.

In 1968, backing Hubert Humphrey, Sinatra had said, "I'll do anything to defeat that bum Nixon." But in 1972, after Sinatra impressively defended himself at a Congressional hearing into organized crime, Nixon called to congratulate him. Flattered, Sinatra donated $53,000 to Nixon's campaign. After Nixon won again, a flap with the Secret Service over security at an inaugural concert caused Sinatra to quit as master of ceremonies. Still, when Watergate burst, his loyalty to Nixon and Spiro Agnew was unswerving. Sinatra loaned the former Vice President over $230,000 and tried to get other friends to contribute to Agnew's legal defense.

"So Sinatra (code name 'Napoleon') was on fine terms with Nixon when I escorted them around New York one night. They started out with drinks at 21. Dick and Pat. Frank and Barbara. Then they went to Jimmy Weston's, on East Fifty-fourth. They had dinner, some more drinks. And then, when they were walking out of the restaurant, this teenager took their picture. Now a lot of papparazzi loiter outside Jimmy Weston's because celebrities eat there. But this was just a kid, a fan, who obviously was thrilled to get this picture of Sinatra and Nixon together. Well, Sinatra, who by then was completely bombed, flew into a rage. He said to me, 'Take his fucking camera!' That, and 'Take the fucker out!' Now beating people up may be standard procedure for Frank's bodyguards, but I didn't go in for it. I ignored him until he said, 'Look, you either take the kid out or *I'll* take the kid out!'

"I said, 'Listen, Frank, just get in the car and settle down.' He got in.

"Nixon, who looked like he wasn't feeling any pain either, said to me, 'That Frank's got a hell of a temper.'

"You'd never see that sort of behavior from Nixon's usual buddies, Bebe Rebozo and Bob Abplanalp. Both of them were extremely reverential toward Nixon. They'd *always* address him as Mr. President. When Nixon wanted to think, Bebe would sit for hour after hour with him without saying a word. He didn't speak until spoken to.

"I always sensed that there was a rivalry between Bebe and Bob. After Nixon left the White House, Rebozo wanted him to move near him in Florida. Abplanalp wanted him to move near him in New York—which he did. The two of them would have little arguments over what the old man would do on his vacation, where they'd eat. Both these guys were classic Nixon types—rags to riches. Bebe, I believe, met Nixon first and was the only person, other than Rose Mary Woods, who'd eat with the Nixons every Thanksgiving. But Abplanalp had made a lot more money (by inventing the aerosol nozzle), and he gave Nixon the wine cellar in his townhouse. Abplanalp was a much more regular guy than Bebe. After Abplanalp bought the property around Nixon's house in San Clemente, somebody asked him what he was going to do with it. He said, 'I'm going to build a ten-story whorehouse on it.'

"That was Abplanalp for you. He had his own chain of islands off Florida, but he was one of the guys. The two of us went gambling one night in St. Martin. He gave me a thousand dollars. He said, 'Here, play with this. If you win, give it back to me. If you lose, no big deal.'

"I made some money. Abplanalp lost a lot—several thousand. I came over to him and said, 'Here, use this.' Nothing like bailing out a mogul.

"Nixon and Bebe and Abplanalp liked the Caribbean. They'd meet up at Abplanalp's island, or he'd have his yacht, *The Star Mist,* meet them someplace. You couldn't believe some of the things that came out of Nixon's mouth when they got him out of his suit and into some swim trunks. One time he saw a local woman carrying a basket on her head and he said to me, 'Now why do you suppose the women have such large asses?' He couldn't get over the nude beaches. He'd say, 'Now why do you suppose they don't wear any clothes?'

"One day a nude woman came up to him on the beach and asked if her husband could take their picture together. Nixon was so taken aback, he said yes. He started to put his arm around her. I saw this happening and went over to the husband. I said, 'Hey, think about this. We don't know who you are. This picture could get flashed all over the world. Why don't you come back when your wife has some clothes on?'

"Nixon did get friendly with one woman on St. Martin. He was staying with Bebe and Abplanalp at a very exclusive resort. Whenever Nixon wanted to go swimming, he'd tell me and I'd put on my swimsuit and check out the beach. After two days, I noticed that whenever I showed up on the beach, this unbelievably beautiful woman in her late twenties would also come out of her cabana—topless. She'd always place herself at a discreet distance from Nixon, but close enough so he could still ogle her. He'd wade out into the ocean and lurk with that nose just covered by the water. Like a crocodile.

"At night, Nixon, Bebe and Abplanalp would eat in the resort's dining room, and this woman would eat by herself right near them. Nixon finally said to Bebe, 'Oh, why don't you invite her over to the table?' So she came over—deeply tanned, dressed in a see-through mesh top. They all had a grand time, and later, in the car, Nixon would say, 'What a wonderfully intelligent woman! Speaks three languages!' He would never directly acknowledge her as desirable.

"Nixon was funny about sex. He's been known to complain that a novel has too much sex in it. But he liked to swear and sometimes he'd try to get into some locker room talk. It didn't always come off. One morning he said to some agents, 'So, did you guys *fornicate* last night?' The agents had to bite their lips to keep from laughing.

"Anyway, back to the story. A few days after this dinner, a huge yacht dropped anchor off the beach. It was beyond belief, almost an ocean liner. It belonged to a European steel magnate, and, *just by coincidence,* the woman knew him. She told Nixon that the steel magnate would like to invite him to lunch aboard the yacht. Out they went.

"About this time, I looked into the resort's records. Turns out the steel magnate was paying for the woman's room. He set all this up to meet Nixon. A lot of oil companies offered Nixon big money to help them get drilling rights in China, and, reportedly, he turned them down. But this steel guy—maybe he had the right approach.

"You'd run into all sorts of people at this resort. Talk about a place attracting a mixed clientele. One day I found David Bowie drinking by himself in one corner of a little bar. This was before Bowie's career took off again. Sitting in the shadows, he looked pretty down—the Thin White Duke trying to avoid a sunburn. Nixon walked past him on the way to his room, and I thought about Bowie's last big hit, 'Young Americans,' with that line where he asked if you remembered *'the President Nixon.'*

"I said to Nixon, 'That's David Bowie over there.'

"He said, 'Who?'

"I said, 'David Bowie, the rock star.'

"He gave his all-purpose response: 'Oh, of course, of course.' What did I expect? Nixon got a much bigger kick out of running into the Andrews Sisters in a little restaurant in Paris. One of them introduced herself, and Nixon invited them over. The place was nearly empty, so we went back into a private room where the Andrews Sisters sang. Richard Nixon on piano.

"Later on, those little musical moments kept sticking in my mind. We went to the Ivory Coast one time. The King of Sanwi invited Nixon there to open a golf course. After we landed at the airport, we boarded a military helicopter that skimmed over this dense jungle that the people called the magic forest. Then all of a sudden we saw this area carved out of the forest, and this incredible palace. Warriors with spears and headdresses came out to greet us. So did the king, who was decked out, head to toe, in gold jewelry. I got to my room in the palace and I could barely lift the ashtrays. Solid gold. I had a gold bathtub with jewel-encrusted knobs. Absolutely absurd wealth.

"At night I'd get away from it by sitting on the edge of the palace's moat. Underneath my feet big crocodiles would lounge on a sand bar, with their mouths open. Servants would feed them live chickens.

"Out in the magic forest I could hear drums. Talking drums they're called. They really reminded me where disco, soul, rock—all of it—began. It was one of those times when music caught up with me. Like when I'd take a boat to the island where Abplanalp's servants lived, to hear reggae. Or when I went with Carter to a memorial for Martin Luther King at the Ebenezer Baptist Church in Atlanta. I was standing in a pew next to Stevie Wonder and listening to that church rock out. That's when I'd realize that for all the action and show biz of the Secret Service, I still missed music. And I'd try to remember why I'd ever left it."

# CHAPTER THIRTEEN

# *An Argument Over Clothes*

MARTIN Luther King Jr. had once said, "A riot is, at bottom, the language of the unheard." After years of giving music a deaf ear, after years of segregating his flamboyant side in an outlying ghetto of his brain, Marty Venker began using that language: his life became a riot. Now that he was living in New York, he began spelunking even more deeply in its dance caverns. Without the hassle of catching the shuttle to D.C., he went out and stayed up any night he wanted. In 1979 the Service ran a standard "Security Update" investigation on Marty. Agents from four field offices spent four months asking Marty's neighbors and colleagues if Marty displayed any criminal or subversive behavior. "No derogatory information developed," the Update had concluded. But . . .

"I was doing some things that, as the agency was always saying, would've caused the Secret Service profound embarrassment. Not so much drugs as outrageous behavior. If it ever got out, if the Service knew what I was into, I would've been fired. Nevertheless, I explored widely. Even chronic nightcrawlers tended to confine themselves either to the new wave scene or the disco scene. Nothing alien was alien to me."

\* \* \*

Janet Paist remembers, "One night at the Crisco Disco I was sitting along the dance floor, when Marty came in with these . . . fringe people. He'd been out in the sun all day with them. He danced with me for a little bit, but then he went away with them. I knew he led this other life. Not only did he have the Secret Service life and friendships with press people like me, but he had this crazy life where he was doing things he wouldn't even tell me about. He had these segments of his life that were not in any way consolidated."

"I *was* secretive about my daytime job with my nighttime friends," Marty admits. "Once or twice someone at a club would say to me, 'God, I swear I saw you on the news last night.'
"I'd look at them like they were crazy and laugh, 'Yeah, sure.'

Out clubbing, he met a petite woman named Rose who japaned her face in vivid colors and who had a flair for designing studded-leather jackets and lavender Casbah ensembles.

We met on Valentine's Day, remembers Rose. "I saw him on this checkerboard dance floor, with his shirt off, wearing a mask and dancing with this really hot-looking girl. We started to see each other casually, going out to clubs with other people. It was a real party atmosphere, so nobody talked about work. We were a pack of people. I didn't know what anybody did, but I loved everybody. We loved each other at night. Marty and I became best friends. I really wasn't that curious about what Marty did, but when I asked him, he said he modeled. I had seen his picture in a catalogue of leather outfits. He'd tell me he had to go to Europe for a modeling assignment, and then I'd get overseas phone calls from him. So I accepted it. He sure never talked about politics. In the back of my mind, I thought maybe he was involved in some seedy underground entertainment."

\* \* \*

"In order to get away from the Secret Service I had to adopt this other personality. I started to resent the Secret Service for taking my life away. I saw too many guys get old before their time. Guys in their thirties talking about retirement all day long. I wasn't going to let it happen to me. I wanted to cram as much living as I could into my time off. I was the guy on the dancefloor at six a.m. I've always wanted to taste. My mother once said, 'I never regretted what I did. I only regretted the things I didn't try.' I guess I took that more to heart than I realized. I overdid everything. I always have. Even my job. When I was doing that, I wanted to give everything I had to it. I felt deep down I wasn't going to retire from the Secret Service. Either I was going to get shot, or I was going to freak out.

"I wasn't always getting enough sleep. But you learned to operate without sleep in the Service. My metabolism might go into shock if it wasn't fighting off at least three hours of jet lag. Looking back, I would've been more alert if I'd been better rested. But for me to feel alert, I also need that mental release. A dance club was like a health spa. Once I'd had my chance to go crazy, I could come back and accept the job again. I felt as if it was my right to wear myself out. The Secret Service didn't care if they put me on a plane to California an hour after I'd gotten back from Europe. So why should they care if I rolled into work straight from the dance floor? That's what I'd do. I'd roller skate to Nixon's townhouse and change into my suit and tie."

The roller skates alone were enough to set Secret Service tongues wagging—especially when other agents factored in that Marty's boss on the Nixon detail was Mike Endicott. Endicott, who'd joined in 1965, had a sharp nose, stout cheeks and the classically hooded Secret Service eyes.

"Endicott had a personality that was 180 degrees different from Marty's," said Jim Kalafatis. "There are guys more flexible than

Endicott. So if there was going to be any friction, here was the type of guy who might take challenging suggestions personally."

Endicott: If some other people on the detail had roller-skated to work, Mike Endicott admits, "I would have questioned it. But not Marty. Marty's lifestyle was New York City all the way. We have some other people in the Secret Service whose lifestyle is New York City . . . Marty used to run with a pretty fast crowd. He used to hang out with Jessica Savitch and he had a girlfriend who was a model. It's hard to live that kind of life when you have to fly off on a moment's notice for three weeks . . . But Marty always reported to work in a condition to do the job. There was never any hint of drinking or drugs. In fact, I've been out with Marty on the road and I don't recall him drinking that much.

"Marty marched to a drum a little bit different than everybody else . . . But there's a lot of me in Marty. From the standpoint that Marty is very creative and I'm very creative, when it comes to the Secret Service's business. Marty had a lot of responsibility and power then. He was not a senior agent, but he had such a creative mind that the people he worked for let Marty do a lot.

"My specialty is protection and logistics, and in those departments Marty had my complete confidence. I could send him anywhere in the world and count on him getting the job done. He was a shift leader and he was fair to the men under him. He listened to them, and I think everybody respected him."

Marty's men were grateful, for instance, when he ignored Secret Service policy and told them they didn't have to stand outside the door of Nixon's townhouse.

"The guard on the sidewalk was only attracting wise guys who would've otherwise passed by without knowing who lived there," says Marty. "Also, it gets cold out there. Anytime agents were freezing, I wondered, How are they supposed to stay alert? How's an agent going to fire his gun if his fingers are like popsicles? At least, put him in a car."

"Like most of the government, the Secret Service favors established procedures," says Endicott. "Marty took creative approaches that were sometimes quite radical. He might disagree, say, on the number of men you'd need for support. Some people may have thought Marty was out of step with the organization. But maybe because I think of myself as a creative person, I found his opinion valuable."

On icy nights other agents might give thanks that they were on Marty's shift; still—was he imagining it?—Marty felt that by now many of them had pegged him as a weirdo.

"Music was taking on a bigger and bigger role in my life. Songs were always going through my head. I was getting so into music that I started to get ridiculed for it on the job. There was no question I was on a different wavelength. One time I was at a airport. Agents were chatting among themselves. I was plugged into one of the first Sony Walkmans, listening to a new San Francisco band—the Dead Kennedys.

"On the night of December 8th, 1980, I was on my way home after working at the New York field office on Nixon's next trip abroad. I had taken the subway uptown, got off at Seventy-second Street and Central Park West. I stopped at a deli on West Seventy-second for a sandwich. Suddenly, there were gunshots outside. I opened the deli's door and saw a limo parked up the block in front of the Dakota apartment building. Striding across the street, I saw a blond woman leaning on a lamppost, crying. I walked up to the Gothic archway of the Dakota and saw people crowded around a body. On the pavement in the courtyard, John Lennon was dying.

"Some people and the doorman helped Lennon into a little office near the arch. A doctor started looking at him. There was a guy sitting on a curb reading a book—*The Catcher in the Rye*—and somebody in the crowd pointed to him and told me, 'That's the guy who did it.' It wasn't long before the cops showed up and took the guy away. I hung around for awhile, but when the crowd got bigger and the street turned into a Be-in, I couldn't take it anymore. I went back to my apartment, which was about two blocks away. I remember lying in my bed, listening to them singing for hours outside the Dakota: 'All we are saying is give peace a chance.'

"Three months after Lennon's death I walked into an ice cream store on Columbus Avenue, where everybody was listening to a radio above the counter. Somebody with an ice cream cone said, 'Did you hear what happened? President Reagan's been shot!'

"I went home and turned on my TV. I saw the footage of the smiling Reagan leaving the Washington Hilton, where he'd just spoken to the same construction union that Gerald Ford had addressed on the day that Squeaky Fromme had pulled her gun. I heard reporters outside calling, 'Mr. President, Mr. President!' I saw Reagan waving his arm above his head, walking toward his Lincoln. Beside Reagan was agent Tim McCarthy, a buddy of mine since we'd both worked in the Illinois field offices. Suddenly, there were two quick gun shots."

Marty saw the six-foot-two McCarthy react to them by splaying his arms and legs, making himself a bigger target. Then Marty saw a Devastator bullet rip into McCarthy's chest—boring twelve inches into his lung, diaphragm and liver—spinning McCarthy to the right and collapsing him onto the pavement. Marty saw his old White House boss, Jerry Parr, push Reagan's head down. Then he saw Reagan flinch, as another bullet nestled one inch from Reagan's heart.

Parr shoved Reagan into the limo, threw himself on top of him and yelled to the driver, "Take off! Just take off!" Other agents and cops jumped on the gunman, handcuffed him, threw a jacket over his head. Marty saw the sidewalk strewn with two other casualties: White House Press Secretary James Brady and D.C. policeman Thomas Delahanty.

"They kept repeating the video over and over and over," Marty remembers. "I sat on my bed, rocking back and forth, shaking."

Right after the shooting, House Speaker Tip O'Neill charged that Reagan's Secret Service detail had been "incredibly lax." Representative Edward R. Roybal, who headed one of the three Congressional committees that probed the attack, said, "There is no question there was a breakdown in security." Roybal said he intended to look into questions of low morale among the agents. Critics asked why Reagan's limo had been parked fifteen feet from VIP exit, and why Reagan hadn't used the Hilton's underground exit. How had twenty-five-year-old John Warnock Hinckley Jr. managed to slip in with the press? How could Hinckley have stayed for several nights just before at the Park Central Hotel (where Marty had lived during his training) while the hotel was packed with Secret Service agents?

Yet in the end, Hinckley's attack earned the Service more cheers than jeers. That Hinckley stayed at the agency's preferred hotel was not a mistake, only an irony. Since the sidewalk outside the Hilton wasn't a restricted press area, no one could be faulted for not checking press credentials. It would have been better if the roped-off area *had* been restricted, if the limo *had* been parked right in front of the door—or better yet, at the underground exit. But Carter had always used the VIP exit without a hitch. A 101-page Treasury Department report found that the Service had "performed well" during the attack. Once Hinckley opened fire, the agents needed only thirteen seconds to whisk Reagan away. Timothy McCarthy had given future agents a textbook picture of how to react. The single most encouraging finding may have been Hinckley's confession that on October 2, 1980, he'd stalked Carter in Akron, Ohio, but wilted when some agents looked him in the eye. The admission that came from the former American Nazi Party member who'd watched *Taxi Driver* countless times—and who'd read up on Oswald, Sirhan, Bremer, and Lennon's killer, Mark Chapman—this admission reminded the agents of how many uncelebrated victories they may have won over the years in other crowds.

All this was consoling. But Hinckley's attack also reminded everyone, especially Marty, how easy it was to kill a President. Critics could ask why Hinckley wasn't put on the Service's watch list after he'd been nabbed in Nashville for carrying three handguns onto an airplane on the same day that Carter was in town campaigning. But airport handgun arrests happened all the time, and without any reason to link Hinckley to Carter, the FBI had no cause to alert the Secret Service. Even if Hinckley had been on the Service's watch list, chances were slim that the Service would have known that he was in Washington, since he told his parents he was bound for California.

Once again, the nation saw that to shoot the President you didn't have to be some *Day of the Jackal*-style professional hit man, just a screwball horny for an actress like Jodie Foster. People like Hinckley didn't care if Congress passed stiffer sentences for attacking the President; Hinckley said he'd been ready to die for Jodie. Legislators could go through the motions of proposing stricter gun-control laws; but the lobbyists would disarm those bills in no time. The Secret Service could try harder to keep the President out of the open air; but the old man and his politics would insist that in a free society the voters were entitled to see their leader.

Reagan had been in office only three months. Yet when he was shot, everybody noticed that people weren't as astonished as they'd been when they'd heard the news from Dallas. Was it any wonder that citizens were deadened to the horror? Since 1963 guns had killed some 400,000 Americans, more countrymen than had died in all of World War II. In the first 174 years since the founding of America, there'd been six attacks on the country's Presidents and Presidential candidates. Starting in 1963, however, assailants had needed just eighteen years to equal that number. Famished for fame, the assailants carried out their work even while mourning the victims of past assassins. Chapman told a doorman at the Dakota how much he idolized JFK, whose portrait had hung on Chapman's television set. Hinckley, who traveled with a guitar, said he'd shot Reagan partly because he was blue over the murder of Lennon.

"I started to wonder what planet we were living on," recalls Marty. "The war we were fighting with these nuts started to seem unwinnable. Like Vietnam. JFK said it himself—there is no stopping someone willing to exchange his life for the President's. I mean, I still believed the President needed protecting. More than ever, *somebody* had to protect him. I just didn't know if it was me. By this time I'd gotten so jaded that the two shootings, back to back, just finished off my last bit of optimism. Lennon's death, especially. I'd been right across the street. Maybe I could've stopped it if I'd been on the other side. I figured I knew as much as anybody about keeping a person alive. But what use had I been? Lennon meant more to me than any politician I'd ever guarded. He was the one who gave the Beatles their edge, their bite. I'd *been* John Lennon in my high school talent show.

"So now one of his fans had killed him. How much more proof did anybody need that the sixties were dead? Nothing was what it once seemed. Even the Kennedys, Jack and Bobby. By now everybody knew about their plots to kill Castro . . . Bobby's wiretapping . . . Jack's sharing a mistress with Sam Giancana . . . all their ruthlessness. That's not to say they were total frauds. They inspired us—me—longer than most politicians. But now my eyes were wide open.

"The point is, my heart wasn't in the job like it used to be. I didn't mention what I'd seen outside the Dakota to anybody at work. Or to anybody that night—I guess I thought even talking about Lennon would've revealed too much about me. So I just kept my mouth shut. I just tried to treat these shootings as news events that didn't involve me. At the same time, I could feel the pressure building. I'd be skating down the streets in the middle of the night and asking myself, Marty, what is going *on* in your life? But I just kept moving. That was my philosophy—keep right on moving. Keep dancing. Forget about it."

His mission became clear: at night he had to blot out his job with louder music, raunchier clothes, kinkier scenes. Every other night was Halloween. When he rolled into work on those glaring-bright mornings, sunglasses became even more essential to his Secret Service uniform. His apartment's wardrobe closet now had two plainly defined sections. On one side, his suits, shirts, ties, oxfords; on the other, his various evening costumes, his unmentionables.

"In the day, I'd wear the most conservative suits I could find. Never any tapered European-cut stuff. Always a white shirt and a dull tie. It made me wonder about other guys I'd see on the street in super-straight nerd suits. What were *they* hiding? I was still getting off on the ruse. I laughed to myself. I almost wanted to get caught. The people on either side of my life wouldn't believe the story.

"I went home to St. Louis for a visit. I looked up my old high school pal, John Glover, who by now had left his job as a city cop to become a prosperous wholesaler of golf equipment and country club toggery."

"Marty came back wearing a leather jacket, leather pants, studded leather wrist things," Glover remembers. "He looked like Billy

Idol—and most of the people I know don't even know who Billy Idol is. *I* would never give Marty the satisfaction of any comment on his appearance. But I'd have him over to our house and invite over our old buddies who Marty used to play ball with. They'd bring over their wives. You could just see them all absolutely freak out. Nobody would say anything until Marty would get up and go to the john, and then they'd start buzzing.

"I think Marty is a split personality. It wasn't apparent so much when he was younger. My wife and I identified it after he became a Secret Service agent. When he had his suit on, he could remember everything. But when he put on his leather jacket and leather slacks, he couldn't remember people we went to high school with."

"Unless I thought they were worth remembering," Marty adds. "I gave a call to Barbara Bowers, my college girlfriend who I'd hoped to impress by joining the Secret Service. As it happened, she'd just broken up with the man whom she started seeing after we'd split up."

"I bet it was ten years to the day from when Marty and I had broken up that he called me," Barbara recalls. "I hadn't heard from him in ten years. We got together. He told me he'd taken Rosalynn Carter to the Pope's funeral. He told me how, at the time, he thought he could die because he'd seen everything he wanted to see in the world. But then two weeks later, the new Pope died, and Marty went through it all again. The most outstanding thing he'd ever seen had just repeated itself. It seemed so typical of Marty. He wanted to try every experience. But then when he thought he'd discovered the ultimate, it turned out to be just another thing.

"He told me he wasn't real happy in the Secret Service. We roller-skated in Forest Park. He was so flashy he stopped cars just with the way he looked on roller skates. It surprised me that he had stayed with the Secret Service all those years—that he'd put aside those moments when he'd want to go crazy. The way he used to pull on his hair over some song—he really was an early punker. What did he do with that personality when he was in the Secret Service? The truth is, it still must have been there."

The ultimate expression of Marty's two natures came when, after he'd been away from the Nixon townhouse for a while, he reported to work wearing that great oxymoron, a conservative wig.

"I was doing odd things to my hair. My own hair was cut real short in places, with a long tail in the back. I remembered the wig idea from my Army Reserve days. Guys who wanted to keep their hair long wore them so they could pass the weekend inspections. I wasn't ready to show up at Nixon's with punked-out hair. It would've opened a whole can of worms. But I still wanted to see how outrageous I could be. I wanted to test the limits. I'd always had this fascination with dual personalities. Ever since I wore my Superman costume as a kid. I liked having two residences. One life wasn't enough for me."

Looking back, it was almost like his undercover surveillance work—when he'd pretended he was a demonstrator. That had been a sort of inverted dress rehearsal for his current masquerade, his pretending he was a straight-arrow. Perhaps the culture of the Service subliminally encouraged the masquerade. Secrets were the bedrock of the Service. Back in 1865, when it was founded to plug the gush of phony money, the Service quietly hired the best experts it could find on the subject: former crooks and counterfeiters. Stealth was the wisdom they brought to the agency, and the legacy they left with it. Before there was an FBI, before there was a CIA, the government gave the Secret Service all its covert investigations: the Teapot Dome scandal, the Ku Klux Klan, Coxey's Army, land frauds and spy rings operating during the Spanish-American War and World War I.

After 1901, when the Service took on the job of protecting the President, its vital tool still was stealth. Its brainy Technical Security branch and its squirrely Intelligence section (the Fantasy Factory) dealt in secret weapons, secret code names, secret passageways and a secret Oval Office taping system. The smallest fact that might help as assassin qualified as a secret. When in doubt, the Public Affairs officers always knew the correct answer for reporters: "No comment."

On the street, besieged by rabid demonstrators, and in the office, encircled by cocky competitors, any agent who might feel a moment of doubt about his ability, about his courage under fire, kept it secret. George Orwell once described his feelings as a policeman serving in British colonial India. Any law enforcer who in his heart questions his own authority over the citizenry, Orwell wrote, "wears a mask, and his face grows to fit it."

Marty tried to keep the Secret Service mask from completely recasting his face. But in the process he ended up donning an even more elaborate disguise. His nighttime mask, his after-dark uniform, may have been of his own choosing, but, it became exhausting. There were so many secrets to keep.

"I started to feel like I was being watched by them. I guess I was hoping to get found out.

"It was getting so I didn't recognize myself. One night I was riding the subway to my shift at Nixon's. It was about eleven-thirty and the only other person on the subway car was this kid who was wearing sunglasses and a really weird smile. He was sitting opposite me, grinning and bouncing his knees up and down really fast. After another minute, he slowly took this long knife out of his pocket. He kept grinning at me. Maybe he just wanted to scare this guy in a suit he thought was a Wall Street yuppie.

"But I didn't feel like playing games that night. So just as slowly, I reached into my suit and pulled out the .357 Magnum. Right away, he lost his smile. Neither one of us said a word, and I put the gun back in my jacket. When I didn't say I was cop or something, he must have thought I was some vigilante. He got off at the next stop.

"That might be the way a lot of New Yorkers' dream of *High Noon,* but I wasn't particularly proud of what I'd done. I never liked guns.

"On the subway or in an airplane, travel failed to transport me as it used to. Even when we'd land in some city I hadn't been to before, I had no interest. The guy from the embassy would be rattling off the sights as we drove in from the airport.

"He'd say, 'Anybody have any questions?'

"I'd say, 'Yeah. How many minutes till the hotel?' I didn't want to see any roadside attractions. It gave me a headache looking through the thick bullet-proof glass—those limos were like fishbowls. The plane could've turned around and come back to the same city every day and it wouldn't have mattered to me. I always kept the blinds drawn in the hotel room. I was like a walking zombie. My behavior was getting pretty erratic. I'd go for months without putting in my travel expense reports. They'd owe me thousands of dollars, but I just couldn't be bothered to fill out the paperwork.

"Most of my years on the job, I felt like an invincible teenager. I couldn't die. An assassination attempt on video could scare me. But on the job, it didn't seem real. You were always wrapped up in the moment at hand. But as the years went on, you started to feel like a pilot who's scared of flying at first, and who then gets blase about it, and then, right before he retires, gets very conscious of each flight.

"Around this time, especially after the Lennon and Reagan shootings, I started to have nightmares. They were always the same. Someone was pointing a gun at me. I'd pull my gun out—in plenty of time—but I couldn't pull the trigger back. It wouldn't fire. Then the other guy would shoot me in the chest. I'd pull open my shirt and look at the hole in my chest. I'd be sort of laughing: 'Look at this. Isn't it wild?'

"At the same time I was also getting sick a lot—bad colds, throat infections. It turned out I had to have my tonsils out. At age thirty-four. The operation becomes dangerous when you're older, but I had them out. I had to take off work. I pretty much lost my sense of taste for over six months."

His tongue had become a spokesman for his body and brain. All over, Marty felt numb to sensation—no matter how much stimulus he provided. Something kept working away at Marty, working the man.

Dr. Bertram J. Newman, the Manhattan internist who recommended that Marty have his tonsils out, had first patched him up after the limo in the Pakistani motorcade ran over his foot. Over the course of five years, Newman had treated Marty for various ailments and learned about the rigors of the Secret Service. By the time he shined a light on Marty's tonsils, he could see that the agent, who used to show up for appointments in a suit, might have problems that went deeper than his throat.

"There was one day when he came into my office on roller skates dressed in a T-shirt and short-shorts, rolling down the hall," Dr. Newman recalls. "You might call that an abnormal coping response—that's a nice way of saying he needed psychiatric help, that he was pushed too far by his responsibilities. Marty and I started to talk about psychopharmacological agents, but he felt he couldn't afford to use them because his reactions would be slower."

Hearing of Marty's recurring nightmare years later, Newman made a classic Freudian interpretation. In one word: impotence. "When you pull your gun—the tool of your trade—and it won't fire, you feel impotent."

How could that be? In New York he certainly was making up for those lonely nights on the road. And the trim, hard-muscled agent never heard any complaints. But that sort of prowess only made Newman sure of his arm-chair analysis: "The reaction to impotence is to prove you're not impotent—put notches on your gun." Marty didn't buy it.

"The dream was a reflection of reality," says Marty. "Taking another person's life is really serious. You have to feel totally justified. Subconsciously, I doubted if I had the will to kill someone. I always wondered if I'd let them kill me first."

Maybe he and Dr. Newman were talking about the same thing. In any case, Marty didn't tell Newman about his dream at the time. Why should he? He knew of another agent who'd had a dream.

"The guy had been seeing a psychiatrist and telling him about nightmares where he'd see himself confronted by a faceless assassin. Apparently he kept having these nightmares, and after a while the shrink called the Secret Service and gave them his diagnosis—that he thought the 'faceless assassin' was the agent himself. Next thing, I saw a memo at the White House with the agent's name and the instruction: 'Do Not Admit.' That told me how sacred the patient-doctor confidence was.

"If other agents shared any of my emotions, I had no way of knowing it. Gallows humor was still as close as we came to talking about our anxiety. There'd be brief flashes of black humor, like when we were driving through Rome for Pope John Paul I's funeral. The streets were lined with people and one of the supervisors turned around from the front seat and said in a real dead-pan voice, 'Marty, at the next intersection I want you to take your machine gun and fire into the crowd indiscriminately.' He had a real dry sense of humor and he knew the pressure that built up while you were waiting for something to happen. But years together hadn't brought many agents close enough to divulge any weakness. Spilling your guts didn't win you any promotions. I wish that just one night we would have sat around and acknowledged that, sometimes, we had the shit scared out of us."

But Marty wasn't much different. He didn't even like it when his boss stopped by his hospital room after Marty had had his tonsils out.

"I didn't want anyone to see me in that condition. I couldn't talk. I had tubes coming out of me. The only person who came to see me was Mike Endicott. Against my wishes."

Marty had so disguised his true nature to Endicott that his former boss would later say, "In my mind there was no question that Marty was conservative in his political views. He was pro-Nixon, pro-Reagan. He was pro-law enforcement." Gradually Endicott had begun to glimpse how internal stress might be arising out of a conflict between, as he saw it, Marty's liberal lifestyle and his other beliefs. In the final weeks of the 1980 campaign, he'd told Marty that the Service needed some extra men on the road.

"We were on an airplane with Nixon. We'd just come back from one trip and they were asking me to go on another. I told Mike, 'I can't do it.'

"He said, 'You've *got* to do it.' He brought it up again when we were in a Greek coffee shop, the American Restaurant, at Sixty-ninth and Broadway, eating with another agent.

"Mike said, 'Do you have other plans?'

"I said, 'No, I just can't do it.' Suddenly I got really emotional. I wasn't expecting to, but my voice started cracking and I kept saying, 'I can't do it. I don't know how much more I can take of this.'

"Mike gave me some days off and I asked him and the other agent if they could keep what happened that night to themselves. They assured me they would. They said it happened to everybody once in a while. My main concern was that it didn't get back to the Director."

Back to the Director? What sort of a maverick was this, who still worried about what the Director thought? It just went to show:— "outrageous" as Marty was at night, he still couldn't carry out the most simply radical act of his life: quitting the Secret Service.

His old girlfriend Debby remembers, "When he moved back to New York we started looking for a condominium. I wanted to get married. And then all of a sudden he decided he could not take the pressure of the relationship. So we saw each other a few times after that, but eventually I said, 'I can't handle this. Let's cool it.' We still talked. He was depressed most of the time. Finally I said, 'Look, this is what you wanted. Why don't you call me when you have something good to say? I'm sick of this depression thing. I'm trying to get over mine. I think you should too.' He always talked about music. He was convinced that his voice was shot. I thought it sounded sort of like Rod Stewart's. He talked about quitting the Service. I kept teasing him that he never would—because at his age, where else could he go and make the same kind of money? I told him he'd never do it."

This ate at him. Down deep he felt the shame of being a part-time punk. A half-assed half-breed. He'd seen too many true protesters willing to risk a beating for him not to pick out a hesitant dissenter in the mirror. The wig he wore to work—was it daring, or just the opposite? How outspoken was the former free-speech activist if his current boss had no doubt that Marty was very conservative. Marty had done well in the Secret Service; he may have saved more lives than he knew about; surely, he'd stored up enough rare moments for a second lifetime. But now that he was tired of the role, why was he leaving it up to the Secret Service to "catch" him?

"I knew that most of the stress I was feeling was self-inflicted," admits Marty. "I was still reconciling the different directions my mind was going in. I wasn't afraid of dying really. I was afraid of the future."

"In August of 1981, ten years after I started my training as a special agent, I set out on my last detail with the Secret Service. A year and a half had passed since Richard Nixon had moved to New York. His 'come-back' was coming along nicely. And now he was taking a two-week vacation in Europe. He started out in Paris, where, in the month that marked the seventh anniversary of his resignation as President, Nixon shook hands with French throngs who seemed to revere him even more than Jerry Lewis. After a few days, he pushed on to Medoc, to see his friend, Baron Phillipe de Rothschild. I strolled with Nixon through the baron's chateau and inspected the Rothschilds' private wine cellar. Nixon and some of his agents then boarded a train to Lausanne, Switzerland. I and my shift headed there by car—tearing across the countryside in rented Puegots and arriving ahead of Nixon at Lausanne's grand hotel, Le Beau Rivage.

"I'd been there before with Nixon. It was one of the places he'd always return to. All the wandering monarchs-in-exile stayed there. It was like their mausoleum, but they must have been summering somewhere else that week. Every morning, right on cue, these waiters—there must have been twenty of them in their starched white jackets—would lay out the linen table cloth and about six pieces of silverwear. They'd set up this tremendous buffet of lobster and seafood and every kind of fruit. They'd drape their napkins over their arms. They'd stand at attention. And then nobody would come into the dining room. Oh, maybe a half dozen people passed through. But they'd order from the menu. Most of the day, in this huge dining room filled with ghosts. At the end of the day, the waiters would throw the buffet in the garbage.

"Nobody swam in the pool. The only time that water ever rippled was when they'd raise the wall between the indoor pool and the outdoor pool. Or when I'd dive in. But there was this one woman who'd always join me at the pool. We'd met when I'd stayed there before. She was absolutely beautiful. Fluent in four languages. She said she was a music student and that her father was a concert violinist. She was very worldly, but she had a sense of humor. We used to laugh every time we saw those waiters setting up that buffet again.

"She and I would lounge around the pool and talk and gradually we started opening up to each other. Well, she told me that she actually was a call girl who slept with the aristocrats and politicians who stayed at the hotel. I told her I was living something of a double life myself. Later on, she invited me to her apartment and we talked some more. We both felt out of place in this rich world—you know, looking down our noses at it, but not leaving it either. There was nothing sexual between us at all. I figured if there was anybody tired of screwing it was her. So the next day, we were down at the pool again and I told her I had to get ready to leave. She said goodbye, and I went into the pool locker room where the other agents were blow-drying their hair.

"I stepped into the shower, and—surprise—she was waiting for me, naked. We started making out, and she pulled back the shower curtain and started waving the other guys in. Their mouths were hanging open, but I didn't even care. We didn't stop. I think the guys got a vicarious thrill out of watching their shift leader burn out."

Maybe it was fitting that the final day of Marty's masquerade should find him buck naked before his men. Maybe it also made sense that, after spending several years switching back and forth from gray flannel to black leather, Marty should have a final argument with his boss over the proper attire of his shift.

"The other agents were sitting in a car in the driveway of the hotel when my friend came out with a towel wrapped around her. She stuck her head in the window and kissed me. Nobody said a word to me about what'd happened. I think they were in shock. I was the one who never left the hotel.

"We headed for the airport. Nixon had taken the train to Vienna, where we were supposed to relieve the earlier shift at four P.M. We should've had plenty of time to make it, but we ran into some bad plane connections, so we didn't get to the hotel in Vienna till almost nine. When the shift finally showed up, Mike Endicott was mad. My men were still in their casual clothes."

"I took a pretty good piece out of him," Endicott recalls. "We had people who had been on for quite awhile. Not that they were complaining. But I was Marty's boss and I told him he had a responsibility to make the relief as expeditiously as possible, and that he didn't have anything to do but travel that day. He didn't care for the criticism. A few words were exchanged."

I said to him, "What are you flipping out about? It'll take us two minutes to change into our suits."

"My shift changed into their suits and we walked Nixon to dinner. I took him into this banquet hall that was about seventy feet long. Nixon was eating by himself at a table. I was about thirty feet away, sitting in a chair. I'd been hyped up all day. And then suddenly I was alone with *him* again. As he ate, we just kept staring at each other. That's when things started spinning. I could hear Nixon's knife and fork *screeching* against his plate. It got to be deafening. Nixon cutting his meat in this depressing city with its overtones of the centuries—dead kings, ostentatious waste. It was like *2001*—that scene where the old man eats the meal.

"I suddenly felt that if I didn't get up from that chair, I never would. I heard a referee counting: 'Seven . . . eight . . . nine.' So I got out a piece of paper and I wrote to Mike asking if I could talk with him when the shift was over. I passed it to an agent in the hall. The agent came back and told me that Mike said if I wanted to talk to him, I should talk to him right now. Somebody filled in for me and I went outside in the hall and told Mike, 'I can't stand one more minute of this. I've got to quit. I'll try to finish my shift, but if you can find anybody to fill in for me, it'd be a big help.' He started getting into the argument about the clothes again.

"He was wrong in what he did," says Endicott, "it wasn't me he offended or hurt. He hurt the other guys . . . That wasn't very considerate."

Marty: "I told him, 'It doesn't have anything to do with the argument we had. I just can't take it anymore.' Mike said that if that's the way I felt, he thought I should leave right away. He started talking again about who was right and wrong about the suits and I said, 'I don't think you understand. As of this moment I don't work for you anymore.' I was trying not to get any more emotional than I already was, but he didn't seem to understand me. So I said something like, 'You can't tell me shit! It's over!' That's when he told me he would contact the U.S. Embassy, that there'd be a ticket waiting for me there."

"I suggested that he should return to the United States. I was taking him off the trip," Endicott remembers, ". . . he said he was going to quit and I said, 'Fine.'"

*   *   *

Marty: "I went to use the free phones in the command post and everybody was real silent because they knew what was happening. I called my mother in St. Louis."

"He wasn't asking for my approval," recalls Viola, "he was just telling me he was going to do it. It sounded to me as if he was getting unhappy. I told him, 'The only thing that ever really shocked me in your life was when you joined the Secret Service. I always thought you were going to go into the arts of some sort.' "

Marty called his new friend Rose, who'd first seen him on a dance floor with a mask on and his shirt off. She still had no idea that he worked for the Secret Service.

Rose remembers that call. "He told me he'd made a real important decision, something that would affect the rest of his life. He told me he was in Vienna and that he was taking the next plane home. He said he couldn't talk to me over the phone. It was very brief. When I hung up the phone, I had a big smile on my face. Because I hadn't expected him to come back for another three weeks."

Marty explains what followed. "After I had gone down to my hotel room to pack, Gary Yauger knocked on my door. Yauger was one of the agents who'd interviewed Sara Jane Moore and who'd decided she didn't pose a serious threat. He and I had met nine years before on the McGovern campaign. He sat down on the bed and told me that I was doing the right thing and not to worry about any criticism that might come down on me. He said he'd come under fire after Sara Jane Moore shot at Ford. He said he'd survived that and that I could survive this. He helped calm me down a little bit. A little later, Mike Endicott came down. He was understanding. I said to him, 'Mike, you knew it was just a matter of time before I showed up to work nude.' "

"I'd seen how Marty had changed," says Endicott, ". . . I told him, 'I think you're absolutely right. I think you should quit.' I had been through some other situations with him where he wanted to quit and at that time I didn't think it was a good idea. I'd discouraged him from quitting. But I now felt it was in his interests, that he was just going to deteriorate in his performance and leave with a black name."

"When I was heading for the airport, everybody was in a state of shock," Marty recalls. "I'd said to the agents who'd worked for me five minutes before that, 'Hey, it was good, guys. Ten years, but . . .' I went to the embassy. They had my ticket all ready. I don't remember if I took a cab to the airport or if somebody drove me. I just remember this unbelievable feeling of relief when I was on the airplane and I felt the wheels lifting off the runway. I felt like a 100,000-pound weight had dropped off my shoulders. I didn't want to get out of the Service the way I had. The moment just overtook me. I looked down and saw Vienna getting smaller, and I started to cry."

# CHAPTER FOURTEEN
## *Skating Backwards*

"IT was more than a month after Vienna that I stopped by the World Trade Center to formally resign. I'd left my gun in Vienna, but I dropped off a cardboard box with my commission book, my handcuffs, my lapel pin, my bullet-proof vest, some other stuff. They asked me to sign some papers. I didn't even read them. I was in such a fog. I was just trying to smile my way through it. I wasn't embarrassed really. But everybody there seemed embarrassed. They barely said a word to me. There was one secretary who I'd gotten to know pretty well over the years. She was so nervous she wouldn't look at me. She kept concentrating on her typing. I made a joke: 'It's all right. I'm not an enemy of the state.' She didn't laugh. She just kept dabbing on her White-Out."

Word had traveled ahead. People in the Secret Service knew Marty was . . . Marty—but agents didn't just quit in the middle of a trip, in the middle of their shift. He must've been pretty wigged out. What was it that happened over there?

"I would hear a few rumors," remembers Chuck Rochner. "Reputations aren't always fair in the Secret Service. Sometimes reputa-

222

tions develop to destroy. I didn't hear a lot. Just the roller skates, his departure and some altercations he had with Endicott. It wasn't something that was overblown. The Secret Service is rampant with rumors that aren't always true. I certainly wouldn't judge. I'd just smile and say, 'Gosh, that's Marty.' "

Steve Garmon, Marty's White House buddy, now assistant director was taken aback. "I heard that he had rather summarily decided to chuck it even before he returned to the States. It surprised me. But it didn't. Marty was given to being whimsical and impulsive as far as what I had seen of him. But that was bizarre even for someone of that nature. He had had a lot of time on the job . . . It's not uncommon for there to be more mystery to any man than meets the eye. I never would have perceived that Marty was that troubled inside. I'd like to think that the ratio of those who survive intact their whole career is commensurate with other professions . . . But there's a stress that is fairly significant. Traveling. Shiftwork is constantly changing. Being away from your family. Everyone reacts to different circumstances in his own way. There are those who find it stressful *not* to travel, just to be with their wife and kids. One man's pleasure is another man's pain.

"Marty probably viewed his role as more demanding than it absolutely had to be. He took the job seriously—oh, yes. He was not hysterical ever. But occasionally it struck me that he needed to float back down to earth. Relax a little more. There are those among us who probably make more of it than it deserves. It is very stressful and demanding. But . . . there are those among us who are a little more fragile than others . . . I don't think that most people in the organization would be so harsh that they would see Marty's leaving as weakness. I'm sure they'd try to be supportive if they had the opportunity. There might be a few who would see it as weakness. But if Marty slipped a little bit, we're sympathetic."

*     *     *

Jerry Parr agrees that "Marty was a very sensitive guy. He did his duty, but I think his focus was elsewhere. It was my sense that he really wasn't a law enforcement type. Some that aren't can keep it up and end up retiring and do quite well. Others don't do as well."

"There are burn-out cases and they're caused by many different things," explains Chuck Rochner. "You can be on the front line too much. You can take your job seriously, do it day after day, year after year. When I left the White House, the last thing I wanted to do was take a foreign trip. It was really tough on me to take that last foreign trip. It was too much. There is a percentage of us for whom enough's enough."

The Secret Service reports that less than three percent of those who become agents leave before retirement; and most of those people drop out within the first year or two. Agents can retire after twenty years if they are at least fifty years old. The average agent leaves at the mandatory retirement age, fifty-five. Many of the top agents start a second career as a security chief for a corporation, where they usually make more than they did in the government. Chuck Rochner started his own security consulting firm after he retired. But Rochner admitted, "I didn't go out under the best of circumstances. And I've kind of resolved it in my mind. It's a very competitive outfit with a lot of hard-charging guys who for some reason really claw to the top."

Rochner said he'd been right in middle of a power struggle between Secret Service director H. Stuart Knight and Robert Powis, the assistant director who'd been guarding Ronald Reagan since the 1976 campaign. Knight tried to demote Powis in 1980 after the Treasury reprimanded Powis for mishandling funds. But Powis cleared his name in court and, backed by Presidential aide Edwin Meese, was named deputy Assistant Secretary of the Treasury. Shortly after Powis became Knight's boss, Knight quit as Director of the Secret Service.

* * *

"There's a lot wrong with the Secret Service," Rochner admits. "Many who stayed on after Marty found that there was only a certain number of leadership positions and most of the agents were over-qualified. Probably the majority of the agents go out bitter in one way or another. It seems as if none of them ever meet their expectations. It's a special group of men, extremely competitive. And I'm no exception; I should have been Director. Most guys felt that way. They really worked hard for that position. Many, many retired with disappointment."

"The Secret Service is a very close family," says Endicott. "I'm sure if there were incidents of nervous breakdowns, they certainly wouldn't publicize them to everybody."

"I knew others beside the agent who dreamt of the 'faceless assassin,'" Marty admits. "There was a period when I was in the New York field office when we heard about a couple of agents flipping out. One guy was found stalking through a forest in New Jersey. He had a gun and he was wearing next to nothing but combat boots. The police found him. Another agent got 'lost in the crowd'—that's what it's called. He just wandered away from the detail and kept going 'Gotta take a break.' The plane took off without him. A couple of these breakdowns happened, by coincidence, around the same time. Naturally our reaction was to laugh it off. Somebody came into the field office one day and made some wisecrack about 'What's happening to this place?' A bunch of us pulled out our pistols, held them up to our heads and screamed, 'Aaaaahhh!!!!' "

Of course there was Clint Hill, the greatest example of Secret Service bravery, and its burden. The day that shots rained down on John Kennedy's motorcade, Hill needed less than two seconds to dash from his follow-up car, to mount JFK's limo and to push the

First Lady into the backseat. There on the blood-soaked upholstery Hill held Jackie as she held her hemorrhaging husband. Even when they got to Parkland Hospital, Jackie continued to press Jack's bloody head against her pink suit. Understanding that she didn't want everyone to see the President's open skull, Hill coaxed her to give Jack up, and then covered the President's head with his own jacket. The thirty-one-year-old agent saw his jacket still shrouding Kennedy as the doctors wheeled away the gurney.

Other agents later tried to re-enact Hill's dash but no one could do it as fast. The Treasury awarded Hill a citation for exceptional bravery and the Service named him head of the White House detail. But Hill was never the same after Dallas. In 1975 he appeared on CBS' "60 Minutes." Even though he'd probably saved Jackie's life, Hill told Mike Wallace and the nation that he felt guilty for not reacting faster. During the interview, Hill broke down in tears again and again. Having reportedly received a medical discharge from the Service, he admitted that he suffered from a severe neurological problem and that he'd been told he needed psychiatric help.

Jerry Parr, who went from the Secret Service to work as a counselor to the dying and the homeless, said, "Clint Hill is probably a person who should have had an opportunity to talk about it more, to ventilate. The organization didn't provide it. I'm not blaming the organization. Sometimes organizations have to grow, like people."

In 1973 agent Jim Connally, who'd had a drinking problem, took his own life. According to Chuck Rochner, another agent took his life "in the late sixties, in Washington, with his own weapon. There were signs that he was beginning to buckle."

Jerry Parr suggests, "The Service ought to talk about fear. I gave my people an opportunity to talk about it after the attempt on

Reagan. Sure there's fear. But a macho organization doesn't like to put it out that it's afraid."

The service has begun opening up. After he handed in his 1979 study on stress among agents, Dr. Frank Ochberg said the agency was doing "a mature job of self-scrutiny." The Service has since tried not to make agents share hotel rooms. It's cut down on the number of days agents can spend traveling during campaigns. There is no strict rule on how long an agent can spend on the White House detail; but most agents are limited to serving from three to five years. The Secret Service can now point an agent—and any member of the agent's immediate family—toward psychotherapists and experts in substance abuse, marital counseling and personal finance.

"As with many law enforcement agencies, I think we're just catching up . . .," says Rochner. "The last ten years, they got a handle on it, or were moving in the right direction. They were actively looking for people who showed stress."

"There were avenues for Marty once he came back from Vienna," says a senior agent. "When our outfit really comes forward is when a guy's having trouble or his family's having trouble . . . I happened to be at the hospital when they wheeled in the son of [former Nixon White House detail head] Bob Taylor. He had been killed in a car accident. The Secret Service staff gave the okay for Bob and his wife to go up to Camp David to recuperate . . . We don't just try to hire the agents—we hire the family. We're looking for a guy who can give 110 percent and still keep his family together. Of course there is an unwillingness on some people's part to come forward and say, 'I have a problem.' "

"Marty's quitting was a matter of stress," admits Mike Endicott, "but we weren't conscious of him having a nervous breakdown

. . . Certainly there was nothing abnormal in his behavior that would cause me to call the Director. If Marty had a breakdown, he certainly didn't convey it to me. There was nothing that led me to believe he was anything other than frustrated with the job and with his social life . . . Many agents like to leave their job at work. But with Marty, it became almost impossible for him to come back to work. It got to the point where he had to decide what he was going to do with the rest of his life . . . Marty was a hell of an agent and one heck of a dedicated employee, but it was probably in his best interests that he left . . . You could see that he was not necessarily comfortable with his colleagues anymore . . . It's just like a marriage that goes bad. Sometimes you just grow apart. Nobody's fault. You just change. Marty changed. . . ."

Many of the Service's family assistance programs didn't exist when Marty felt his nerves jangling. But those reforms were almost beside the point, since Marty wasn't in the least inclined to walk into any official confessional.

"The thought of getting 'counseled' never crossed my mind," says Marty. "I felt so different from the rest of them. I didn't have a wife. I didn't have an alcohol problem. What advice could they give me? I just didn't want to be a Secret Service agent anymore. So, . . . I had a nervous breakdown. I was okay for a couple of weeks after Vienna. I partied some. But all of a sudden, after all that running around, it was like I'd smashed into a brick wall. I couldn't get out of bed. After all those days when I didn't need any sleep, now I couldn't stay awake. When I opened my eyes, I'd just stare at the ceiling above my bed. I can't even remember what I thought about."

So here was the Secret Service's free spirit. Recruited by a Treasury agent who had killed himself, Marty now had the energy of a corpse. Like the quarterlies he'd once interrogated, he too was badgered by macabre dreams; he too had come to feel as if he was being watched; and now he too couldn't leave his cell.

"We come in contact with characters all the time whose behavior has slipped an inch to the right or left of normal," explains Steve Garman. "While we hope that it won't happen internally, we recognize that it *could* happen."

"Marty seemed all right when we first got together again, at a club," Rose remembers. "But we didn't have time to be alone and talk. So we made plans to go out a few days later. Then when I called him to get together, he said he couldn't go out. He said that every time I called. I decided to see what was happening with him. I went over to his building and pressed his buzzer downstairs for a few minutes and finally he buzzed me in. He opened the door of his apartment and he really looked neglected. He hadn't shaved. He hadn't bathed. He'd stumbled back to his bed and passed out. There were newspapers and Chinese take-out cartons all over the place. Garbage piled up. I'd sit there and read while he slept. He'd wake up and say a few words, 'Sorry I'm like this . . .' Then he'd pass out again. He'd told me he'd quit his job, but I just figured that meant he wasn't going to model anymore. I thought he was physically sick. I thought he might have hepatitis, like some of our friends. Every couple of days I'd come back with some groceries. And after about a month, he started staying awake long enough to shower. He'd get half-dressed. But most of the time we still didn't make it out."

"On one of my first ventures out among the living," Marty recalls, "I visited Dr. [Bertram] Newman. Newman diagnosed me as suffering from something akin to post-traumatic stress disorder." It was common among the veterans of the war Marty had managed to avoid.

\* \* \*

" 'Nervous breakdown' is such a generality," says Dr. Newman. "It means different things to different people. Marty was suffering from a severe depression as manifested by agoraphobia—not being able to appear in public and escaping into sleep rather than trying to be the airborne ranger he was trained to be. Basically, he lost the will to keep punching, keep slugging. Marty would only use me for crisis intervention, not for the management of the whole thing."

"Newman prescribed some anti-depressant pills," Marty recalls. "They only left me more depressed when they wore off. Newman recommended a psychiatrist, but I still remembered the shrinks I'd met on my quarterly interviews, and didn't go. I wish I had. It would've been much easier."

Marty's mom sent him an airplane ticket so he could come back to St. Louis for her birthday. After she saw her son, she said, "I think it was time for him to quit. He was nervous—well, not nervous exactly. He was changed. You can't read Marty very well. You don't really know what's going on inside. When he comes home here, no matter how bad he feels, he won't say it. But I got the feeling he had been unhappy and he didn't feel good."

John Glover saw him on that visit. "Marty had a crew cut and army fatigues. He was extremely thin, unshaven, not talkative at all. He didn't look like Billy Idol, he looked like a mental case from *One Flew Over the Cuckoo's Nest.* When he'd speak to me he was incoherent. I would try to make him laugh, remind him of the old days, but he was just very depressed. He was lost, completely lost. I think it was New York that did it to him. I told him he should try to get some kind of disability compensation from the Secret Service. But he never followed up on it."

\*   \*   \*

WNBC-TV anchorwoman, Sue Simmons, the only friend with whom Marty shared his eyewitness account of John Lennon's death remembers, "I'd seen Marty the night after Lennon was killed, and there'd been an urgency in his face and voice. We were all upset about the shooting to a degree—we'd all bought Beatles records. But it seemed to be a personal thing for Marty. He had to tell me from A to Z how it happened. It puzzled me. I'd sensed he was having some problems in the Secret Service when he told me about stressful situations. But it was tough to talk to him about it, because I felt he'd tell me when he wanted me to know. I must not have been aware of how disturbed he was because I remember being stunned when I heard he'd quit. After that I knew he was in a delicate state. I'd always thought of him as the stoic agent who was always calm and in control. Now he seemed to cry easily. We had a friend who was at his apartment one night when Marty got some kind of anxiety attack. This friend couldn't handle it, and she just jumped up and left."

"I was out of the Service, but I was still in some purgatory between the old me and the new me. I had mood swings. Once I got my energy back, it came back full force. I was all keyed up. My body wanted something to do. I felt most at home on the streets. All night long I'd roller-skate under the amber crime lights, jumping on and off curbs like they were limo running boards, watching the Manhattan sewer covers sail beneath my wheels. I'd have my headphones on, listening to music. Half the time I'd skate backward to see who was following me. I had this feeling that the Secret Service might be watching me . . . to see why I'd left so abruptly.

"I started hitting the nightclubs again with a vengeance. I danced past the hour when Nixon was heading out on his constitutional. I started looking up old friends. I went over to Jessica Savitch's apartment one night and Warren Beatty was there. I'd met him years before on the McGovern campaign, but he just thought I was some freak Jessica hung out with. That was fine with me. Jessica was going through some hard times of her own. Five months after her second marriage, her husband had hung himself in their Washington townhouse. Jessica would sit on my lap and flirt. But it seemed like she just wanted someone to hold onto her."

Savitch had recently attracted the attention of a Nebraska farmer-turned-taxi driver whom the Secret Service had arrested a few weeks after Hinckley shot Reagan. The farmer had written letters implying that he might kill the President to "win the love" of Jessica. In another two years, when she was thirty-five, the anchorwoman would die in a drowning accident. "Marty," she'd written inside the autobiography that she gave her old Secret Service source, "you can secure my anchor anytime."

"I was still searching for my own ballast. I set out to make up for lost time. No urge would be submerged. I was finally free of all responsibility. I was cramming in all the days and nights I'd missed. As money ran low, I made a 'career move' and got a job showing off my body—for a couple of months I worked as a stripper. All the roller skating had kept my body in shape, so I figured, why not get paid to dance? I really wasn't conscious of why I was doing it at the time, but I guess it was my reaction to the past disguises. I wanted to disrobe—shed secrets."

"The first time I knew Marty was my kind of guy," says Sue Simmons, "was when he got up to dance at a party and ended up in his underwear. Red briefs. That was his sense of humor and how he liked to relax. When Mary couldn't relax around a particular set of friends, they weren't his friends anymore. He has a very low threshold for hassle."

*     *     *

"Marty and I and some other people would go around trying to get banned from clubs," Rose recalls. "I remember one night we came to Magique, that glitzy disco on the Upper East Side. Marty was on his roller skates and he climbed on top of a bank of speakers. Then he started pulling down his lavender harem pants. For some reason the owners of these places never talked to him, they always singled *me* out. The manager brought me up to his office and told me, 'There are other places where you can go and do things like that.' He started listing all the raunchy clubs we normally went to."

"I enjoyed being a party terrorist," Marty admits. "I liked upsetting people's equilibrium. But after a while even the most bizarre spectacles became routine, and all the raunch left me feeling confused. It all became repetitive and depressive. I don't regret anything I did. But I realized that nudity can also be a disguise. I wasn't getting off on this stuff anymore. None of this behavior was answering the basic question of what I was going to do with my life."

# CHAPTER FIFTEEN

# *"Last Night a DJ Saved My Life"*

ONE smelling salt had been able to snap Marty out of his deep sleep.

Rose remembers that, "Playing records just started out as something we'd do when I'd come over to his apartment and he didn't feel well enough to go out. I'd bring over some things I thought he should hear. We didn't have the same taste back then. I was strictly into punk and new wave. Marty would listen to that, and he'd also play me some of the funk he grew up on."

"When I started going out again, I didn't just dance. I'd hang out around the DJ booths. I'd ask the names of records. I'd study how the DJ worked. I'd get a little bit from everyone. One guy's technical skill at meshing beats. Another guy's lyricism. I'd watch how over the course of a night somebody good could establish a certain mood and carry it through to its logical conclusion."

No doubt the college frat rat thinks back on a DJ as the dude at keg parties who in between swigs of brew slapped down a forty-five by the Beach Boys and then one by the Stones and then one by the Monkees—like a guy punching the buttons of his AM car radio on

234

a Saturday-night cruise down Main Street. There still are DJ's who play golden oldies in New York, at clubs favored mostly by white, cleancut, upwardly mobile professionals. But that wasn't the sort of DJ Marty had his eye on. No, the disc jockey who pulled Marty close to his booth, where the ex-agent could see his own reflection in the plexiglas—that DJ was a shrewd performer who didn't buy nostalgia and who liked the sound of the future and the sight of a motley crowd pushed out of control.

The New York nightclub DJ was almost twenty-five years old when Marty quit the Service. It was back in the fifties, filmmaker Roger Vadim claimed, that he'd bestowed the name *"discotheque"*— French for record library—on the small Parisian clubs where *disquaires* entertained. The Peppermint Lounge, which opened in 1957 on West Forty-seventh Street, was among the first Manhattan clubs to have hi-fi equipment. A DJ kept patrons like Jackie Kennedy and John Lennon twisting when acts like Chubby Checker and Joey Dee left the stage. Later, in the sixties, DJ's at clubs like the Dom and the Electric Circus kept the Warhol crowd tripping to Hendrix and the Doors.

Disco took its first baby steps as early as 1970, when Sanctuary opened in an abandoned church and DJ Francis Grasso began twirling his black vinyl hosts on what used to be the church's altar. A number of gay clubs—Le Jardin, Flamingo—refined disco's Mars violet decor at the same time that singers like Gwen McCrae and Betty Wright were burnishing the soulful moaning that would incite dry-humping in dancers of all persuasions. Disco climaxed when Studio 54 opened in 1977. Co-owner Steve Rubell paid DJ Richie Kaczor a nice round $54,000 a year and used Kaczor's booth as an exalted nursery for celebs like Truman Capote, Liza Minelli and Andy Warhol (who by then had recovered from a 1968 assassination attempt). Of course by 1980 the IRS had banished Rubell and his partner Ian Schrager to a country-club prison. After that, uptowners tried again to behave themselves in public. The gay clubs became the lone outposts where DJ's still decorated the room with lush "high energy" music. Disco, as people once knew it, was dead. Yet on the downtown punk scene, in shadowy rock quarries like the Mudd Club and Danceteria, the DJ's were working more bodies than ever.

In 1976, when the punks first started to snarl, you couldn't buy many punk records because hardly anybody would let the mangy buggers into a studio. But as punk combed its hair and grew into the sundry experimental forms generally known as new wave, more independent record companies in the U.S. and in Europe started pressing the music in small batches. Major record labels distributed some of the more accessible new wave bands. But few radio stations in America would play even those acts sanctioned by the majors. If you wanted to hear alternatives to the music sprayed out of the ceiling speakers at Burger King, you had to go to new-wave night-clubs. Since the DJ's at those clubs were the foremost living scholars of this avant garde movement, dancers relied on the DJ's to separate the Thrashing Doves from the Meat Puppets, to choose between the London version and the Munich version of a song's Extended Dub Re-mix.

By 1981 several of the New York clubs which showcased new bands had closed or were about to. Perhaps the newer new bands just weren't as riveting as the older new bands, or maybe there weren't enough club owners with the knowledge or courage to give any of the bands a shot. But one thing was sure—the attention span of the New Yorker wasn't getting any longer. Clubgoers would walk out in droves if they didn't instantly connect with this *particular* brand of sonic minimalism being jack-hammered into their ears.

So more and more, the DJ was replacing the band as the featured attraction of the nightclubs. To practical club owners, the advantages were clear. The DJ was usually, though not always, cheaper than a band. The DJ might at least listen if a club owner stormed up to the booth and shouted, "What is this shit you're playing?" With the DJ, the club owner didn't have the problems of getting half a dozen musicians to start on time.

If the DJ was good, if he or she had a musical sense that reassured the people with the familiar and challenged them with the new, then the night could become one uninterrupted trance of dance. That DJ could caress and knead and chop-chop that body of flesh like a fat lady's on a massage table. The power of the DJ derived partly from the way that making records had changed. Since the mid-seventies, many of the most popular new dance "bands" hadn't made for much of a show, because many of their "players" were machines. The real genius behind a hit was often a studio producer, and his work usually came across best in a club with a state-of-the-art sound system.

Just like a band, a DJ could develop an avid following. In his 1979 song "D.J." David Bowie recognized that the record spinner could develop a messianic complex as big as the recording star's. The fervor that downtown new wavers showed for their DJ's was anorectic, though, next to the devotion that black dancers slathered upon mix-masters *way* uptown. In the ghetto disco, the DJ's role of doling out achingly romantic and erotic music earned him a place in the songs themselves. "Last Night a DJ Saved My Life," by In Deep, had the record-spinner mending a woman's broken heart as the "handy man" of earlier rhythm and blues had once done. *"There's not a problem that I can't fix,"* the song's DJ assured, *"cause I can do it in the mix."*

Nobody took DJ-ing more seriously than the residents of the outer boroughs, especially the Bronx. Up there, on every playground, in every project, on every floor of every project, they had their own DJ. Somebody would have a block party and the DJ would come and plug his sound system into a street lamp. Maybe it was because they had to fight honking car horns that these street DJ's had no taste for the candied orchestrations of discotheque music. What they liked was the harder, grimier, nastier funk of Sly Stone, James Brown, Rufus Thomas, and George Clinton—people who made records that

flew at you like sewer covers. The part of these records that the street
DJ's liked best was the percussive break, the section where the
drummer or the conga player really hammered on the dancers' hips.
Certain DJ's pioneered a technique for stretching these breaks. Master blasters like Kool DJ Herc, Grandmaster Flash, and Afrika
Bambaataa would put two copies of the same record on two turntables and then race back and forth between them, cueing up the funky
break on one disc and then the other, so that the ecstatic pounding
just went on and on and on.

"Break beat" or "hip hop" music was what they called it, and DJ
Herc became one of the first people to "rap"—rhyme in time—over
it. Herc and some others also perfected the art of "scratching." By
rhythmically moving the turntable's tone-arm needle back and forth
in one record groove, the DJ created a coarse keening sound.
Scratching turned the turntable itself into a new kind of instrument:
a sort of cross between a violin and a drum.

When they were working the "wheels of steel," the ghetto DJ's
could move quicker than a knife-wielding Japanese chef. In the
course of two minutes, they might "cut up" a half dozen obscure
records, mixing in unlikely slices of heavy metal rock, the TV theme
from "The Flintstones," a speech by assassin's victim Malcolm X,
and several flavors of drumming. And as if there was any question
that all this was as much of a "live" show as any band, some DJ's
would do their scratching with their backs turned to the turntables,
or with their lips pressed to the vinyl. Dancers who witnessed a hip
hop DJ slapping together his aural collage could become so spell-
bound that they'd forget to dance.

A few downtown new wavers heard about the ghetto renaissance,
and they invited Bam and Flash to spin at the Mudd Club and other
clubs below Fourteenth Street. Other downtowners tasted one chunk
of the funk and that was it. Before long, SoHo galleries were showing
graffiti art. London fashion designer Vivienne Westwood was knocking off the baggy sheepskin fashion of black "homeboys." West-

wood's boyfriend Malcolm McLaren—the Paris riot vet who'd started the Sex Pistols—spotted hip hop as the natural heir to punk. McClaren raced up to the Bronx to recruit some talent for a record. He was followed by all sorts of recording stars. Even former folk rockers like Hall and Oates wanted a ghetto DJ to etch their record with scratch effects.

Something good came out of this. Gradually, the record industry's distinctions between a black record and a white record began to be overpowered by the simpler category of the *dance* record. One curvy dancer who hung out on the club scene persuaded a couple of DJ's— Mark Kamins and Jellybean Benitez—to take her to the studio and dress up her scrawny voice with the absolutely *defest* production. Then her DJ friends played her records at Danceteria and the Funhouse, where dancers, who couldn't quite place the race of her voice, kept asking, "Who's that girl?" Before long, guys who used to buy drinks for Madonna Ciccone saw her pouting on the cover of *Time* magazine.

So more record execs started making friends with DJ's, giving them test pressings of new songs and listening very carefully to what the DJ's thought of those songs. The number of people going out to clubs was rising. Steve Rubell estimated that around the time of his success at Studio 54, four thousand people a night went out clubbing; by 1987 he put the figure at more like forty thousand. And the uptown-downtown showdown to entertain those people was something sweaty. "So you wanna be a DJ?" rapped Malcolm McLaren's World Famous Supreme Team.

Marty Venker did.

"I wanted to pick up where I'd left off—go back to where I'd last felt creative. Play dance music. Back in St. Louis, when I used to watch Benny Sharp play, I saw everything I needed to know about exciting a crowd. At the same time, being a DJ was a whole new thing. It was a different technology, and it brought in all the other music I'd heard since St. Louis. By this time I'd danced in so many clubs I figured I knew the good DJ's from the bad ones.

"On the other hand, I said to myself, this is idiotic. You're almost *thirty-six* and you're going to start *this?* What makes you think you're any good? It doesn't even pay anything. You're gonna starve. But then I said, hey, nobody's *ever* too old for music. Every day for ten years I'd been facing the possibility of dying. And if it taught me anything, it was that you have to live for the moment.

"So one day I walked into an electronics store. I bought two professional-style, direct-drive Technics MK II turntables. A Numark mixer. And a headphone. I set it all up in my apartment, I put on two records and I started to mix. The turntables came with a thirty-six-hour guarantee. That's pretty much what I played for— thirty-six hours straight. I'm sure the neighbors were thrilled.

"I got busy, practicing sixteen hours a day. I taught myself all the possible ways to intercut two records: how to subtly dissolve one beat into another, how to dramatically wipe from percussion to horns, how to phase in snatches of a song's lyric—and how to firmly grip the turntable's platter and *sc-sc-sc-scratch.*"

"He started making me tapes," remembers Rose. "My friends heard them and said, 'This is really good.' Marty had a friend who was a DJ. They'd have a forty-eight-hour DJ blast-off. The other guy's girlfriend and I would listen to one of them for a while, then the other would take over. We'd time the beats-per-minute of songs with a stopwatch and we'd catalogue them. We'd make them coffee, keep them going. I remember Marty had these two records. He said he knew he could make them fit together. I don't know *why*—there were lots of other records. But he was determined to make them fit. I'd fall asleep and wake up and the two records would still be playing. I never, ever, want to hear those records again."

*   *   *

"I'd go all over looking for records," says Marty. "Manhattan had been picked pretty clean, so I went up to the Bronx, looking through basements. One time I was back in St. Louis and I asked this old guy at a record shop if he had any of those twelve-inch records they made just for disc jockeys. He said I could look downstairs. Man, there was a gold mine down there. The guy gave them to me for fifty cents apiece. But I'd pay anything if I felt I needed a record. Fifty dollars for an original pressing of 'Soul Makossa.' A hundred and fifty dollars for a copy of 'I Dig You' by Cult Hero. I'd go shopping for imports at the stores that catered to DJ's and drop five hundred dollars in an afternoon.

"I started making my nighttime rounds in the day, applying for work at the clubs. I knew the bigger clubs were out of the question, so I went around to the after-hours places. Even they told me every night was booked, but they asked me to leave a tape. I think they just liked to have tapes for their cars.

"The clubs had their inner circle. Every year, some new sucker came along with money to burn and the conviction that he knew what was wrong with the clubs in New York today. Usually what was wrong was that *he'd* gotten tired of shivering outside the velvet ropes of somebody else's club. So the money man, the backer, found the ruins of some club that time had forgotten and he hired some veterans of the nightscene to make his club different from anything the world had seen before. The backer usually got burnt and learned his lesson. But the coterie of people whom various backers hired to *conceptualize* the clubs, to create a fabulous VIP room, to decide who got in—these impresarios were relatively permanent.

"Though they migrated from club to club, they could be more clannish than the elders of a colonial New England village. These creatures who walked by night could meet you ten times and still never utter your name. And when they came to hiring a new club's DJ, well, of course they considered more than whether they liked the

records an applicant played. Was he attractive? Did he have good dish? Had he been *around?*

"I applied to *For the Record,* a 'pool' that, for a membership fee, passed along new record company releases to some of the city's top DJ's.

Judy Weinstein, head of *For the Record* remembers, "He gave me his background about the Secret Service and I didn't believe him. I thought he was crazy, a nut job. He didn't look like a DJ. Age-wise. But he was such an item, and as I got to talking with him, I knew he was telling the truth. He told me he didn't want anybody to know about the Secret Service. Of course that's what I was most interested in. I told him he had a lot of competition out there—a lot of guys who'd been doing what he was trying to do for a long time. The odds were against him. He hadn't been on the scene."

"I didn't have much money left. I used to make about $45,000 a year, and I'd made a decent profit selling my townhouse. But I'd blown most of what I'd saved. I spent a lot on records and partying and I gave a lot away to friends who needed money. By then I was sharing my one-bedroom apartment with six other people, including Rose and her two sons. I was trying to avoid going on welfare. I knew some people who were on it, and it looked to me like picking up those couple of coupons only made them feel worse about themselves.

"But I'll be honest. It got to the point where some of that food in garbage cans started looking pretty tempting. I had to ask my mother to send me some of my old Army Reserve fatigues. Believe me, this wasn't some fashion statement. I just didn't have any money to buy clothes. But Rose has this talent. She can make a dish rag look stylish. She sewed ornaments on the uniforms. She moved the epaulets around. She showed me how to make the best of what we had.

"I had a chance to make good money again. I got a call from an agent I'd known in the Secret Service. He said he and some other agents were starting their own private security firm. He asked if I wanted to come aboard. I said, 'Not interested.' He asked me what I was doing, and I said, 'Something with music.'

"He said, *'Music?'* Like we had a bad connection.

"I said, 'Thanks anyway. Good-bye.'

"By this time my brother Bud was part of the top management of the Worthington Corporation and would soon head the pump manufacturer's European operations. My brother Steve was a successful civil engineer. I sensed that people in my family were absolutely mortified by how I was living. I'd gone from owning a townhouse and a Corvette to *this!* They didn't say it. But I felt it."

"When I heard about his DJ ambition, I thought it was kind of a hairbrained idea," recalls Steve Venker. "Here's a guy who has a *master's* degree, and he wants to be a disc jockey? It seemed he was getting a little old for that. I think our mother was worried about him. She didn't know how he was going to make a living. My dad had pretty much the same reaction."

"Fortunately, about four months after I bought the turntables, I got my first job as a DJ. It was at a swingers club. I didn't care what kind of club it was. They paid me fifty dollars a night. I needed the experience of seeing how a live audience reacted to what I was playing. They were definitely a live audience. Some of them would dance in the nude. Most wore a towel or some leather get-up. Obviously, they didn't just dance. I used to get a kick out of changing a record to make them go faster. Sort of like saying *mush!* to a team of huskies.

"I'd been playing for the swingers for about six months when I started to get some breaks. I played a night at Danceteria. I also heard about a new club. Peter Gatien was this Canadian guy with an eye-patch who had a hot club in Atlanta called Limelight. He was going to open another Limelight in this huge old church. I showed up for my audition. There were a couple of girls who said they'd listened to about eighty DJ's before me and they told me to start spinning and that they'd stop me after about twenty minutes. So I hauled my records up four flights of stairs, up to the booth they'd built above where the altar used to be. I was almost at the ceiling of the church, with stained-glass windows all around me. I started spinning. After twenty minutes nobody came up, so I kept playing. Almost an hour went by and finally one of the girls came up and said, 'You got the job.' They had forgotten about me because they'd all been dancing downstairs.

"I wasn't the only DJ they used. I got the second night of opening week. I have to say I was getting a little ahead of myself. I had to pretend I knew things about this big sound system that I didn't know. It was lucky I didn't blow the speakers. I played Limelight three nights and it was a thrill, but then the girl who hired me said Peter Gatien only wanted to pay me $150 a night, instead of the $300 she'd promised me. I didn't think that was right, even though I know now I was a crazy to ask for $300. So I decided to concentrate on another club where I'd gotten an offer. I'd just opened, and, of all the things, they called it Kamikaze."

Kamikaze was started by four guys who'd wanted to open an after-hours joint till they found what used to be a sheet metal factory. "When I first walked in and saw the size of the place," co-owner Kirke Walsh said, "it took my breath away." Besides the old factory, the club took over a private garage that had previously housed one of the Shah's Mercedes sedans and the bulletproof limo of Marty's departed protectee, Nelson Rockefeller. Stuck where it was, on the forbidding block of Nineteenth Street between Ninth and Tenth Avenues, the club got its name, Walsh said, "because we thought anyone who'd come way over there had to be a kamikaze."

The club had some impeccably hip credentials. Its upstairs gallery-lounge had been the loft of that irrepressible Sex Pistol, Johnny

Rotten (who was then going by his given name, John Lydon). One of the club's first doormen was Stephen Saban, a Roman-nosed wit on his way to becoming the Walter Winchell of downtown society at *Details* magazine. And tending bar was a cocky actor who played the harmonica and cracked jokes and who also went by his given name Bruce Willis. Willis—a.k.a. Bruno—ended up beating out some 3,000 actors to become Cybil Shepard's costar on ABC's Emmy-winning series *Moonlighting*. Even when he was shaking cocktails, Bruno seemed to sense his destiny. Lighting man Tim Alger recalled, "I used to bathe the bar in this ill white light. So Bruce would say, 'Change this light! I look terrible.' I didn't care. I'd just turn into a vicious queen and say, 'Honey, I'm lighting the orchids, not *you*.'"

Of course, for Marty Kamikaze had one attraction: a cavernous room where a fifteen-foot-high DJ booth overlooked a 4,275-square-foot floor—the largest dance floor, at that time, in Manhattan. The lighting system had been designed by Brian Thompson, who did Studio 54. "I took one look at the room," Marty recalls, "and I said, 'This is for me.'"

"Marty made an appointment and came into my office," remembers Kirke Walsh, who had a staff of around seventy people. "I looked him over and I thought, Wait a minute, this guy's not a kid. I figured he'd probably had all kinds of experience as a DJ. But then he said he'd only spun one other place. I said, 'What!?' He said he wanted a career change. I said, 'What did you do before?' He said, he'd been a Secret Service agent. I said, 'Get outta here!' To me, that was really weird."

"I told Kirke I'd appreciate it if he'd keep this to himself. And he said OK. I wanted to blank out my past. I didn't want it coloring people's impression of me as a DJ. The beauty of the nightclub world is that you can get away with that. Maybe it's because so many night people have shady pasts—nobody wants to raise too many questions."

Walsh needed someone to play Thursdays and Fridays. Those nights had been the fiefdom of one of downtown's most fashionable DJ's, Johnny Dynell, who dressed in sequined American flag outfits and who, as a rapper, had cut a few of his own records.

"Johnny went off and got married. And when he left, the room started to get in trouble. I told Kirke I could turn things around. It was a big break because some people were still showing up expecting to hear Johnny. So I played for four weeks while he was on his honeymoon, and the club kept its momentum. Johnny came back, but after a few weeks Kirke decided to try out different DJ's on Fridays. I got some of those Fridays.

"I'd get to the club around nine-thirty or ten. A few people would be drifting in, having a drink. When I first started, I'd panic: 'Oh, God, it's ten-thirty, and nobody's dancing.' Then I got to understand, it's too early. There's nothing more depressing than walking onto an empty dance floor that's getting bombarded with head-banging music. People want to talk at the start of the night, not battle with the DJ. But even if there were five people in the room, it was important to me that they had something interesting to listen to. So I'd put on some ambient minimalist record, like Philip Glass or Steve Reich. I liked 'E2–E4,' by Guetsching. Once we had seventy-five people or so on the floor, I'd look at Timmy Alger over on the lighting booth and I'd say, 'Well, are you ready to go to work?' And then we'd do it."

Night manager Tom Birdy admits, "I used to be amazed. I'd be up in the booth with Marty and he'd tell me, 'Watch this, Tom. I'm going to bring them in now.' And then he'd pull everybody in from the back bar. It was like he was herding livestock."

*   *   *

"What I'd do was move from instrumental to vocals, bring up the volume and start sending them little signals. I'd phase in one lyric, like, 'It's party time'—that, subconsciously, people knew wasn't on the original song. I'd play two copies of the same record—to give the song a much bassier and spacier sound than people had heard before. And I'd start up the roller coaster.

"I changed as a DJ. When you first get started, you want to impress people with your seamless overlays. That's the traditional art. But after a while I realized that I wanted to take the crowd through more mood swings, make them feel every dip in the energy. People will dance all night long if, every so often, you give them a break. So I'd take them up and up, increasing the beats-per-minute till their hearts were pounding. Then I'd bring them all the way down, usually with reggae, which a lot of DJ's will only play very early or very late. It's important to bring the crowd all the way down, because then every record they hear on the way back up seems to have more power.

"One of the worst things you can do is play something very fast, and then drop down to midtempo. People will barely notice the change. They'll just think, Oh, this song's not as good. You have to watch that crowd like a bubbling stew. You can turn down the heat, but if it stops boiling—if too many people walk off the floor—you're in trouble. It's hard to get them back after you've lost them once.

"Around four A.M. the dance floor would still be packed, but I'd have hundreds of people almost standing still. I'd bring them down gently. I'd turn down the bass and play something with a bright sound, where the drum high-hats blended into the clinking of glasses at the bar. Then the lights would slowly come up, like the sun rising. It's a real civilized way to end an evening."

All week long Marty would tinker with new mixes at home. At night he'd try them out, sometimes working three turntables at once, darting from one to another, keeping the records in sync like a juggler spinning plates on sticks. He'd jam—scratching and cutting up familiar ditties like a sax player taking apart "My Favorite Things." Marty's ideal was integrating "black" and "white" records that weren't supposed to get along. He'd pull out a classical record like Gustav Holst's "The Planets" and make it a satellite of "Supernature," the ethereal disco stomp by Cerrone. He'd moderate a dialogue between funk queen Jocyln Brown's "I'm Gonna Get You, Baby" and "I Touch Roses," by new wavers Book of Love. He'd cross-pollinate the guitar lines of Gang of Four's "To Hell With Poverty" and Santana's version of *"Oye Como Va."* In essence, Marty would create his own commentary, a third song: "That was how I'd talk through the vinyl."

The crowd would talk back.

The hyperactive inmates of New York, who serve much of their sentence on earth bolted inside cramped apartments, can go stir crazy. A dance floor is their exercise pen. Up in his guard tower, next to the man with the searchlight, Marty encouraged the prisoners to attempt a midnight escape. When he was at the top of his form, Marty would hear them down below in the darkness screaming, barking, chanting their disco calliope chant—*"oo-ooh, oo-ooh."* It was as it had always been: the drummer and his tribe: call and response.

Party promoter Chris Halliburton remembered a Kamikaze event he threw for playwright David Rabe, "We had everybody from investment bankers to transvestites to ballet dancers to graffiti artists. Marty got everybody to take off their masks and go wild. At one point people started getting up on platforms, taking their shirts off, tying their ties around their heads like sweatbands. Marty was just sitting up there laughing."

*     *     *

"When I first heard a crowd screaming from the dance floor, I thought they were mad at me. I thought maybe they were going to march up and drag me from the DJ booth. But just like when I was in the Secret Service, when the crowd started screaming, I'd remove myself mentally from the situation. I'd get lost in myself. I started to get better when I stopped planning and started feeling. Instead of worrying what do *they* want to hear next? I'd ask myself, What do *I* want to hear next? I'd make myself a dancer."

Tom Birdy remembers, "The place would be going crazy and Marty would be up in his booth with some strange outfit on, doing a dance. We had a lot of wild acts perform, but on a nightly basis Marty was the wildest."

Before he came to Kamikaze, Tim Alger had operated two of New York's largest light constellations: Studio 54 and the Saint (which in the sixties had been Bill Graham's fabled Filmore East).

"I used to want to be a DJ," says Alger. "I had maybe a thousand records. But besides records, you need a strong emotional makeup. If you put on a record and the dance floor clears, it can be shattering. The Saint had the toughest audience in the world, because to gay people the music was the most important thing at the party. They knew every song, beat by beat. They'd applaud at the end of the night for a good performance, but they could also be vicious queens. To them, you're as good as the last beat in your last mix. A record once skipped when a DJ at the Saint was playing. He left the DJ booth and he never came back.

"A lot of the straight DJ's don't try as hard. But I've never worked with anyone better than Marty. He has a great feeling for making the evening have a beginning, a middle and end. He definitely knows how to make people pay attention. He was always very good at trying to make the light and the music come together. He'd say, 'I'm going to stop the music dead and then go into *this* weird sound.' Musically, he was easily two years ahead of his time. I was not the most progressive listener. I was strictly a disco diva. But he even got me into rap music. He took a lot of people through an evolution."

Not everybody, of course. Kirke Walsh observed, "Bruce Willis would go out of his way to sing in a very loud voice a song that wasn't being played. I once said, 'Bruno, would you cut it out? Be cool!' " Marty hadn't worked long at Kamikaze when Willis, who went on to record an album of his own soul-singing, climbed up to the DJ booth.

Recalling the incident Marty said, "He'd always say the same thing, 'Hey, man, play some Motown. Play some James Brown.' I did it for him once or twice, but after that you just wanted to say, 'Please, ask for anything else.'

"However, I must've been doing something right. When four A.M. came and the club turned on its go-home lights, a thousand dancers would still be on the floor shouting for more. After six months of playing on alternating Fridays, I won Kamikaze's regular Friday and Saturday slots. Shortly after that, I also got Wednesdays. I was making $200 a night—a higher per diem wage than I'd earned in the Service, where I'd worked far more hours. Of course I didn't have any overtime or expense account or Federal benefits. And some weeks I'd spend so much on records that I was almost working for nothing.

"But I was enjoying myself. I developed calluses on my hands from working the wheels of steel. I remembered how the steel strings of my guitar used to give me calluses. It felt good to have them back."

On any given night at Kamikaze there was no telling what sort of extravaganza Marty might be providing on the soundtrack. Mayor Koch had a birthday party there. There was a post-concert bash for

Prince. "He didn't show up," said Marty. "Or maybe he did. There were so many little clones with mustaches and eyeshadow he could've sneaked in and nobody would've noticed." One New Year's Eve a forty-piece orchestra accompanied the unparalleled "One Man Show," of Miss Grace Jones. "She peeled out of a gorilla suit," Marty recalled. The usual luminaries put in appearances: Mick Jagger, Rod Stewart, Robin Williams, Harvey Keitel, Jack Nicholson. Kirke Walsh's girlfriend, Stacie Teele, curated art exhibits that sometimes featured the canvases of celebrity dabblers like Kurt Vonnegut and Tony Bennett. There were also more serious shows, one of the largest New York exhibits of abstract painting in years, and some controversial ones, like "Hitler is Marching," a retrospective of the work of anti-Nazi collagist John Heartfield.

"We had an Art Disposal Night. Some artist spray-painted coveralls for the club's staff and they gave away about seventy paintings. The whole thing was presided over by New York's Commissioner of Sanitation. Another night, Frankie DeCurtis, the doorman, rented a bunch of paper shredders and brought in all sorts of prints and photographs—everything from Man Ray to Currier and Ives. By three A.M., whatever Frankie hadn't given away got shredded. Rose went up on stage and threw the prints into the shredder. Everytime she tossed some more art in, I blared this record of chainsaw noise. I might point out this was years before Oliver North had *his* shredding party.

"One time one of the art curators put up this electric mobile. This thing had four or five sails about eighteen feet long, and it was supposed to revolve above the dance floor. Well, they mounted it on the ceiling and it revolved for maybe half an hour. Then it started smoking. People thought it was part of the art, but the fact is, it was starting to catch fire. They unplugged it. Another artist installed these ten-foot-tall fiberglass flowers all over the dance floor. The dancers got so worked up one night that they started swinging from these flowers and bending them. The artist freaked out. But what could I say? It's a dance floor, not a museum.

"There were a couple of intergalactical affairs. One was 'Morons From Outer Space.' We had big glowing models of Pluto and Saturn dangling over the floor. Rockets were going off. A guy in a spacesuit hung for about five hours in a black room. There was the night we had a fashion show where guys on big Harley choppers drove around on the dance floor. Another night, we had a stripper come out and set her body on fire. Not her body, really—actually, it was a flammable costume that she peeled off. It wasn't like we even needed to *hire* strippers. Girls would climb up on these big cubes on the floor and start taking off their shirts. I'd pull out this sex talk record I found. This sultry woman's voice would say, 'I see you there everynight in the corner, watching me in the dark . . .'

"No question, it got wild down there. Guys walking around on their hands. Our resident drag queen bartenders, dressed up like Madame Pompadour, dancing on the bar. Then you had the dark corner with the ladder that lead up to the DJ booth. Every weekend, I swear, some couple would be getting it on on the steps. I'd say, 'Uh, excuse me.' Every time I wanted to go the bathroom, I'd have to witness this interruptus ritual.

"We also started getting the homeboys. I'd look down and see kids breaking and popping and moonwalking, spinning on their heads, doing the worm. I knew what'd make 'em bug them out, and I threw it down for them."

Tim Alger felt, "Marty was a lot blacker than some of the "buppies"—the black urban professionals. The nights when we'd have mostly homeboys or buppies, and when Marty was making them go wild, I'd black out the dance floor and shine a white light on the DJ booth. The people would look up and point at us. 'Look at those two white boys!' "

\*   \*   \*

On a couple of nights, Kamikaze held rap shows. Metal detectors were set up at the door to check for guns and knives. Bouncers who were used to dealing with street gangs were hired to do the frisking. "The bouncers only found one knife on a crowd of over a thousand people," reported Tom Birdy. Still, early in the evening, as blacks, whites, Chinese, and Puerto Ricans swapped stares, something like an electrical storm could be felt below the DJ booth.

"One gang would be watching to see how the other gang reacted to a song," Alger remembers, "and Marty would play up on the gang energy. I guess it could have been dangerous. Sometimes it would get scary, but we'd love it."

"The best way to get two gangs to chill out is to get them dancing together. Give them a good time. I'd play rap, but it wouldn't be in-your-face rap where they just keep boasting, 'I'm baddest! I'm the toughest!' That stuff was funny when it first came out, but enough already. I'd play the rap that makes you dance but also makes you think—back then, things like 'The Message' by Grandmaster Flash and 'It's Like That,' by Run-D.M.C. I'd play Latin rap and Jamaican rap and any of the two-tone bands like UB40—'Sing Our Own Song'—any of the crossover groups that refused to stay in one musical gang. Punk-funk—I loved that: 'World Destruction,' that antinuclear assault that John Lydon cut with Afrika Bambaata. Of course I'd play James Brown. They used to bill him as 'The Only Man Who Could Quell A Riot,' and it's probably still true. I'd play 'Free Nelson Mandala,' by the Special AKA and then I'd mix into the instrumental side of Sting's '(If You Love Somebody) Set Them Free.' I'd also throw in different kinds of African and Third World music—you know, to remind people that the earth didn't end at the tip of Manhattan."

\*   \*   \*

Tom Birdy remembers, "Those rap nights were tense but they were pretty nice. One thing was for sure—there were no complaints about the music."

Marty liked the nights "when the crowd was at its wildest, when things *almost* got out of hand. On those nights I would look down on the dance floor and in the strobe-light that flickered like the grainy Zapruder film, I would see the dancers lunging at each other, convulsing: On the nights when the crowd really surged beneath me, it was almost like my DJ's earphones could pick up messages from the past.

"Certain songs had a special meaning for me. I'd do a special mix using John Lennon's 'Just Like Starting Over.' Almost every night I'd play a song by New Order called 'Temptation,' which back then hadn't been released in the U.S. It's a beautiful song and it sort of became my signature. When I put it on, people knew it was me up there. The lyrics always remind me of that night I flew out of Vienna:

> *Up, down, turn around*
> *Please don't let me hit the ground*
> *Tonight I think I'll walk alone*
> *I'll find my soul as I go home.*"

The former Soul Seeker would play "Temptation" and then do something he couldn't do in the Secret Service—he'd join the crowd. "I'd come down from the booth and I'd dance with them."

"He does tell a story with his music," says Rose. "I just close my eyes and get into it. Maybe it's just because I know Marty, maybe I'm just a set of cliches, but I go down all sorts of mental roads when I hear him."

It wasn't till five months after he'd quit the Service that Marty told Rose what he used to do.

\* \* \*

"Rose and I had gone out with some friends to their cabin in Pennsylvania. We'd had a great day, and that night, when we were in bed, when there was a snowstorm outside, I told her the basics. She didn't press me for details.

"I said, 'Don't you have any questions?' She said, 'Not really.'

"That's one of the reasons I was so attracted to her. I used to be an interrogator. I used to be surrounded by interrogators. But Rose didn't care about anybody's past.

Rose said she wasn't shocked. "I didn't think he'd been deceiving me. I'd know he'd quit *some* job and that he was going through something. I just always felt that when he wanted to say something, I'd listen. I found out more as time went on. We rented a house out on Long Island with a bunch of people. Anybody who didn't have a place to sleep, who didn't have any direction in their lives, Marty would say, 'Come and live with us.' He was always picking up strays—pregnant dogs and homeless people. It was like a punk commune. The neighbors on the block would see all these wild-haired people coming in and out at all hours of the day and night and they'd give us funny looks. Anyway, we started running out of things to wear, so me and one of our friends went down to the basement, where Marty had his boxes of old clothes. We opened the boxes and there was all this Secret Service stuff inside. We started rummaging through it. We'd say, 'Oh, wow, look at these pens from the White House.' Then we came across all these fake ID cards. A driver's license and passport with Marty's picture and somebody else's names. Our friend was more freaked out than I was. He said, 'I don't understand this guy. Who the hell *is* he?'

"I started thinking that maybe the people in Washington were still checking up on Marty. Particularly when you thought about all the crazy stuff he'd been into. I was under the impression that you couldn't just *walk away* from the Secret Service if you had secrets.

Marty told us to relax. He said they'd given him phony ID's so he could work undercover at demonstrations. He gave the ID's and his gun holster and stuff to my two little boys. After that, Marty and I started talking more about the Secret Service. We'd try to figure out if I'd been a demonstrator at some rally where he'd been an agent. Sometimes we'd pull one of the stereo speakers into the den and Marty'd tell little stories about the Presidents. He'd do the Nixon voice and the Carter voice. We'd all laugh. But that's when I started to see how much living Marty had done."

Except for Rose, Kirke Walsh and July Weinstein, Marty hadn't told any of the nightclub people about his old job. Gradually, though, he started indulging in some private jokes. Finding a recorded collection of Richard Nixon's speeches, Marty attached the voice of Searchlight to the clickety-clack percussion of Kraftwerk's "Trans-Euro Express." The doomed President developed a scratchy throat in Marty's version of the 1972 inaugural oath: "I, I, I—I, Richard Nixon, do solemnly swear . . ."

"In the two years since I'd quit the Secret Service, I had exercised full rights as a chameleon. Rose and her friend used to change the color of my hair all the time. I'd just say, Do whatever you want. They'd make it cherry, platinum, whatever. At the opening night of Area, I hit it off with Eurythmics' star Annie Lennox—after we discovered that we sported almost identical flaming orange crewcuts. You could just bet that any one of these hairstyles would've prompted my former Secret Service colleagues to tackle me if I ever tried to slip too close to Ronald Reagan. So it was the ultimate perversity that, one Halloween, I showed up to spin wearing—no!—a suit and a tie."

Tom Birdy remembers, "This one Halloween we had people giving tattoos. We had a real gypsy palmist named Sister Sara telling fortunes. And the costumes—oh, it'd take an hour to describe them. But at the beginning of the night, Marty came in looking like Sam Normal. He stood right next to me and I looked out of the corner of my eye and I thought, Oh, shit, it's a salesman or something. So I walked away. But the guy kept following me around. Finally, he said, 'Hey Tom, it's me. It's Marty.' I said, 'Holy shit, what are you *doing?*' "

"Everybody freaked," says Tim Alger. "They were all asking, 'Who's that guy in the DJ booth?' "

# CHAPTER SIXTEEN

# *Young Americans*

MARTY'S Halloween costume showed how he could laugh now about his past. All the same, putting that uniform on again was like telling trouble where to find him.

Two years after Marty started spinning at Kamikaze, after he'd become the club's house DJ, after he'd built up a following of his own, a posse of suits and ties tracked him down. Down that god-forsaken block of West Nineteenth Street there rolled a motorcade of taxis, and out of those taxis emerged—starched and pressed and armed with briefcases—*the yuppies*!

Kamikaze's owners had tried to lure the king cats of the down-town scene into the club. Back when Kamikaze opened in 1983, quite a few veterans of the scene—artists, writers, directors, actors, pho-tographers, designers—were finally making good. Former busboys and cooks like Julian Schnabel, Jean Michel Basquiat, and Keith Haring were commanding astonomical sums for their paintings in the booming art market. Among the other downtown talents who'd been—or were getting—noticed far above Fourteenth Street were David Byrne, Laurie Anderson, Spalding Gray, Jay McInerney, Tama Janowitz, Jim Jarmusch, Susan Seidelman, Ann Magnuson, John Lurie, and Stephen Sprouse.

In the late seventies there'd been a number of inventive clubs where these subterraneans went, not just to drink and dance, but also to watch and star in dada vaudeville shticks worthy of Marty's voice-activated mental patients. As it happened, some of the most beloved of these nightspots—the Mudd Club, Club 57, Berlin, The Continental—were shutting their doors just as Kamikaze was taking flight. Kamikaze had hoped to draw this same arty crowd with its gallery and theme nights. But Kirke Walsh, who'd run three previous clubs, had to admit, "What did we know about art?"

Kamikaze couldn't quite compete with the inspired camp happenings at the East Village's Pyramid Club—chronicled in *People* magazine, no less. And even tougher competition lay down the road in TriBeCa: at Area, a tireless in-house staff of artists and set designers spent between $30,000 and $60,000 every six weeks to revamp the club's interior around such themes as religion, food, body oddities, confinement and suburbia. At least, in Marty, Kamikaze had a DJ who played the same cutting edge music that dancers heard at Area, Pyramid and the great downtown clubs of yore.

Frankie De Curtis, Kamikaze's doorman and sometime curator says, "One of the reasons those Thursday night art openings didn't work was because Marty didn't play on Thursdays. I wanted him to, but he couldn't step on the toes of the Thursday night DJ."

Since he'd started, Marty had been pulling more and more downtown dance fanatics into the club. Tim Alger observed, "He built up the number of people who'd come back and pay. They'd ask at the door, 'Who's playing?' If it was Marty, they'd come in."

Marty had some ideas about how to keep Kamikaze from going into a nose-dive. "You asked yourself one question: what was the oldest dance club in New York? Answer: the Paradise Garage. It opened in 1976 and year after year, it survived the trendoids. That's because it didn't waver. It always kept the music fresh and it knew who its audience was.

"Just like Kamikaze, it was a big space to fill—an old parking garage. Not only that, the place didn't even serve liquor. But people paid $300 a year for a membership and, on top of that, $10 at the door. All you had to do to be a member was love music and love to dance. The Garage had some incredible dancers. It also gave some big stars their early breaks—Madonna, Whitney Houston, Patti La-belle, Gwen Guthrie, Grace Jones, Sylvester. These people came back later, too, because of the crowd.

"But the real star was the DJ, Larry Levan. Larry invented 'the Garage Sound'—which is hard to describe except to say that it's some of the darkest, densest, most hypnotic music you'll ever hear. Larry plays things you will *never* hear any place else. Mick Jagger, Duran, Duran—anybody who wants to be on the cutting edge of dance music—they bring Larry their unreleased session tapes. He takes them apart and makes them into something new—live, right before your ears!

"I didn't play exactly the same kind of music as Larry Levan, but I felt we could do the Garage thing at Kamikaze—build a loyal clientele around music. Not just around me, but me and other DJ's who wanted to experiment. I knew there was audience for that."

Kamikaze's owners, however, couldn't wait for Marty's following to swell. They had to pay salaries, rent, taxes, insurance. They'd been dazzled by the size of the old sheet metal plant, but they hadn't quite foreseen how dead their twelve-hundred-capacity club would look even with three hundred people milling around in it. New Yorkers could now choose from a number of sprawling sound-and-light cir-cuses. The underground club scene had become big business.

Like its competitors, Limelight and Visage, Kamikaze had to have its own public relations staff. The staff had a mailing list broken down by subculture: the East Village bohemians, the Concorde-fresh Euro-trash, the Seventh Avenue fashion victims, the buppies, the gays and the art crowd (A, B, and C lists).

But even with these many lists, Kamikaze's owners decided they had to rely on freelance party promoters. These promoters promised that, for a cut of the bar or the door, they'd have the club jumping with people. One of the first party promoters was none other than that radical scourge of the Chicago Democratic Convention, Jerry Rubin. By the late seventies, the author of *Steal This Book* had clipped his hair, wiped off his war paint and gotten himself a job as a Wall Street stockbroker. Suited up, Jerry was throwing eighties-style love-ins called "networking" parties, where Young Urban Professionals swapped business cards.

Before long, the yippie-turned-yuppie saw raiders waging takeover attempts on *his* crowd. Other promoters began sending out invites to recent graduates of Ivy League colleges, to young comers at the investment houses, to anybody who'd signed in at their last party. Yuppie promoters typically liked to use the birthday of some debutante as a premise for a party, but the flimsiest excuse would do. One Kamikaze party was simply in honor of "Guys Who Wear Yellow Suspenders and Girls Who Wear Pearls."

When you received (or found) an invitation to one of these things, it meant that you, as an instant VIP, were entitled to enter Kamikaze without paying the fifteen-dollar cover charge—at least before a given hour. Of course, at Kamikaze's bar the drinks cost a good deal more than you'd pay at the corner Blarney Stone. But the yuppies, rich from riding a bull market that seemingly would never quit bucking, didn't haggle over drink prices. And that suited Kamikaze's owners and bartenders like Bruce Willis just fine. "Bruno never liked the artists," laughed Kirke Walsh. "They didn't tip."

Those yuppies tipped plenty. But when these canary-suspendered lads and their pearl-chokered dates brought their drinks back from the bar, they knitted their brows. Who should they find sitting in the booth next to theirs but a bunch of swarthy, prickly haired people in leather!

Kamikaze had another face-off of the gangs. The only difference was, in this throwdown Kamikaze's DJ—never mind his Halloween costume—wasn't neutral.

"All week long I would screen some fifty new domestic releases from my record pool. I would spend at least a hundred dollars a week on imports. I would pick favorites from my home discotheque, which was growing toward 10,000 records. And then . . ."

Tim Alger explains, "The promoters would be sending out thousands of invitations for 'Let's Bring Back Elvis Night.' The night of the party, these promoters would get to the club and find out that Marty didn't have any Elvis. They'd say, 'What kind of DJ doesn't have Elvis?' "

"Marty'd come in all excited about some new mix," recalled Frankie DeCurtis, "but the promoter's invitation would say 'The Best Dance Music of the Fifties, Sixties, Seventies, and Eighties.' Marty would play that older stuff. But at about eleven, he'd get to the eighties, and that's where he'd stay. That caused a little disturbance."

"What would get me was the yuppie who'd come up to the booth with his tie undone and sweat pouring down his face and who'd say to me, 'Why don't you play some music people will *dance* to?'

"I was there to entertain people. But that's why I was against requests. Someone was paying me for my instincts and taste. You don't interrupt a singer and say, 'Don't sing *that* song, sing *this* song!' If you don't like the singer, leave the club. When *I'm* out dancing at a club, I don't want to know what the next song will be.

I want to be surprised. That's why you go out. Even good requests interrupt a DJ's train of thought. You'd be amazed how often, when somebody asks for a record, how I'll already have it on the turntable, ready to play. Requests aren't for clubs, they're for weddings and bar mitzvahs.

"At first I tried to cooperate. I'd play music that the yuppies liked and that my crowd would tolerate. I *do* play old songs. I know as well as anybody how an old song can dredge up memories that'll just about make you cry while you're dancing. But, see, my frame of reference, it's different from people who just started going out to nightclubs when they heard about them on MTV. I'd play underground cult classics that the diehard club people remembered. If Timmy blacked out the dance floor and I put on Tanya Gardner's 'Heartbeat,' the club people would scream after the first three beats. The art of the DJ is connecting the past with the future—showing people how nothing's really new. All this new 'house' music coming out of Chicago and London—I like to overlay it with something like 'Dirty Talk' by Klein and MBO. Those people were making 'house' years ago. So these young bankers would ask me to play old soul music. Okay, I know something about that. But let's not hear 'Baby Love' for the ten-millionth time. Let's hear some *new* old soul music. I'd play them some rare groove things from Memphis and Philadelphia that never made it onto white radio. I'd do a whole set. But that wasn't enough for the yuppies.

"It's not like I had anything against bankers and accountants. God knows I could use some good advice on handling money. I didn't hate everybody who wore a suit and tie. I know first hand that somebody else can be living inside that suit, choking in that starched shirt. The fact is, I wanted to reach that person. I didn't want to just preach to the converted. I wanted to make that yuppie take off his clothes and say, 'I don't know what this song is, but it feels *good!*' I mean, I really would look at the yuppies and see myself at twenty-five—when I was working around the clock to become a *professional,* when I had to have my Corvette and my townhouse, when I thought I knew it all.

"After a while, I think I got a lot of the yuppies into my music. But some of them were so closed-minded, such followers. The records they asked for—Elvis, the Beatles, Bruce Springsteen—you know at one point somebody had to go to a club and hear those guys for the first time. Somebody took a chance on them, even though maybe they didn't have their chords down and maybe you had to listen to their songs a few times before you liked them."

Tom Birdy observed, "Most of the time it was the promoters doing the complaining. They were young guys who in the day worked at a brokerage firm or went to med school. They thought they knew how to run a disco. They'd say, 'Well, I've been to *plenty* of clubs.' Yeah, right. Early in the night, when people would be talking and having a drink, the promoters would find me and say, 'Tom, the lights are too bright, the music's too slow.'

"I'd say, 'I know. It's only ten-thirty.' They'd say, 'Yeah, but people might leave.'

"Every twenty minutes they'd be after me for something else. Marty tried to be nice and give them something like they were asking for. But finally, when their promoter party ended at the agreed time, at midnight or whatever, I'd say, 'Marty, do your thing.' He'd smile and say, 'Thank you very much.' And he'd let loose. The place would go crazy. Then the promoters would come up to me and say, 'See, we knew what we were talking about, huh?'

"I'd met these little dictators before," Marty scoffed. "The White House had these young staff snots who'd ask you to run down and get them a Coke. Fuck that. I wasn't their Coke machine and I wasn't going to be their juke box. You know, a dance floor has a very simple electoral system. The plebiscite votes, and the returns come in immediately. If a song sucks, the dance floor clears. If the dance floor stays packed, the song must be doing its job. The DJ gets to stay in office.

But this was years before Wall Street got hit by the insider trading scandals and the stock market crash. And so you'd get these twenty-five-year-olds who thought they were geniuses, who had this attitude: I want it all and I want it *now!* They'd be upstairs in the gallery, trading insider tips or scoring some blow—and then they'd decide they wanted to dance. But they had to dance to Wham! And it had to be now!

"One night this yuppie girl invited herself into the booth and started screaming into my ear, 'Can you play Tears for Fears?' Now I'd been playing Tears for Fears on imports for a year. But by then, they were all over AM radio. Good band, but they'd already made it. Other bands deserved exposure. Anyway, I couldn't resist. I put a mike up to this yuppie girl's mouth and said, 'What'd you say?' Her voice went out to the crowd and the people who knew what I was up against started laughing. You know what song she wanted? 'Everybody Wants to Rule the World.' "

There were nights when Kamikaze threw the world into bold relief. Like the night when 250 artists donated work to raise money for the homeless. The organizers of the show thought it only right that the homeless themselves should be able to view the art. But the scene that resulted—it was worthy of a photograph by Wegee.

Tom Birdy remembers that night. "That same night we had a small yuppie party. People from some bank rented part of the club. I remember there was this one character at the bar, a real swell, you know, with an ascot and a crest on his jacket. He turned around and saw bag people coming in off the street, bellying up to the open bar. I thought he was going to choke on his cigarette holder. This bag lady came up and asked him if he could spare a quarter. Actually, the bag people didn't drink that much. But they managed to get upstairs where the food was. While they were putting little sand-wiches into their shopping bags, the yuppies were flipping out. This one woman looked like she was going to have a nervous breakdown. She was crying in a booth, playing with her pearls. This one ragged guy came up to her and said, 'Lady, those are beautiful pearls.'

"It did get to be a problem at the end of the night. About twenty of them—the homeless, that is—went to sleep on the dance floor. At four I had to wake them up and move them along. They ended up sleeping on the street outside after the limos had taken off."

"But the yuppies weren't always so frail," insists Marty. "I guess I'd come full circle the night we had the yuppie riot. I think it was a college reunion party. As usual, the promoters sent out something like 5,000 invites, but this time half the people actually showed up. I was spinning and I could see that the club was over its fire capacity. Meanwhile, there were hundreds of people outside, trying to get in. Tom Birdy told the bouncers at the door not to admit anybody else."

"People kept asking if they could come in to look for their friends," says Birdy. "A lot of them were getting mad because they claimed they got there before ten, so they shouldn't have to pay. It was cold out there, and certain people started getting rowdy—screaming, knocking down the wooden police horses. Unhooking the velvet ropes. Some of them started throwing beer bottles. The bounc-ers finally pulled down the steel doors. Then people couldn't get out. They started to panic. We must've had 1,800 of them inside. Eventu-ally, the bouncers restored order. But there was about an hour there of real high tension."

Marty had to admit "part of me got pumped up when that riot energy spilled onto the dance floor. But I wasn't pleased when I heard about that shit at the door. I've seen how scared people get when they're trapped in a crowd. Look, I wasn't out there. I can't say if the bouncers antagonized anybody. But for the record, we didn't have that kind of trouble on the rap nights. The homeboys chilled."

"Bankers who made gang lords look polite? Right. Surely, there was a wide range of personalities in between the yuppie who wilted at the sight of a bag lady and the yuppie who whipped beer bottles at bouncers. But some kind of turf war was afoot here. I wasn't alone in feeling that some of these people you might call conformists weren't conforming to downtown codes."

"The yuppies were the kind of crowd the club wanted," Birdy explains. "We wanted 'nice' people. But sometimes these nice people became very bizarre in that they became very demanding—with Marty, with everybody."

Alger admitted, "The yuppies were some of the rudest people. Rose used to be abused. She's such a sweet person. But these yuppie boys would get stupid drunk and verbally abuse her. She'd have to find the darkest corner to dance in."

"These guys in button-down shirts would say, 'Hey, punk chick,' says Rose. "One guy kept grabbing at me and trying to lift up my skirt."

The security of Marty's underground paradise had been violated. The gray-suited people who sauntered past the velvet ropes were pissing him off as much as the nitwits he used to see along the parade ropelines—the pushy people who didn't notice that they were strangling the spectators in wheelchairs.

"I'm not against rich people. I know rich people who are *very* hip. I'm against arrogance. Blacks, gays, Hispanics, punks—they all came to Kamikaze. But it was the yuppies—at least some of them—who wanted to impose their white suburban fantasy wherever they went. There were nights when we'd almost have a fist fight breaking out in the DJ booth. Promoters would come up with their big friends and say, 'You *are* going to play that record.'

"I'd say, 'Get out of the DJ booth. If you have a complaint, go to the management.'

"So a couple of minutes later one of the owners would come up to talk to me. What could he say? He'd see 800 people whooping it up. Nights when everybody was going wild—that's when some of those yuppies would complain the most. It seemed like it infuriated them to see all these 'pathetic' freaks enjoying themselves. Worst of all, other yuppies were joining in and actually dancing to that 'shit' I was playing. Life is such a B movie. It was the old story of the frat boys against the greasers. Your music is the way you view the world."

"Sometimes Marty would get so frustrated with them that he'd get violent with the music," says Alger. "He'd say, 'They want to hear *this?*' Okay! And he'd turn up the volume so it'd hurt their ears. Or he'd go even further into left field and play some German industrial music."

"They used to ask for Madonna *all–the–time,*" Marty complains. "I played Madonna a long time before she ever made it to MTV. But by then club people were sick of hearing 'Like a Virgin.' So when the yuppies would ask for it, I'd play it at thirty-three r.p.m. instead of forty-five. She sounded like Joe Frazier. Another time I mixed the Virgin song with that sex-talk record. Funny thing—Madonna came up to the booth one time, and what'd she ask for? 'The Dominatrix Sleeps Tonight.' I knew it was just a matter of time before she went for the whole B&D route, wearing the tassle corset and everything."

* * *

He also knew it wouldn't be long before the yuppie promoters began to plot a coup.

Frankie De Curtis remembers, "The crowd the promoters invited might not even show up. You *would* make more at the bars with promoter invites, but the hardcore dance people, they'd come back and bring friends. You'd develop regulars. I was a supporter of Marty's because I saw the number of paying customers at the door. Clear as day, the numbers would drop off when he didn't play. But the owners started to feel Marty was sabotaging the promoters."

"I saw that even though I'd left the Secret Service, I hadn't escaped politics. Several of the promoters were solidly behind me. But there was this one yuppie promoter named Mitchell who kept telling me to play oldies. One night he actually had the nerve to bring me records. He said, 'Here, put these somewhere so you can play them later.'

"I said, 'OK,' and I put them in the trash can.

"He said, 'You're driving all my people out of the club.'

"I said, 'Good.'

"After that, he wanted me out. He complained to one of the owners, a guy named John. I heard about it, so one night when I was spinning I got out the Nixon record. I found Nixon's Watergate explanation, the part where he talks about confronting the Attorney General, where he says, 'I talked to Mr. Mitchell, and he said he had no knowledge.' I kept playing the part where Nixon says, 'I asked him, John, did *you* do it?' Frankie De Curtis cracked up. He started pulling other people who knew what was going on onto the dance floor. I kept scratching it: 'John, did *you* do it? John? John?'

"After a while I saw how deep this music problem went. The promoters and certain people in charge didn't like the crowd I was attracting. I was getting the homeboys and breakdancers. Timmy and I would get excited watching these people go crazy. We'd be all

proud of ourselves and the energy we'd worked up. But then we'd
see a couple of the owners and their faces would be like stone. I used
to tell one of the owners, 'Hey, the yuppies don't want to just be
around yuppies. They want to look over and see some freaks, some
breakdancing. Give them something they can't get uptown.'

"But this one owner laid it out plain for me. He said, 'Marty, we
don't want this to turn into a black club.' "

"A yuppie crowd can spend money," explains Kirke Walsh. "But I
had no objections to the crowd Marty was pulling in. His personal
friends were very funny. They had the leather and the spikey hair,
but they were very nice once you got over your initial fear of them.

"We all loved Marty. He's a very wonderful and charming guy.
He worked really hard and he did build an audience and fill the
room. He had a purpose and an aim. And if a club owner has the
patience, he can stick it out with a DJ and build the club around him.
I have the utmost respect and admiration for Marty's stick-to-it-
iveness.

"However, Marty only worked a few days a week. And when you
have a club, you have to be willing to change hats. With few excep-
tions, clubs don't dictate the policy, it's the people who come in. You
have an idea in your head of the crowd you want, but then you find
out you're not going to *get* that crowd. We had a big club. It had
a lot of expenses. In order to survive—especially with the insurance
crunch—we'd have promoter parties. Marty was a DJ, he wasn't an
owner of the club. He was inflexible. I attributed that to his inexperi-
ence. If he'd been around longer, he would have changed hats."

But Marty couldn't go through another costume change. Quite
possibly no one has ever made a bigger drama than Marty out of
putting on a goddam record. Yet for reasons the owners couldn't
possibly glean, Marty found it impossible to tailor his taste to the
taste of certain suits and ties. After two years Tim Alger knew almost

nothing about the background of this DJ who was pushing middle age. But Alger saw that Marty "physically and emotionally couldn't play those oldies and pop songs. It was like asking an artist to paint another way. He couldn't do it. That was one of his downfalls. But he was the one DJ I worked with whose performance came right from the heart. He was always *right there.*"

"I just started turning more and more nights down, and after a while they stopped offering. We understood each other."

Three months after Marty's last gig at Kamikaze, the club closed. "It finally got so mainstream and dull that everybody cool left," said Alger. "And when they left, the yuppies moved on—I guess to places like Heartbreak and Shout and the Surf Club, where they didn't have to fight with the DJ."

Kirke Walsh explained Kamikaze's crash. "The insurance companies went nuts. Our landlord wanted us to carry a $3 million liability policy. We used to pay a premium of $40,000 a year. Suddenly, it shot up to $270,000, with—get this—a $1 million deductible! I would say that seventy-five percent of the clubs in New York aren't insured."

Marty did all right. He played private parties given by Kamikaze promoters who liked the fact that they didn't know half the records he played. He jumped around the progressive clubs: Area, where he quickly had the bartenders dancing on the bar. The Saint, where— small world—he played a party for Amy Carter (code name "Dynamo"), who by then had traded her caterwauling violin for a picket sign denouncing the CIA. Marty's favorite club after Kamikaze was the World—a former Jewish catering hall at Avenue C and Second Street, where most yuppies feared to tread. The World was an enchantingly cheesy slum that featured some of the most provocative groups in America and England—including Big Audio Dynamite, the Art of Noise, the Pogues, the Beastie Boys, and, in one of their last appearances, the Dead Kennedys.

Frank Roccio, one of the World's owners who didn't have a problem with Marty said, "Marty's always been quite professional. He's a real open guy. He doesn't take himself so seriously, as DJ's often do. They can sometimes mix technically accurate stuff but not care if the audience isn't responding. DJ's can get so introspective. I remember years ago at the Nu Musik Seminar there was panel on DJ's. And Sean Cassette, who used to spin at Hurrah's, told everybody, 'I'm not there to entertain, I'm there to *educate.'*

"I don't think Sean worked another day in his life. That's an exaggeration. But let's face it, people come to a nightclub to meet people. To suggest that people were less important than the DJ's need to tell them something is ridiculous. Marty's got the least ego of DJs I know. He's very self-assured, and he'd ask us what we thought. He was open to criticism. It's a pleasure to work with him."

Marty was gaining some purchase in the industry. *Details,* hipdom's missalette, was printing his fave record picks in its "Deejayvue" column. Producers, singers and record promoters kept dropping by his booth to get his feedback on test pressings. David Jurman, National Director of Dance Music Promotion for Arista, said, "Marty's definitely one of the top DJ's in New York. He plays a unique hybrid of music. He easily flows from rap to hip hop to rock to reggae, and somehow he makes it all work."

Studio 54 creator Steve Rubell had been keeping on eye on Marty when he was at Kamikaze. "You can build the most beautiful club, get great lighting, architecture, and put millions into it. But if you don't have a great DJ—no one will come."

In 1984 Rubell was in the process of opening his first club since getting out of prison. Drawing on an estimated $10 million bankroll,

Rubell and his partners hired Japanese architect Arata Isozaki, as well as artists Basquiat, Clemente, and Scharf, to turn Fourteenth Street's old Palladium concert hall into the most spectacular club in the world. In the months before it opened, Rubell had also been talking to Marty about playing opening night at Palladium. Rubell said that Mick Jagger had heard Marty's audition tape and liked it. In the end, Rubell opened instead with Jellybean Benitez. Jellybean, Madonna's old boyfriend, was better known.

Moreover, there had been that point when Rubell, who liked to make requests, had asked Marty if he would play Bruce Springsteen? Marty had said no. Still, Rubell allowed later, "Marty's one of the two or three most versatile DJ's I know. I'd always be open to working with him."

Marty, however, did end up playing at Nell's. Nell's was the uptown-meets-downtown social smash that Rubell had hoped Palladium would be. A throwback to the days of the Stork Club and El Morocco, Nell's was a dimly lit supper club with dark-wood paneling, crystal chandeliers, overstuffed sofas and understated engravings. Whereas Palladium had a shopping mall capacity of 3,500 people, Nell's was an egg shell that could hold only 400.

Its size let the owners of Nell's be very discriminating. Sting, Bianca, Warhol and Claus von Bulow made it past the velvet ropes. But even Cher and Don Johnson, those dreamboats of the trailer-park, met the brush off. And even regulars who paid $200 a year for membership had to watch the guests they brought with them. Nell's sentries would scribble a damning "no-no" in the guest book next to the name of any *arriviste* who didn't have the right look. Too many no-no's could spell a member's expulsion.

The club snubbed conspicuous yuppies, favoring instead Europeans who never let their cigarettes drop below their wrists, as well as other patrons who, though they wore the black uniform of the artist, didn't look like they were struggling. "These Downtown people are the most upwardly mobile people I've ever met," Rubell told interviewer Brad Gooch. "They're all into their careers, their money."

"I call them the Bohemian Billionaires," says Marty. "I played Nell's a couple of times, and I will say that Nell Campbell did stop by the booth to say what I was playing was *wonderful.* But the place she runs isn't my idea of a club. One time I ran over to the bar to ask for a glass of water. The bartender said, 'That'll be four dollars.'

"I couldn't believe it. I said, 'I'm DJing here tonight.'

"She said, 'I'm sorry. That's the policy.' I got a drink from the bathroom tap.

"Nell's is supposed to be comfy and conducive to conversation. But I've never seen so many attractive people shooting each other such cruel looks. What would they do if someone deformed snuck in? The truth is, I think they scare each other. If one of them tries to talk to another without an introduction, they're ready to call a bouncer. I swear, if Anastasio Somoza were still alive, he'd be at Nell's.

"I don't know, maybe it's because I jumped in and out of so many limos in the Secret Service, but when I see those limos lined up outside a club, I go someplace else. To me they're like a funeral cortege. They mean the club is dead. Cause that's when the superrich show up—when they know it's safe to get out their limos.

"I like clubs that used to put on airs but can't afford to anymore. So everybody gets in. It's like the people seizing the dictator's palace and turning it into a gymnasium. Palladium's like that now—all the people from the boroughs who used to get turned away are partying down. And the music's better. I remember I played at Studio 54 three nights in 1985, after Halston and Bianca were long gone. It was a thrill to be in that DJ booth, especially since, on one of the nights, they had some rappers performing. Naturally there were a lot of homeboys in the audience. I knew what they wanted to hear. And I had them screaming. But once again the management was going for a yuppie crowd—which was why the lighting guy said to me, 'You know, as wild as this crowd is, I think you're going to be fired.'

"I didn't care, but he was right. End of the night, I said to Studio's new owner, Mark Fleischman, 'Pretty good reaction, huh?'

"He said, 'You don't understand. After tonight, none of these people will get in again.'

"I'd rather stick to the dance floor and let the scenemakers make their scene without me. Most of them aren't interested in music, anyway. They want their picture taken. They want to look *fabulous!* I suppose a nightclub needs those people. They're part of the theater. But these types who fancy themselves celebrities just because they're 'nightpeople'—they're a little hard to take seriously after you've done time with Richard Nixon. There were nights at Kamikaze when some people came through who I'd first met on the White House detail. David Bowie. Muhammad Ali. I kept Stevie Wonder and his wife dancing till about five in the morning. Those people were sort of reassuring to see again. It just went to show, maybe my life had some continuity after all."

# CHAPTER SEVENTEEN
## An Emotional Agent

"AFTER the White House, though, I'm sort of celebritied out. I hate to see people tyrannized by their image—stars and would-be stars who set themselves apart. I don't know, maybe I set myself apart from the yuppies. Maybe I like being a DJ because it lets me sit up high and batter people with my taste. But I try to stay open. I know it can work both ways. I remember when the Vietnam war was going on and I cut my hair for the Reserves. It kept me from going to Canada. But suddenly there were hippies who wouldn't talk to me. I said to myself, Hey, are these people against the war or against short hair?

"I guess that's always been my conflict: being an outsider inside a group. But I always liked being on some team—the Soul Seekers, the staff at Kamikaze, the Secret Service. I was proud to be a part of the Secret Service. Otherwise I wouldn't have stuck around as long as I did. I finally got tired of the job, but no one's to blame for that. The farther I get from that job the more respect I have for some of those agents. A lot of people base their impression of the Presidency on how one agent treated them. They have to be strong and in-timidating and tactful and charming. You just got to hope the right emotion pops out at the right time."

* * *

After Marty had quit, his agency kept on fighting the old battles. When President Reagan visited West Germany in 1985, Jewish protesters and members of French President Francois Mitterand's delegation charged that the Secret Service's had treated them brusquely. The same year the White House Correspondents Association released a three-month survey of its members. The study charged that John Hinckley's attack had given Secret Service agents an excuse to push and shove reporters and keep them from asking questions of Reagan. "This pattern of petty harrassment," the study claimed, "imposes additional stress on members of the press corps.

Of course members of the Secret Service had been feeling some stress of their own. Under the deficit-cleaving cuts of the Gramm-Rudman Act, the Service's budget fell from $293 million in 1985 to $281 million in 1986. Critics said it was about time that "the Sacred Service" felt the axe. The agency, which worked with $5 million and 525 employees in 1963, *had* picked up the jobs of guarding candidates and dignitaries; but still, said the deficit-reducers, a nearly eleven-fold budget jump between 1970 and 1984 was enough to make even the Pentagon envious. Officials inside and outside the agency disagreed on whether the country should save money by shaving protection for ex-Presidents and their families. Former director Stuart Knight favored cutting loose some spouses and children, but his foe Robert Powis testified against pinching pennies "in this age of terrorism." Former Presidents would have only received protection for five years under a 1986 Senate bill. But that bill was defeated, and in 1988 with a new campaign underway, the Service saw its budget boosted to a new high of $364 million. Currently, ex-Presidents still receive protection for life; their spouses do too, unless they remarry; their children receive guards till they're sixteen. (Agents guarding Michael Reagan fueled a bitter feud in the Reagan family when they claimed that Michael was a kleptomaniac. Eventually, the Service admitted that Michael's agents had exaggerated some and the agency agreed to fire them.) In 1985 Richard Nixon voluntarily asked the government to call off its guards. Seeming to forget his past attempts to escape his protectors, Nixon said his sole reason for ending the relationship was to save the taxpayers $3 million a year. Now he relies on the retired Mike Endicott, who relies on a few men to back him up.

Agents have continued to defend the "foreign digs." Ariel Sharon was no longer Israeli Defense Minister when he came to New York in 1984 to wage his libel suit against *Time* magazine. But when the Secret Service learned of a possible Palestinian terrorist plot to assassinate him, it sent Sharon twelve agents and an armored car. Twice, in 1982 and 1985, it looked as if agents would have to risk their lives for Moammar Khadafy. Both times the Libyan dictator ended up cancelling his visits to the UN, claiming that CIA assassins were out to get him.

In 1981, Khadafy reportedly ordered "hit teams"—allegedly trained by former Green Berets and directed from Libya's embassy in the U.S.—to kill President Reagan. A rumor perhaps, but the Secret Service nevertheless tightened security around the President. It battened down the hatches at the White House again in 1983. The CIA had reportedly learned of another hit team through Manucher Ghorbanifar, the Iranian businessman who acted as a middleman in the secret 1985 shipment of U.S. arms to Iran. Ghorbanifar reputedly got wind that a five-man Iranian commando squad had been formed and that it was planning a Thanksgiving Day kamikaze assault on the White House. The attack was to be in the style of the Beirut truck bomb massacre that left 241 soldiers dead. Composite sketches of the Iranian commandos were circulated around Washington. The Secret Service set up a concrete barrier at the southwest gate, parked seven sand-filled trucks at other entrances and reportedly readied ground-to-air missiles.

Later, the agency took other precautions at the White House. A $771,000 "garden pavillion" was built to check all tourists for weapons. The agency tried to ban traffic on streets surrounding the White House; it succeeded in turning East Executive Avenue into a pedestrian mall. It also tried—but failed—to stop a developer from adding three floors to an office building that would give a sniper a gimlet view of the White House.

Miscellaneous marauders continued to storm Fort President. Protesters hurled bottles of blood at the front door of the mansion—even as Reagan recuperated from the Hinckley shooting. A nude man drove his car into a gate. Another man came charging with a samurai sword. Numerous homeless people tried to hop the fence. All this clearly put a strain on the Service's uniformed guards. In 1987, the guards shared the sidewalk with the picketers they usually kept out. The guards' placards read: "I'm a target every day, why can't I get better pay?"

In 1984, on the sidewalk behind the White House, a Secret Service agent shot and wounded a young man who'd brandished a sawed-off shotgun. The next day the White House announced that visitors could only enter the grounds through two gates, and that just about everyone but Cabinet members would have to have their briefcases searched and pass through metal detectors. Nevertheless, nine months later—and just a few hours before Reagan took his oath for a second term—a Denver meter reader named Robert Latta snuck into the White House with the Marine Corps band. Arrested on the floor below the Reagans' bedroom, Latta turned out to be unarmed. But doctors who later examined Latta said the former mental patient had heard voices that told him, "You blew it."

Secret Service sources said threats against the President more than doubled in the week after John Hinckley opened fire. Authorities hauled in three "copycats," one of whom had already been convicted for threatening to kill Presidents Johnson, Nixon and Ford. A week after the Hinckley shooting, agents arrested a fourth threat-maker named Edward Michael Richardson. The Service found no evidence that Richardson knew Hinckley. But they were both jobless drifters who'd been living at about the same time in Lakewood, Colorado. Richardson had also been fixated on *Taxi Driver* actress Jodie Foster. Armed with a .32-caliber pistol, Richardson had seen Foster perform at a Yale University theater that was crawling with cops and Secret Service agents. "I will finish what Hinckley started," Richardson told Foster in a letter. "RR must die. He [Hinckley] has told me so in a prophetic dream . . . Sadly though, your death is also required. You will suffer the same fate as Reagan and others in his fascist regime. You cannot escape. We are a wave of assassins throughout the world."

Richardson was right on that last count. The charismatic Reagan seemed to have a lunar effect on a tidal wave of assassins. Though Hinckley later wrote the President to say, "I'm very sorry . . . I thank God no one died," the threats kept flooding in. A number came from Vietnam vets. According to Federal prosecutors, one came from James Lewis, convicted in 1982 of trying to extort one million dollars from Johnson & Johnson after seven people died from taking cyanide-laced Tylenol. (Informants said Lewis had planned to send up remote-control model airplanes to disrupt Secret Service radios.) In 1983, before Reagan left on a Far East trip, the Service screened reports of separate assassination plots in the Phillipines, South Korea and Japan. That same year, agents finally arrested an auto wrecker known as "The Cat," who'd stalked Reagan and New York Senator Alfonse D'Amato. For two years "The Cat" had been calling the White House and taunting authorities with letters that trotted out security details unknown to the general public. He also sent "arms-length" snapshots of his intended victims at political events—and a lot of pictures of cats. In 1984, agents questioned *Hustler* magazine publisher Larry Flynt, who said on TV, "I have confessed to putting a contract out on President Reagan's life. I want to kill him."

Whether you put it down to Reagan or the psychosis of the times, the agents faced as much menace as ever. (They made 374 arrests in 1987.) At least they had a few things going for them. The Service now had a grand total of 4,300 employees, including 1,925 agents. The agency had also continued to come up with nifty technology like the white bulletproof tent that covered Pope John Paul II when he stepped out of his Popemobile during his 1987 U.S. visit. The year before the Service had signed a $35 million contract with Telenet Communications to set up a satellite network that would link Washington with its one hundred field offices around the country. Since 1983 the Service has been able to run the names of suspected assassins through the gigantic FBI computer that was once restricted to people actually accused of a crime.

The Service's most significant "advance," however, may have been its strict refusal to let its once-shot President do the sort of curbside handshaking that used to be the essence of politics. Mounting terrorism, horrible as it is, has simplified the Service's task: it just doesn't let "the Man" out anymore. Newspapers don't publish his schedule. And as spokeswoman Jane Vezeris commented, "Obviously, if the Secret Service had its way, we'd like to see someone in a totally secure environment, never coming in contact with the public. We would love it."

At least one senior agent observed, however, that "I think a lot of the guys feel as I do, that if the job got any easier, it would be boring. But then, there's always the unknown." Yes, there's that. The Presidential candidates still gambol through the nation's shopping malls. And the home study assassins can keep up with them—taking advantage of the Super Saver fares and killing the flight time by reading about John Hinckley's request for an unescorted Easter visit home or his letters to serial killer Ted Bundy.

The 1988 campaign called for the largest protection budget ever— $30 million to guard a field of twelve candidates. Pat Robertson and Jesse Jackson received so many threats from sickos jumping the gun that the Service gave the two candidates early protection. During the 1984 campaign, Jackson drew 311 death threats (fourteen of which resulted in arrests). By May of 1988, the man who claimed he'd knelt beside the dying Reverend King counted at least one hundred threats. One of the most serious came from a neo-Nazi couple that hailed, like the conspirators against King, from Marty's home state of Missouri.

Those who've watched the job of the Secret Service grow over two decades seem to see today's agents as at once better and worse says one longtime agent: "We're getting fewer and fewer guys with a military background. But we're getting a sharp breed. The process of hiring is better organized now, and you have more steps to go through. We're getting a real high-caliber guy." And yet some of the vets—the guys who rode with the Kennedys and who used to make $3.36 an hour and squeeze by on a $12 travel allowance—those guys say they've seen the Secret Service lose something as it's grown in size. They say that the Service has a yuppie rebellion of its own."

"I think the agents who are out there now aren't as tough as we were," reflects Jerry Parr. "I just frankly think that. Tough in the sense that now they've *got* a lot. They get overtime, they get support. We didn't have any of that. I'm not saying it was right. But we had to grin and bear it. I told them, 'There are a couple of young men and women in the Middle East. And they don't worry about their overtime. They aren't worrying about their government car. They're focused on a goal, maybe malevolent. So you better worry about them. Because they're dedicated.' "

Mike Endicott feels that, "Before the baby boomers, there was still a sense of respect and dedication. The reward for doing a good job didn't necessarily have to be financial. But the kids today are different. Each generation has wanted their children to have it better. And today, boy, do they have it better . . . My generation—we'd never question an order. You might worry if it was wrong, but you did it.

You might talk about it later. Today, they question *everything*. You can't give them an answer like 'that's just the way we do it,' or *'because*—because I'm the boss.' "

Marty neglected even to put in for his expenses, and he probably leaned farther leftward than the Service's Reagan Youth. Yet maybe these younger agents have inherited Marty's skeptical bent—his generation's insistence on asking *why*.

"No," insists Endicott, "I would never say Marty challenged authority in the sense of the newer kids—just to challenge it. Marty had a creative mind. When he asked why, it was to say, 'There's a better way to do this.' "

No doubt Marty's breakdown testifies that the Service's yuppies have every right to complain. All the same, older agents can't help but listen to their grousing and hear the wheezing exhaustion of the brilliantined hero who was Ronald Reagan's ace agent Brass Bancroft. The old romance, the sheer *esprit de corps* that rode on the running board of the agency's guilt—*that* was what used to give agents their second wind.

Chuck Rochner admits, "We all knew there were things we wanted to change, but this new agent would take you to the wall—making sure he got his rights. When I came on, it was a privilege to work, just to have the job."

"There's still a mystique about the Secret Service," said Endicott. "I think the guys today love it every bit as much as the guys of my generation . . . But the organization has changed. The Secret Service is impersonal today. Everybody fears the teletype machine. In the old days, you'd get a phone call, and you'd at least have the chance to say, 'How about sending John this time? I need to stay home.' When you're dealing with the logistical numbers they have today, there isn't the same latitude."

Marty may have seen the last days of a Secret Service that put up with his sort of eccentricity, or the hijinx of that departed bon vivant, Brooks Keller.

Endicott remembered traveling with Nelson Rockefeller on a fact-finding mission in 1969. "I flew into—I think it was Haiti—on military aircraft. It was somewhat early in the morning, and this guy met us—dressed in a white suit, white Panama hat, speaking French. I didn't know he was a Secret Service agent for two days. Brooks Keller was a different, unique individual. He was in the Secret Service at a very exciting time. Every organization has its Brooks Keller. Sometimes the guy lasts a long time, sometimes he doesn't. Brooks Keller, in addition to being very colorful, was very talented. The last years of his career, he was a liaison between the New York field office and various other agencies. And you couldn't have had anyone better. But the modern Secret Service is much more structured and formal. Brooks was a more informal guy. Brooks Keller would have a very difficult time surviving in the Secret Service today."

All the better, then, that Marty got out when he did—before the agency got starchier, and while he still had a vivid picture of Americans melting at their President's touch. But it just went to show: even if he'd stayed in the Service, those second-guessing yuppies would have found him. As it was, even though he'd gone underground, he still wasn't that far from danger.

"I was playing at Kamikaze the night the cops came in and arrested a guy who'd killed a callgirl. They arrested the killer right on the dance floor."

For more than two years, starting in 1981, Marty's bosses at The World worked with the FBI on an undercover sting operation at an illegal after-hours club called the Continental. World co-owner Arthur Weinstein used to wear a radio transmitter under his jet-black cummerbund while he made payoffs to cops. One of Weinstein's associates was a Soviet emigre named Victor Malinsky. On the night Weinstein and his partners opened Le Pop, Malinsky was shot dead outside the club. Malinsky, a successful cocaine dealer, had been talking with the Secret Service about working as an undercover informant in an international counterfeiting ring."

Grandmaster Flash used to say that in the Bronx clubs where he DJ'd, he couldn't make too many mistakes, or else he could get himself shot. How thoughtful, really, of the new owners of Studio 54 that they should install not only a battery of metal detectors at the club's door, but also bullet-proof glass around its DJ booth.

It was no joke. The Roxy, once the castle of rap and hip hop, closed its doors after repeated stabbings and violence made its insurance premiums jump to over $500,000 a year. Even Marty's beloved Paradise Garage, though it drew a less warlike crowd, got a reputation as a trouble spot. Bowing to neighborhood pressure, the Garage's landlord, after eleven years, refused to renew the club's lease. On the Sunday night that the club closed, Larry Levan spun for something like twenty-four hours and the regulars cried and hugged each other. They also heard that, outside the Garage the night before, two people had been killed and that a third was recovering from a gunshot wound.

"I guess some people might say I had a safer job when I worked for the Secret Service," suggested Marty. "But most people who come to a nightclub are there to have a good time, to make friends. I can tell the illin' b-boys who aren't listening to a note of music, who are there to rip people off. Nobody hates club violence more than the people who love the music. One of the most brilliant DJ-producers around—Scott La Rock—got shot in 1987. New York is what it is—a violent city where people get murdered every day. It happens in the streets, in the subways. Sometimes it happens in the clubs. The people who think the music causes the violence might want to consider something else—that maybe the music is what's keeping it from getting worse."

Frank Roccio, Arthur Weinstein's partner in Le Pop and The World, didn't know for a long time that Marty had been a Secret Service agent. "We were all quite surprised. If I'd known, I would've called Marty to come down and help us with security. I bet he still has a little of that old stuff in him."

"You'd think, here's this guy who learned judo and who used to carry an Uzi, but he always seemed appalled by violence," recalls Kirke Walsh. "He didn't seem to have a bad bone in his body. He was a real cool cat. I think I only saw Marty get upset once. About three beads of sweat came out. I think he was mad at a promoter."

"I want to stay as far away from danger as possible," Marty insists. "I'm a total pansy. I'm very skittish about loud noises. One night when the dance floor was going crazy, somebody set off a string of firecrackers. I almost shit in my pants. Another night Rose and my friend Jeff and I had just sat down with some friends at a restaurant in Chinatown. All of a sudden these guys in the next booth started getting into an argument. One guy stood up and broke a couple of plates, and next thing I knew, he pulled out a gun and shot another guy at his table. Everybody in the restaurant stampeded. I grabbed Rose and we ran down to the basement, which, naturally, had no exit. We hung out there till things quieted down upstairs. When we came back up, we saw the guy who'd been shot stretched out on our table. It looked like it'd been a .22. We were driving home and I felt this pain in my ribs. I checked to see if I'd been shot. I guess I just hit my side on a bannister. But the whole incident brought back alot of memories I'd just as soon forget."

Jim Kalafatis thinks that Marty "must be crazier than ever today, because he doesn't have that Secret Service image to portray."

"But that's probably why I act *less* crazy," Marty says. "In some ways, I've become the average Joe I might have been had I never left St. Louis. I hate to travel."

His record pool friend Judy Weinstein says, "I keep trying to send him overseas. I get calls from people who need a DJ in Tokyo, St. Thomas, all over. But he won't go." The former libertine is now an advocate of safe sex. He rags relentlessly about stupid dust heads who still do coke or smack, or try crack. At a time when college students play a tag game called "Assassination," Marty doesn't like to see kids in his neighborhood fooling around with toy guns.

"I have calmed down. I don't feel that need to become two people. I don't have to be conservative during the day, so I don't have to be so flamboyant at night. I'm glad. It got to be exhausting."

"I got back in touch with Marty after he'd been playing at Kamikaze for awhile," said former roommate Debby. "I was a little surprised. I saw him with the bleached blond hair and a cherry pony tail. Yet sitting down, having dinner with him, he was the same person. I was never very into the nightclub scene. But I went to visit him in his DJ booth and it looked like he was on top of things. He always was, no matter what he did."

\*   \*   \*

"In many ways he's the same. Except he seems more lovable to me this new way. It's as if he's come out of that guarded mode," says Sue Simmons.

Hearing that her old beau had slowed down, Barbara Bowers sighed, "Oh, how sad."

Not to fear. As self-reliant as he feels today, certain urges still overtake him. Just recently Marty shaved off all his hair.

"Don't ask me why, I just felt like it. Musically, I'm still at the barricades. I'm still traveling with my ears. A friend and I started up a company that imports records from England, Germany, Belgium, Spain, Sweden, Yugoslavia, Greece, Israel, India, South Yemen and a couple of countries in Africa. We ship the world's music to cities all across America. The business is showing excellent profits. That's probably because we aren't just salesmen, we're DJ's. We know which records to buy."

And if the business finds Marty doing the sort of cost-projections that he once considered "selling your soul," it's also pushed him toward the next logical step—making records himself. The latest insurrection in the music industry is being led by studio producers who've mimiced DJ scratching techniques, using digital samplers. The sampler is a sort of silly putty that can copy any sound in nature. It then creates a musical scale based on that sound. In 1987, a couple of producers who call themselves M/A/R/R/S sampled bits of half a dozen underground club hits, added some live guitar and arranged it all in a collage titled "Pump Up the Volume." Not many fans know what M/A/R/R/S looks like, but the group's record topped the U.K. and U.S. charts for months. Marty, who placed a huge order for the record before any U.S. label picked it up, has been noodling with his own sampling ideas in a twenty-four-track studio on Long Island.

*        *        *

"Sampling is the art of theft and it's hitting the record companies like the punks wanted to, because it rejects the majors' whole star system. See, the sampler lets you lift what may be the one good horn section on a George Michael song. You can do that under the fair use provisions of the copyright laws, so long as you keep the sample to a couple of seconds. Painters have been doing this sort of thing for years. But the record company lawyers are filing all kinds of suits. They say sampling steals from the original artists. Actually it's reviving their sales. And what did John Lennon say? 'Art is anything you can get away with.'

"But I don't just sample. I work out melodies on a guitar and we play around with drum machines and a synthesizer. We have a deal with some Jamaicans who run this studio. They give us free studio time and we trade ideas. Their thing, obviously, is reggae, so they've turned us onto some really crucial bass. But I gave them this idea for laying some Yemenite chanting over one of their rhythm tracks. It had them all bugging out.

"Stuff like that really excites me—splicing cultures together. I've been working on this one track where I drop in lines from this taped interview with a black kid who was arrested in a Harlem riot in 1968. This kid was explaining how the cops would only send you from the jail to the hospital if you could show you were injured. In his cell, he wanted to make his bruises look more convincing, so he said, 'I opened up the bruise blood to come out to show them.'

"We laid that tape loop over a real hard drum pattern I programmed. After a while, when you keep repeating that phrase—'come out to show them'—it starts to lose its specific context. And it starts to describe any kind of oppression you might feel. That hammering beat turns it into a sort of command: 'Come out to show them! Come out to show them!' For *me* anyway.

"We're working on something else that uses phone calls from listeners on a late-night radio talk show. Very severe callers, threatening to kill the host. I mean this is raw emotion, not a singer trying to act emotional. Venomous people saying, 'I hope you go blind.' And: 'All atheists should be lined up and shot.' They're sort of like the calls to the White House we used to get, or the letters from the quarterlies. The one that really gets to me is: 'You must be a disgrace to your whole family!' Then I drop in on somebody saying, 'Yeah! Yeah!' "

Marty's brother Steve remembered feeling for years that there was among the three Venker sons "a lot of competition about who had more money, who was progressing in his job. But it's just not important to Marty anymore. Just being at peace and being with Rose's kids and doing what he wants—that's what's important to him."

Viola Venker agrees. "Now that Marty's gotten back to music, you can imagine the difference in him. He's happy as a lark. He says, 'Mother, you can't imagine how good it feels to get up in the morning and go do something you really want to do.' What more can you ask for a person?"

Some people might consider Marty a wimp who couldn't hack it in the Secret Service. But his old boss has a different take.

"Marty was probably too creative for the job," suggests Mike Endicott. "People didn't think of Marty as a quitter. It takes courage to quit a job when you're making something like $45,000 a year and you don't know where you're going. Studies show that one of the greatest causes of stress in your life is starting a new job."

Doctor Bernard Newman said, "What really helped pull Marty out of his depression—more than my pills—was Marty being the person that he is. He had enough underlying guts, and enough underlying insight to pull himself out."

\* \* \*

"I didn't always feel so brave while all this was going on. It took me a long time to take off that suit. After I left, it took me five months before I felt like telling Rose what I used to do. Believe me, I'm sure not any yogi master of self-control. I still have plenty of insecurities. But this whole breakdown thing made me stronger. I found out that just because you've burned out in one career doesn't mean you can't start another career. You have to keep taking risks. I know that's not always easy. A lot of people have families to feed and bills to pay. But sometimes you can swing it—particularly if you don't get as weird as I got. If you can find some job you love to do, you might just find that instead of always feeling tired, you've got bundles of energy. You weren't spent after all."

Tom Wicker once described the burn-out that a generation of Americans felt in an *Esquire* essay titled "Kennedy Without End, Amen." In 1977, as the country ebbed toward electing Ronald Reagan, Wicker wrote that Americans looked back upon the smudged image of JFK, "as to their own lost dreams. [Kennedy] is the most fascinating might-have-been in American history, not just for what he was in his time but for what we made of him—not because of what we were but because of what we thought we were, and know now we'll never be."

But, as of 1988, Marty Venker says, "I'm happy where I am. I'm doing what I originally wanted to do back in 1968."

Some might see Marty's quitting the Secret Service as emblematic of the loss of liberal energy after the sixties. Having gone into the Service to defend the political system, Marty did, for the most part, give up on it. Maybe it was too late from the start. The 1968 assassinations that nudged him toward enlisting were really the final curtain on Camelot. It just took Marty, and many others, a while to realize it. Marty foreswore party allegiances so that he could unflinchingly protect pols of all stripes. But clearly it was a moot point. In Marty's ten years in the Service, neither the Democrats nor the Republicans produced a Presidential candidate who much tempted him to swerve from the agency's apolitical ideal.

"I'm still cynical about politicians. How can you blame me when you have over 110 Reagan officials accused or indicted for conflicts of interest, and when you have Gary Hart making a bigger fool of himself than even I could've imagined in '72."

And yet only a dumbass idealist could expect so much of lawmakers who have to answer to more special interest groups than Marty ever faced as a nightclub DJ.

"I still feel passionately about political issues. If anything, I think I'm more aware of racism and poverty than when I went into the Service.

"There's nothing like working in a city where everybody wants to go to an *exclusive* club to see the prejudice that exists not just between races, but within races. It isn't just the club owners, it's their customers. The other night I was out at a club and I looked down on the dance floor. The dancers had separated themselves by color. The whites were on one end and the blacks were on the other end and the light browns were in between. Three little clubs.

"It's only now that I've run up against the kind discrimination that other people have known for generations. One summer Rose and I decided it'd be fun to go camping—head upstate with Rose's two boys and a couple of our friends. So we drove for hours. Finally we pulled up to this private campsite. The guard there looked at me and Rose and our friends with our colored hair and he said, 'Sorry, this camp's for *families.*' Families? The kids—Jason and Marc—they were right in the car.

"I said, 'Hey, what do you call these people in the back seat?'

"He didn't care. We finally found one camp that'd take us. But they kept checking up on us, like we were the Manson family. And they put us in a part of the campground that was a goddam junkyard. I was trying to show the kids nature and all we saw were rusted-out car bodies. Garbage everywhere. We had to hide in our tents because of the goddam raccoons crawling around. All because of the way we looked.

"Next time somebody said, 'Let's go camping,' I would say, 'Well, then we have to wear our wigs.' If they said, 'We don't want to,' I said, 'No wigs, no camping.'

"I've dropped a long way from eating three-thousand-dollar meals with Richard Nixon. I really wish now I hadn't given away *quite* so much money. Eating rice and beans and sleeping on a concrete floor gets a little old after a while. I still can't even get a charge card. But you know, I still love rice and beans, and I'll tell you something else—dropping down to zero gave me a view of the world I never got flying around on Air Force One. I may have thought I was a 'soul-man' back when I was a college boy, but I didn't know shit about soul. After I left the White House, that's when I found out about people who've lost their jobs and lost their homes and lost their minds.

"And that's when I also found out that you can remake yourself."

It's a strange bird that rises from the ashes of its own burn-out. The kamikaze DJ puts little trust in establishment politics, and yet, at forty-two, he has a teenager's faith in the power of art to revive people and unite them.

"A song can drill a message into a person's heart in a way a political speechwriter has got to envy. You look back. Slave songs. Sea chanties. Union songs. Marine drill chants. Antiwar protest songs. Almost every group has had its music to spur people on. People always remember a prayer they can sing.

"The Beatles changed the way people thought about fashion, sex, drugs. And politics. That's why Nixon's people had the FBI try to nail John Lennon on a drug charge before the '72 Republican Convention. Apparently, they were afraid he was going to lead an anti-

Nixon rally in Miami. Never mind that the Beatles told everybody to put away their pictures of Chairman Mao. By '72, Nixon was hugging the Chinese.

Nowadays you've got the Republicans and the Democrats both trying to get Bruce Springsteen on their bandwagons. "Music's *still* changing people's thinking. Paul Simon—there's a sixties singer who kept his ears open. His 'Graceland' album got millions of people here listening to African music and talking about apartheid. All those events of the last few years—Band-Aid, Live-Aid, Farm-Aid, the Sun City record—you know, there were a lot of celebrity egos showing off, and there were questions about how far the money went, but it showed that music could still rally people behind a cause.

"I'm looking for today's anthems. Like rap. People could've used rap in the sixties, on the freedom marches. A lot of record company people thought rap'd die after a year. But instead of dying, you have Run-D.M.C. shipping platinum. That's because the best rappers kept re-inventing the form. They borrowed from German electronic music, from heavy metal, from reggae. They also didn't just keep boasting about what studs they were. They saw their friends turning into junkies, getting raped in prison, and shooting each other in the face—and they said how stupid it was, in a very clever way.

"Rap is the billboard of the underclass. You can make a rap record for five hundred dollars. So now you have more and more guys writing down rhymes instead of sticking up stores. And you have girl rappers—who are some of the smartest—putting those would-be studs in their place. You even have Jesse Jackson cutting an anti-apartheid rap with people from the Bronx and from Nigeria. Rap comes from a harsh world that some people don't want to deal with. Some people—white and black—leave the dance floor when I put it on. But over the years, I've watched how more and more people, yuppies included, stick around for those rap songs. And they know the words! So I keep playing rap.

"But you don't always have to clobber people with heavy lyrics to get the message across. I play African and Middle Eastern records. People don't know what the lyrics mean, but the spirit comes through and it makes them feel, I believe, more *worldly,* part of the planet they read about in the newspaper.

"That could be the first step toward picturing reform. A song can't all of a sudden change how a person feels about some issue. But it can start to change how a person feels about himself or herself. A dance floor is a stage where, with the lights down low, and fortified with some wine, a person can pretend to be somebody better. He or she can feel stronger, more beautiful, more noble, than during the day."

"Some of the most uplifting songs I play have a message no more, and no less, demanding than *reach up and respect yourself.* Now you can argue that people snap out of that dreamworld when they get off the dance floor. But I happen to know that a person will keep humming a good song long after they've walked out the door and into the night. If music could pull me out of my career, I think it can at least give other people a tune to whistle in the dark."

"People on a dance floor may segregate themselves into different colored clubs. But as the night wears on, you can see the borders disintegrating. The colored lights make it hard to tell what race that guy with the purple face is. So many people keep jumping in and out of the sweaty pool that you lose track of your partner and gradually you feel your pelvis pulling you toward that freak to the left. The music is so loud, nobody can hear you. So you start to sing that song they're playing. You start to hear your own voice coming out of the speakers. You get the vague sense that everybody's looking at you and thinking how cool you dance. How you must be a dancer. So, nonchalantly, you lift your eyes to check. But nobody's looking at you. Over there, some other people—they're all jerking in time with you, brother, they're all singing *your* song!

"What I see and hear in clubs makes me hopeful. I don't remember, back in the sixties, seeing dance floors as integrated as I see today.

"Sometimes I'll cut the sound in the middle of a song. Hundreds of people will finish the verse. They'll all be screaming, 'Free Nelson Mandela!' Some of them, for a second, will look embarrassed. But then I'll turn the sound back up and they'd all laugh and jump back into their song. You know, it's just records I'm playing. I'm grateful when the people applaud me, but *they're* the performance. When they lose their inhibitions, they all feel like they could have a second career as a singer or a dancer. That's why I like my job. We're entertaining each other. We're a tribe. Clapping our hands and wailing and stomping our feet. We're a congregation."

"Music is an emotional agent. A lot of DJ's are pretty jaded," says Judy Weinstein. "With Marty, you feel his heart would be broken if he had a bad night."

Like a political rally, a dance floor is a demonstration where feelings run high, where believers and dissenters trade suspicious looks, and where there always exists the danger of guns. The fantasy of the republic may be punctured at any moment. Marty has always liked working the perimeter of these events, standing in the limelight at times, and yet performing his best when he's blending into the crowd—working as a secret servant.

He has a public space in mind, a place along the Hudson River, where he'd like to promote an outdoor throwdown that would raise money for the homeless. "I'm talking to the city about it. Wait'll you see the view from this spot. Incredible." He'd like to open a club of his own. Kirke Walsh advises him against it. But he insists, "I think it says something that the Paradise Garage stayed open for eleven years, when the natural lifespan of a New York club is something like two years. A lot of that Garage crowd, right now they're wandering around, looking for a new place."

He remembers vividly how, before they would head over to the Garage, quite a few members of that lost tribe would gather beneath his booth at Kamikaze.

"One of the last nights I played there was unforgettable. After two and a half years, I was hitting the crowd with some pretty radical beats. I knew I wasn't doing what the owners and promoters told me. But I felt a responsibility not to cop out on the people I'd courted. I saw a lot of familiar faces down there. The energy on the floor was as jacked up as I'd ever felt it. I think they could tell I was going for it. And I felt like, if you kick them out, you kick me out. We all go out together—Kamikaze-style. Tears started rolling down my cheeks. But you know, it wasn't like leaving Vienna. Or like that night in college, at the Last Chance Bar, when I watched Bobby Kennedy dying on TV. That night when I was spinning, I was really delighted by the faces down there."

They were wild-eyed, sweaty faces, but they were different from the perspiring face that he had stared down that cold night in Chicago—different, too, from the vague face of the dream assassin who used to blow gaping holes in his chest while he slept.

On one of those last nights, in one of those brief, shining moments when Kamikaze seemed like Camelot, looked down on those faces and put on the S.O.S. Band's *a cappella* version of "Just Be Good to Me." He cradled his earphone against his cheek. He let the record's echoed female voice sing the first line: "Friends . . . tell me I am crazy." All of a sudden, he stopped the record dead and scratched the needle wildly in the first groove. The crowd roared. He let the record play just one word: "Friends." Then again: "Friends."

His friends started calling up to him, and he called back to them. "Friends," said the dance floor's speakers.

The dancers whistled and clapped. Marty's thumb nudged the bass lever upward. He waited two seconds. Then he unlocked his hand from the vinyl. The beat *ripped.* A girl *shrieked.* And a thousand happy lunatics were once again unleashed upon the world.